Modern Critical Views

Chinua Achebe
Henry Adams
Aeschylus
S. Y. Agnon
Edward Albee
Raphael Alberti
Louisa May Alcott
A. R. Ammons
Sherwood Anderson
Aristophanes
Matthew Arnold
Antonin Artaud
John Ashbery
Margaret Atwood
W. H. Auden
Jane Austen
Isaac Babel
Sir Francis Bacon
James Baldwin
Honoré de Balzac
John Barth
Donald Barthelme
Charles Baudelaire
Simone de Beauvoir
Samuel Beckett
Saul Bellow
Thomas Berger
John Berryman
The Bible
Elizabeth Bishop
William Blake
Giovanni Boccaccio
Heinrich Böll
Jorge Luis Borges
Elizabeth Bowen
Bertolt Brecht
The Brontës
Charles Brockden Brown
Sterling Brown
Robert Browning
Martin Buber
John Bunyan
Anthony Burgess
Kenneth Burke
Robert Burns
William Burroughs
George Gordon, Lord
   Byron
Pedro Calderón de la Barca
Italo Calvino
Albert Camus
Canadian Poetry: Modern
   and Contemporary
Canadian Poetry through
   E. J. Pratt
Thomas Carlyle
Alejo Carpentier
Lewis Carroll
Willa Cather
Louis-Ferdinand Céline
Miguel de Cervantes

Geoffrey Chaucer
John Cheever
Anton Chekhov
Kate Chopin
Chrétien de Troyes
Agatha Christie
Samuel Taylor Coleridge
Colette
William Congreve & the
   Restoration Dramatists
Joseph Conrad
Contemporary Poets
James Fenimore Cooper
Pierre Corneille
Julio Cortázar
Hart Crane
Stephen Crane
e. e. cummings
Dante
Robertson Davies
Daniel Defoe
Philip K. Dick
Charles Dickens
James Dickey
Emily Dickinson
Denis Diderot
Isak Dinesen
E. L. Doctorow
John Donne & the
   Seventeenth-Century
   Metaphysical Poets
John Dos Passos
Fyodor Dostoevsky
Frederick Douglass
Theodore Dreiser
John Dryden
W. E. B. Du Bois
Lawrence Durrell
George Eliot
T. S. Eliot
Elizabethan Dramatists
Ralph Ellison
Ralph Waldo Emerson
Euripides
William Faulkner
Henry Fielding
F. Scott Fitzgerald
Gustave Flaubert
E. M. Forster
John Fowles
Sigmund Freud
Robert Frost
Northrop Frye
Carlos Fuentes
William Gaddis
Federico García Lorca
Gabriel García Márquez
André Gide
W. S. Gilbert
Allen Ginsberg
J. W. von Goethe

Nikolai Gogol
William Golding
Oliver Goldsmith
Mary Gordon
Günther Grass
Robert Graves
Graham Greene
Thomas Hardy
Nathaniel Hawthorne
William Hazlitt
H. D.
Seamus Heaney
Lillian Hellman
Ernest Hemingway
Hermann Hesse
Geoffrey Hill
Friedrich Hölderlin
Homer
A. D. Hope
Gerard Manley Hopkins
Horace
A. E. Housman
William Dean Howells
Langston Hughes
Ted Hughes
Victor Hugo
Zora Neale Hurston
Aldous Huxley
Henrik Ibsen
Eugène Ionesco
Washington Irving
Henry James
Dr. Samuel Johnson and
   James Boswell
Ben Jonson
James Joyce
Carl Gustav Jung
Franz Kafka
Yasonari Kawabata
John Keats
Søren Kierkegaard
Rudyard Kipling
Melanie Klein
Heinrich von Kleist
Philip Larkin
D. H. Lawrence
John le Carré
Ursula K. Le Guin
Giacomo Leopardi
Doris Lessing
Sinclair Lewis
Jack London
Robert Lowell
Malcolm Lowry
Carson McCullers
Norman Mailer
Bernard Malamud
Stéphane Mallarmé
Sir Thomas Malory
André Malraux
Thomas Mann

Modern Critical Views

Modern Critical Views

RALPH WALDO
EMERSON

Edited with an introduction by

Harold Bloom

Sterling Professor of the Humanities
Yale University

CHELSEA HOUSE PUBLISHERS
New York

PROJECT EDITORS: Emily Bestler, James Uebbing
EDITORIAL COORDINATOR: Karyn Browne
EDITORIAL STAFF: Sally Stepanek, Linda Grossman, Claudette Gayle, Jerry Ralya, Peter Childers
DESIGN: Susan Lusk

Cover illustration by Peterson Design. René Magritte illustration, "The False Mirror," 1928.
Courtesy of Museum of Modern Art.
Composition provided by Collage Publications, Inc., New York, N.Y.

Printed and bound in the United States of America

10 9 8 7 6 5

Library of Congress Cataloging in Publication Data

Emerson, modern critical views.
    Bibliography: p.
    Includes index.
    Contents: The question of means/Stephen E. Whicher—
Emerson the prophet/Sacvan Bercovitch—The circles of
the eye/James M. Cox—[etc.]
    1. Emerson, Ralph Waldo, 1803–1882—Criticism and
interpretation—Addresses, essays, lectures. I. Bloom,
Harold.
PS1638.E415   1984   814'.3   84-27406
ISBN 0-87754-604-5

Contents

Editor's Note

This volume gathers together a representative selection of our most useful contemporary criticism of Emerson, written from 1973 to the present. The single exception is an excerpt from Stephen Whicher's *Freedom and Fate*, which is the precursor work to much that has been written on Emerson in the last decade. Sacvan Bercovitch and James Cox, two central scholars of American literature, place Emerson in his American context. David Porter provides an advanced study of Emerson's poetry, as Barbara Packer does for his finest single essay, "Experience." The editor's essay complements his Introduction as an exposition of Emerson's religion of Self-Reliance. Julie Ellison's analysis of structural patterns in Emerson's essays is an intricate demonstration of his subtle links between style and idea. Finally, Richard Poirier provides an eloquent defense of Emerson as a theorist who remains more challenging and pragmatically useful than any current European interpreter of interpretation.

Introduction

Emerson is an experiential critic and essayist, and not a Transcendental philosopher. This obvious truth always needs restating, perhaps now more than ever, when literary criticism is so overinfluenced by contemporary French heirs of the German tradition of Idealist or Transcendental philosophy. Emerson is the mind of our climate, the principal source of the American difference in poetry, criticism and pragmatic post-philosophy. That is a less obvious truth, and it also needs restating, now and always. Emerson, by no means the greatest American writer, perhaps more an interior orator than a writer, is the inescapable theorist of all subsequent American writing. From his moment to ours, American authors either are in his tradition, or else in a counter-tradition originating in opposition to him. This continues even in a time when he is not much read, such as the period from 1945 to 1965 or so. During the last twenty years, Emerson has returned, burying his undertakers. "The essays of Emerson," T.S. Eliot remarked, "are already an encumbrance," one of those judicial observations that governed the literary academy during the Age of Eliot, but that now have faded into an antique charm.

Other judicial critics, including Yvor Winters and Allen Tate, sensibly blamed Emerson for everything they disliked in American literature and even to some extent in American life. Our most distinguished living poet, Robert Penn Warren, culminated the counter-traditional polemic of Eliot and Tate in his lively sequence, "Homage to Emerson, on Night-Flight to New York." Reading Emerson's essays in the "pressurized gloom" of the airliner, Warren sees the glowing page declare: "There is / No sin. Not even error." Only at a transcendental altitude can Warren's heart be abstract enough to accept the Sage of Concord, "for / At 38,000 feet Emerson / Is dead right." At ground level, Emerson "had forgiven God everything" because "Emerson thought that significance shines through everything."

Sin, error, time, history, a God external to the self, the visiting of the crimes of the fathers upon the sons: these are the topoi of the literary cosmos of Eliot and his Southern followers, and these were precisely of no interest whatsoever to Ralph Waldo Emerson. Of Emerson I am moved to say what

Borges said of Oscar Wilde: he was always right. But he himself always says it better:

> That is always best which gives me to myself. The sublime is excited in me by the great stoical doctrine, obey thyself. That which shows God in me, fortifies me. That which shows God out of me, makes me a wart and wen. There is no longer a necessary reason for my being.

One might say that the Bible, Shakespeare and Freud show us as caught in a psychic conflict, in which we need to be everything in ourselves while we go on fearing that we are nothing in ourselves. Emerson dismisses the fear, and insists upon the necessity of the single self achieving a total autonomy, of becoming a cosmos without first ingesting either nature or other selves. He wishes to give us to ourselves, although these days supposedly he preaches to the converted, since it is the fashion to assert that we live in a culture of narcissism, of which our smiling President is the indubitable epitome. Emerson, in this time of Reagan, should be cited upon the limitations of all American politics whatsoever:

> We might as wisely reprove the east wind, or the frost, as a political party, whose members, for the most part, could give no account of their position, but stand for the defence of those interests in which they find them- selves. . . . A party is perpetually corrupted by personality. Whilst we absolve the association from dishonesty, we cannot extend the same charity to their leaders. They reap the rewards of the docility and zeal of the masses which they direct. . . . Of the two great parties, which, at this hour, almost share the nation between them, I should say, that, one has the best cause, and the other contains the best men. The philosopher, the poet, or the religious man, will, of course, wish to cast his vote with the democrat, for free trade, for wide suffrage, for the abolition of legal cruelties in the penal code, and for facilitating in every manner the access of the young and the poor to the sources of wealth and power. But he can rarely accept the persons whom the so-called popular party propose to him as representatives of these liberalities.

Emerson writes of the Democrats and of the Whigs (precursors of our modern Republicans) in the early 1840's, when he still believes that Daniel Webster (foremost of "the best men") will never come to advocate the worst cause of the slaveholders. Though his politics have been categorized as "transcendental anarchism," Emerson was at once a believer in pure power and a prophet of the moral law, an apparent self-contradiction that provoked Yvor Winters in an earlier time, and President Giamatti of Yale more recently. Yet this wise inconsistency led Emerson to welcome Whitman in poetry for the same reasons he had hailed Daniel Webster in politics, until Webster's Seventh of March speech in 1850 moved Emerson to the most violent rhetoric of his life. John Jay Chapman, in a great essay on Emerson, remarked that, in his polemic against Webster, Emerson "is savage, destructive, personal, bent on death." Certainly no other American politician has been so memorably denounced in public as Webster was by Emerson:

> Mr. Webster, perhaps, is only following the laws of his blood and constitution. I suppose his pledges were not quite natural to him. He is a man who lives by his memory; a man of the past, not a man of faith and of hope. All the drops of his blood have eyes that look downward, and his finely developed understanding only works truly and with all its force when it stands for animal good; that is, for property.

All the drops of his blood have eyes that look downward; that bitter figuration has outlived every phrase Webster himself ventured. Many modern historians defend Webster for his part in the compromise of 1850, by which California was admitted as a free state while the North pledged to honor the Fugitive Slave Law. This defense maintains that Webster helped preserve the Union for another decade, while strengthening the ideology of Union that culminated in Lincoln. But Emerson, who had given Webster every chance, was driven out of his study and into moral prophecy by Webster's support of the Fugitive Slave Law:

> We are glad at last to get a clear case, one on which no shadow of doubt can hang. This is not meddling with other people's affairs: this is hindering other people from meddling with us. This is not going crusading into Virginia and Georgia after slaves, who it is alleged, are very comfortable where they are:—that amiable argument falls to the ground: but this is befriending in our own State, on our own farms, a man who has taken the risk of being shot or burned alive, or cast into the sea, or starved to death, or suffocated in a wooden box, to get away from his driver: and this man who has run the gauntlet of a thousand miles for his freedom, the statute says, you men of Massachusetts shall hunt, and catch, and send back again to the dog-hutch he fled from. And this filthy enactment was made in the nineteenth century, by people who could read and write. I will not obey it, by God.

As late as 1843, Emerson's love of Webster as incarnate Power had prevailed: "He is no saint, but the wild olive wood, ungrafted yet by grace." After Webster's defense of the Fugitive Slave Law, even Emerson's decorum was abandoned: "The word *liberty* in the mouth of Mr. Webster sounds like the word *love* in the mouth of a courtezan." I suspect that Emerson's deep fury, so uncharacteristic of him, resulted partly from the violation of his own cheerfully amoral dialectics of power. The extraordinary essay on "Power" in *The Conduct of Life* appears at first to worship mere force or drive as such, but the Emersonian cunning always locates power in the place of crossing over, in the moment of transition:

In history, the great moment is, when the savage is just ceasing to be a savage, with all his hairy Pelasgic strength directed on his opening sense of beauty:—and you have Pericles and Phidias,—not yet passed over into the Corinthian civility. Everything good in nature and the world is in that moment of transition, when the swarthy juices still flow plentifully from nature, but their astringency or acidity is got out by ethics and humanity.

A decade or so before, in perhaps his central essay, "Self-Reliance," Emerson had formulated the same dialectic of power, but with even more exuberance:

Life only avails, not the having lived. Power ceases in the instant of repose; it resides in the moment of transition from a past to a new state, in the shooting of a gulf, in the darting to an aim. This one fact the world hates, that the soul *becomes*; for that for ever degrades the past, turns all riches to poverty, all reputation to a shame, confounds the saint with the rogue, shoves Jesus and Judas equally aside. Why, then, do we prate of self-reliance? Inasmuch as the soul is present, there will be power not confident but agent. To talk of reliance is a poor external way of speaking. Speak rather of that which relies, because it works and is.

Magnificent, but surely even the Webster of 1850 retained his Pelasgic strength, surely even *that* Webster works and is? Emerson's cool answer would have been that Webster had failed the crossing. I think Emerson remains *the* American theoretician of power—be it political, literary, spiritual, economic—because he took the risk of exalting transition for its own sake. Admittedly, I am happier when the consequence is Whitman's "Crossing Brooklyn Ferry" than when the Emersonian product is the first Henry Ford, but Emerson is canny enough to prophesy both disciples. There is a great chill at the center of his cosmos, which remains ours, both the chill and the cosmos:

But Nature is no sentimentalist,—does not cosset or pamper us. We must see that the world is rough and surly, and will not mind drowning a man or a woman; but swallows your ship like a grain of dust. The cold, inconsiderate of persons, tingles your blood, benumbs your feet, freezes a man like an apple.

This is from the sublime essay, "Fate," which leads off *The Conduct of Life*, and culminates in the outrageous question: "Why should we fear to be crushed by savage elements, we who are made up of the same elements?" Elsewhere in "Fate," Emerson observes: "The way of Providence is a little rude," while in "Power" he restates the law of Compensation as "nothing is got for nothing." Emerson too is no sentimentalist, and it is something of a puzzle how he ever got to be regarded as anything other than a rather frightening theoretician of life or of letters. But then, his personality also remains a puzzle. He was the true American charismatic, and founded the actual American religion, which is Protestant without being Christian. Was the man one with the essayist, or was only the wisdom uncanny in our inescapable sage?

II

A biography of Emerson is necessarily somewhat redundant at best, because Emerson, like Montaigne, is almost always his own subject, though hardly in Montaigne's own mode. Emerson would not have said: "I am myself the matter of my book," yet Emerson on "History" is more Emerson than history. Though he is almost never overtly autobiographical, his best lesson nevertheless is that all true subjectivity is a difficult achievement, while supposed objectivity is merely the failure of having become an amalgam of other selves and their opinions. Though he is in the oral tradition, his true genre was no more the lecture than it had been the sermon, and certainly not the essay, though that is his only formal achievement, besides a double handful of strong poems. His journals are his authentic work, and seem to me poorly represented by all available selections. Perhaps the journals simply ought not to be condensed, because Emerson's reader needs to be immersed in their flow and ebb, their own experience of the influx of insight followed by the perpetual falling back into skepticism. They move endlessly between a possible ecstasy and a probable shrewdness, while knowing always that neither daemonic intensity nor worldly irony by itself can constitute wisdom.

The essential Emerson begins to emerge in the journals in the autumn of 1830, when he was twenty-seven, with his first entry on Self-Reliance, in which he refuses to be "a secondary man" imitating any other being. A year later (October 27, 1831) we hear the birth of Emerson's *reader's Sublime*, the notion that what moves us in the eloquence, written or oral, of another must be what is oldest in oneself, which is not part of the Creation, and indeed is God in oneself:

> Were you ever instructed by a wise and eloquent man? Remember then, were not the words that made your blood run cold, that brought the blood to your cheeks, that made you tremble or delighted you,—did they not sound to you as old as yourself? Was it not truth that you knew before, or do you ever expect to be moved from the pulpit or from man by anything but plain truth? Never. It is God in you that responds to God without, or affirms his own words trembling on the lips of another.

On October 28, 1832, Emerson's resignation from the Unitarian ministry was accepted (very reluctantly) by the Second Church, Boston. The supposed issue was the proper way of celebrating the Lord's Supper, but the underlying issue, at least for Emerson himself, was celebrating the self as God.

Stephen Whicher in his superb *Emerson: An Organic Anthology* (still the best one-volume Emerson) gathered together the relevant notebook texts of October 1832. We find Emerson, sustained by daemonic influx, asserting: "It is light. You don't get a candle to see the sun rise," where clearly Jesus is the candle and Emerson is the sunrise (prophetic, like so much else in early Emerson, of Nietzsche's *Zarathustra*). The most outrageous instance of an inrush of God in Emerson is the notorious and still much derided Transparent Eyeball passage in *Nature* (1836), which is based upon a journal entry of March 19, 1835. But I give the final text from *Nature*:

> Crossing a bare common, in snow puddles, at twilight, under a clouded sky, without having in my thoughts any occurence of special good fortune, I have enjoyed a perfect exhilaration. I am glad to the brink of fear. . . . There I feel that nothing can befall me in life,—no disgrace, no calamity, (leaving me my eyes,) which nature cannot repair. Standing on the bare ground,—my head bathed by the blithe air, and uplifted into infinite space,—all mean egotism vanishes. I become a transparent eyeball; I am nothing; I see all; the currents of the Universal Being circulate through me; I am part or particle of God.

Nature, in this passage as in the title of the little book, *Nature*, is rather perversely the wrong word, since Emerson does not mean "nature" in any accepted sense whatsoever. He means Man, and not a natural man or fallen Adam, but original man or unfallen Adam, which is to say America, in the transcendental sense, just as Blake's Albion is the unfallen form of Man. Emerson's primal Man, to whom Emerson is joined in this epiphany, is all eye, seeing earliest, precisely as though no European, and no ancient Greek or Hebrew, had seen before him. There is a personal pathos as well, which Emerson's contemporary readers could not have known. Emerson feared blindness more than death, although his family was tubercular and frequently died young. But there had been an episode of hysterical blindness during his college years, and its memory, however repressed, hovers throughout his work. Freud's difficult "frontier concept" of the bodily ego, which is formed partly by introjective fantasies, suggests that thinking can be associated with any of the senses or areas of the body. Emerson's fantastic introjection of the transparent eyeball as bodily ego seems to make thinking and seeing the same activity, one that culminated in self-deification.

Emerson's power as a kind of interior orator stems from this self-deification. Nothing is got for nothing, and perhaps the largest pragmatic consequence of being "part or particle of God" is that your need for other people necessarily is somewhat diminished. The transparent eyeball passage itself goes on to manifest an estrangement from the immediacy of other selves:

The name of the nearest friend sounds then foreign and accidental: to be brothers, to be acquaintances, master or servant, is then a trifle and a disturbance.

This passage must have hurt Emerson himself, hardly a person for whom "to be brothers" ever was "a trifle and a disturbance." The early death of his brother Charles, just four months before *Nature* was published in 1836, was one of his three terrible losses, the others being the death of Ellen Tucker, his first wife, in 1831, after little more than a year of marriage, and the death of his first born child, Waldo, in January 1842, when the boy was only five years old. Emerson psychically was preternaturally strong, but it is difficult to interpret the famous passage in his great essay, "Experience," where he writes of Waldo's death:

An innavigable sea washes with silent waves between us and the things we aim at and converse with. Grief too will make us idealists. In the death of my son, now more than two years ago, I seem to have lost a beautiful estate—no more. I cannot get it nearer to me. If tomorrow I should be informed of the bankruptcy of my principal debtors, the loss of my property would be a great inconvenience to me, perhaps, for many years; but it would leave me as it found me,—neither better nor worse. So is it with this calamity; it does not touch me; something which I fancied was a part of me, which could not be torn away without tearing me nor enlarged without enriching me, falls off from me and leaves no scar.

Perhaps Emerson should have written an essay entitled "The Economic Problem of Grief," but perhaps most of his essays carry that as a hidden subtitle. The enigma of grief in Emerson, after all, may be the secret cause of his strength, of his refusal to mourn for the past. Self-reliance, the American religion he founded, converts solitude into a firm stance against history, including personal history. That there is no history, only biography, is the Emersonian insistence, which may be why a valid biography of Emerson appears to be impossible. John McAleer's biography sets out shrewdly to evade the Emersonian entrapment, which is that Emerson knows only biography, a knowledge that makes personal history redundant. What then is the biographer of Emerson to do?

Such worthy practitioners of the mode as Ralph Rusk and Gay Wilson Allen worked mightily to shape the facts into a life, but are evaded by Emerson. Where someone lives so massively *from within*, he cannot be caught by chroniclers of events, public and private. McAleer instead molds his facts as a series of encounters between Emerson and all his friends and associates. Unfortunately, Emerson's encounters with others—whether his brothers, wives, children, or Transcendental and other literary colleagues, are little more revelatory of his inner life than are his encounters with events, whether it be the death of Waldo or the Civil War. All McAleer's patience, skill and learning cannot overcome the sage's genius for solitude. A biography of

Emerson becomes as baffling as a biography of Nietzsche, though the two lives have nothing in common, except of course for ideas. Nietzsche acknowledged Emerson, with affection and enthusiasm, but he probably did not realize how fully Emerson had anticipated him, particularly in unsettling the status of the self while proclaiming simultaneously a greater overself to come.

III

The critic of Emerson is little better off than the biographer, since Emerson, again like Nietzsche and remarkably also akin to Freud, anticipates his critics and does their work for them. Emerson resembles his own hero, Montaigne, in that you cannot combat him without being contaminated by him. T.S. Eliot, ruefully contemplating Pascal's hopeless agon with Montaigne, observed that fighting Montaigne was like throwing a hand grenade into a fog. Emerson, because he appropriated America, is more like a climate than an atmosphere, however misty. Attempting to write the order of the variable winds in the Emersonian climate is a hopeless task, and the best critics of Emerson, from John Jay Chapman and O.W. Firkins through Stephen Whicher to Barbara Packer and Richard Poirier, wisely decline to list his ideas of order. You track him best, as writer and as person, by learning the principle proclaimed everywhere in him: that which you can get from another is never instruction, but always provocation.

But what is provocation, in the life of the spirit? Emerson insisted that he called you forth only to your self, and not to any cause whatsoever. The will to power, in Emerson as afterwards in Nietzsche, is reactive rather than active, receptive rather than rapacious, which is to say that it is a will to interpretation. Emerson teaches interpretation, but not in any of the European modes fashionable either in his day or in our own, modes currently touching their nadir in a younger rabblement celebrating itself as having repudiated the very idea of an individual reader or an individual critic. Group criticism, like group sex, is not a new idea, but seems to revive whenever a sense of resentment dominates the aspiring clerisy. With resentment comes guilt, as though societal oppressions are caused by how we read, and so we get those academic covens akin to what Emerson, in his 1838 journal, called "philanthropic meetings and holy hurrahs," for which read now "Marxist literary groups" and "Lacanian theory circles":

> As far as I notice what passes in philanthropic meetings and holy hurrahs there is very little depth of interest. The speakers warm each other's skin and lubricate each other's tongue, and the words flow and the superlatives thicken and the lips quiver and the eyes moisten, and an observer new to such scenes would say, Here was true fire; the assembly were all ready to be martyred, and the effect of such a spirit on the community would be

irresistible; but they separate and go to the shop, to a dance, to bed, and an hour afterwards they care so little for the matter that on slightest temptation each one would disclaim the meeting.

Emerson, according to President Giamatti of Yale, "was as sweet as barbed wire," a judgment recently achieved independently by John Updike. Yes, and doubtless Emerson gave our politics its particular view of power, as Giamatti laments, but a country deserves its sages, and we deserve Emerson. He has the peculiar dialectical gift of being precursor for both the perpetual New Left of student non-students and the perpetual New Right of preacher non-preachers. The American Religion of Self-Reliance is a superb *literary* religion, but its political, economic and social consequences, whether manifested Left or Right, have now helped place us in a country where literary satire of politics is impossible, since the real thing is far more outrageous than even a satirist of genius could invent. Nathanael West presumably was parodying Calvin Coolidge in *A Cool Million*'s Shagpoke Whipple, but is this Shagpoke Whipple or President Reagan speaking?

America is the land of opportunity. She takes care of the honest and industrious and never fails them as long as they are both. This is not a matter of opinion, it is one of faith. On the day that Americans stop believing it, on that day will America be lost.

Emerson unfortunately believed in Necessity, including "the offence of superiority in persons," and he was capable of writing passages that can help to justify Reagan's large share of the Yuppie vote, as here in "Self-Reliance":

Then again, do not tell me, as a good man did today, of my obligation to put all poor men in good situations. Are they *my* poor? I tell thee, thou foolish philanthropist, that I grudge the dollar, the dime, the cent I give to such men as do not belong to me and to whom I do not belong. There is a class of persons to whom by all spiritual affinity I am bought and sold; for them I will go to prison if need be; but your miscellaneous popular charities; the education at college of fools; the building of meeting-houses to the vain end to which many now stand; alms to sots; and the thousand-fold Relief Societies;—though I confess with shame I sometimes succumb and give the dollar, it is a wicked dollar, which by and by I shall have the manhood to withhold.

True, Emerson meant by his "class of persons" men such as Henry Thoreau and Jones Very and the Reverend William Ellery Channing, which is not exactly Shagpoke Whipple, Ronald Reagan and the Reverend Jerry Falwell, but Self-Reliance translated out of the inner life and into the marketplace is difficult to distinguish from our current religion of selfishness, as set forth so sublimely in the recent grand epiphany at Dallas. Shrewd Yankee that he was, Emerson would have shrugged off his various and dubious paternities. His spiritual elitism could only be misunderstood, but he did not care much about being misread or misused. Though he has been so oddly called "the philosopher of democracy" by so many who wished to claim him for the Left, the political Emerson remains best expressed in one famous and remarkable sentence by John Jay Chapman: "If a soul be taken and crushed by democracy till it utter a cry, that cry will be Emerson."

IV

I return with some relief to Emerson as literary prophet, where Emerson's effect, *pace* Yvor Winters, seems to me again dialectical but in the end both benign and inevitable. Emerson's influence, from his day until ours, has helped to account for what I would call the American difference in literature, not only in our poetry and criticism, but even in our novels and stories—ironic since Emerson was at best uneasy about novels. What is truly surprising about this influence is its depth, extent and persistence, despite many concealments and even more evasions. Emerson does a lot more to explain most American writers than any of our writers; even Whitman or Thoreau or Dickinson or Hawthorne or Melville serve to explain *him*. The important question to ask is not "How?" but "Why?" Scholarship keeps showing the "how" (though there is a great deal more to be shown) but it ought to be a function of criticism to get at that scarcely explored "why."

Emerson was controversial in his own earlier years, and then became all but universally accepted (except, of course, in the South) during his later years. This ascendency faded during the Age of Literary Modernism (*circa* 1915–1945) and virtually vanished, as I remarked earlier, in the heyday of academic New Criticism or Age of Eliot (*circa* 1945–1965). Despite the humanistic protests of President Giamatti, and the churchwardenly mewings of John Updike, the last two decades have witnessed an Emerson revival, and I prophesy that he, rather than Marx or Heidegger, will be the guiding spirit of our imaginative literature and our criticism for some time to come. In that prophecy, "Emerson" stands for not only the theoretical stance and wisdom of the historical Ralph Waldo, but for Nietzsche, Walter Pater and Oscar Wilde, and much of Freud as well, since Emerson's elitist vision of the higher individual is so consonant with theirs. Individualism, whatever damages its American ruggedness continues to inflict on our politics and social economy, is more than ever the only hope for our imaginative lives. Emerson, who knew that the only literary and critical method was oneself, is again a necessary resource in a time beginning to weary of Gallic scientism in what are still called the Humanities.

Lewis Mumford, in *The Golden Day* (1926), still is the best guide as to *why* Emerson was and is the central influence upon American letters: "With most of the resources of the past at his command, Emerson achieved nakedness." Wisely seeing that Emerson was a Darwinian before Darwin, a Freudian before Freud, because he possessed "a complete vision," Mumford was able to make the classic formulation as to Emerson's strength: "The past for Emerson was neither a prescription nor a burden: it was rather an esthetic experience." As a poem already written, the past was not a force for Emerson; it had lost power, because power for him resided only at the crossing, at the actual moment of transition.

The dangers of this repression of the past's force are evident enough, in American life as in its literature. In our political economy, we get the force of secondary repetition; Reagan as Coolidge out-Shagpoking Nathanael West's Whipple. We receive also the rhythm of ebb and flow that makes all our greater writers into crisis-poets. Each of them echoes, however involuntarily, Emerson's formula for discontinuity in his weird, irrealistic essay, "Circles":

> Our moods do not believe in each other. Today I am full of thoughts and can write what I please. I see no reason why I should not have the same thought, the same power of expression, tomorrow. What I write, whilst I write it, seems the most natural thing in the world; but yesterday I saw a dreary vacuity in this direction in which now I see so much; and a month hence, I doubt not, I shall wonder who he was that wrote so many continuous pages. Alas for this infirm faith, this will not strenuous, this vast ebb of a vast flow! I am God in nature; I am a weed by the wall.

From God to weed and then back again; it is the cycle of Whitman from "Song of Myself" to "As I Ebb'd with the Ocean of Life," and of Emerson's and Whitman's descendants ever since. Place everything upon the nakedness of the American self, and you open every imaginative possibility from self-deification to absolute nihilism. But Emerson knew this, and saw no alternative for us if we were to avoid the predicament of arriving too late in the cultural history of the West. Nothing is got for nothing; Emerson is not less correct now than he was 150 years ago. On November 21, 1834, he wrote in his journal: "When we have lost our God of tradition and ceased from our God of rhetoric then may God fire the heart with his presence." Our God of tradition, then and now, is as dead as Emerson and Nietzsche declared him to be. He belongs, in life, to the political clerics and the clerical politicians and, in letters, to the secondary men and women. Our God of rhetoric belongs to the academies, where he is called by the name of the Gallic Demiurge, Language. That leaves the American imagination free as always to open itself to the third God of Emerson's prayer.

STEPHEN E. WHICHER

The Question of Means

To bring to the test of experience his vague but powerful ambition to be a doer was the chief service performed for Emerson by the wave of social reform that arose in the late thirties and early forties in New England. The reformers called on him to perform exactly the kind of action he recognized a duty and claimed a potential capacity to perform—and when confronted with the actuality of his ambition, he discovered that it was something which he had no aptitude or wish to do, and which threatened the very liberation to which his faith had opened the way. As a consequence, the whole atmosphere of his faith underwent a pervasive change, as he adjusted his beliefs to protect the old values in the new situation. Not that the issue of reform alone caused this change. His original faith had been attuned to a millennialism which time and experience alone inevitably did much to weaken. In point of fact, we can see other contributing circumstances which increased the instability of his initial hopes, until the question of action forced on him by the reform movement precipitated their revision.

The kind of action Emerson understood best was that of the preacher. His proper role in society, he felt, was that inspired communication of truth which he called eloquence. '. . . it is the end of eloquence,' he held, 'in a half-hour's discourse,—perhaps by a few sentences,—to persuade a multitude of persons to renounce their opinions, and change the course of life.' This ambition was particularly strong in the early 1830's, while he still hoped sometime to replace his old church with a 'little chapel of the truth.' Then he imagined, 'The high prize of eloquence may be mine, the joy of uttering what no other can utter, and what all must receive'; and at moments he felt 'budding the powers of a Persuasion that by and by will be irresistible.' Here was a mode of greatness which he could aspire to with some color of plausibility. 'If I could persuade men to listen to their interior convictions, if I could express, embody their interior convictions, that were indeed life. It were to cease being a figure, and to act the action of a man.'

There is some evidence that the Divinity School *Address* in 1838 was involved emotionally more than he knew with this personal sense of mission. It had perhaps the deepest roots in his thoughts of any of his lectures, being an exposition of the spiritual religion for the sake of which he had abandoned the pulpit. The substance of the address was explicit in the journals in 1833, and already by 1835 he had formed an intention to 'write & print a discourse upon Spiritual & Traditional Religion. . . .' The address came as close to the irresistible truth he felt called on to announce to his generation as any of his utterances. Had he not written, 'When anyone comes who speaks with better insight into moral nature, he will be the new gospel; miracle or not, inspired or uninspired, he will be the Christ . . .'?

He was correspondingly affected by its hostile reception. Though outwardly unruffled and even amused, inwardly he was definitely perturbed, as the repeated self-defenses in his journals show. The reception of his address was the sharpest hint yet given him from the actual that its limitations were not to be lightly ignored. Inherently a contradiction of fact, the faith in his potential mastery was constantly exposed to the erosion of experience, which daily reminded him that the mountains he had declared to be moving were still in place. The reception of the *Address* was an angular intrusion of fact into the smooth world of his thoughts, which, while rousing him to an unprecedented vigor of defiance, helped to undermine in the long run his capacity to identify the ideal and the real.

His sharpest immediate response was a renewed defiance of society. In the solitude of his study he rose in the insulted majesty of the Soul and prophesied against his critics.

> . . . The world lies in night of sin. It hears not the cock crowing: it sees not the grey streak in the East. At the first entering ray of light, society is shaken with fear and anger from side to side. Who opened that shutter? they cry, Wo to him! They belie it, they call it darkness that comes in, affirming that they were in light before. Before the man who has spoken to them the dread word, they tremble and flee. . . . The wild horse has heard the whisper of the tamer: the maniac has caught the glance of the keeper. They try to forget the memory of the speaker, to put him down into the same obscure place he occupied in their minds before he spake to them. . . . But vain, vain, all vain. It was but the first mutter of the distant storm they heard,—it was the first cry of the Revolution,—it was the touch, the palpitation that goes before the earthquake. Even now society is shaken because a thought or two

have been thrown into the midst. . . . It now works only in a handful. . . .
But the doom of State Street, and Wall Street, of London, and France, of
the whole world, is advertised by those thoughts; is in the procession of the
Soul which comes after those few thoughts.

The passage is a magnificent eruption of the apocalyptic fire that smoldered in
the heart of this son of the Puritans.

    Yet he was stirred to this peak of aggressiveness partly by a certain
shock to his confidence, as its whole context in the journals suggests. Some
years later, he allegorically and ironically reviewed the affair in his poem
'Uriel,' for which the passage just quoted may well have been the germ. The
stress in the poem falls on the two points I wish to bring out: the revolutionary
nature of Uriel's utterance, and the lapse of Uriel himself that followed it.

    The address itself was calculated to give no offense, on grounds of
vocabulary at least, to a Unitarian audience. To compensate for the audacity
of his purpose, perhaps, he instinctively emphasized the regularity and
morality of the inner life with which he would replace external forms. That
freedom, and not just a higher law, was the intent of the spiritual religion
advocated in the Divinity School *Address* is made clear in 'Uriel.' There Uriel
is not the discoverer of a new principle of order, but is subversive of all order.

> One, with low tones that decide,
>
> Gave his sentiment divine
> Against the being of a line.
> 'Line in nature is not found;
> Unit and universe are round;
> In vain produced, all rays return;
> Evil will bless, and ice will burn.'

    True, the tone of the poem is ironical. Uriel is the deadly child in the
house who does not know better than to speak the truth in company. The old
war gods are right: such a menace must be removed at once. Emerson
ironically accepts the respectable definition of good and evil and deliberately
leaves out of account the higher order which in fact he had advocated to
replace the false conventions of his society. But in so doing he reveals what
his address glossed over, his sharp consciousness that his gospel *was* disruptive
of the actual social order. Uriel is the enemy of all worldly authority, and one
can read between the lines that he delights in the confusion his treason
caused.

    His lapse, in turn, is no repentance. The self-knowledge that withers
him is a knowledge of his impotence. Perhaps he is not ready to speak,
perhaps he is 'grown too bright,' but certainly his society cannot bear to hear
him; his hour is not ripe. He stands outside his conventional society in the
freedom and the solitude of outer space. The most he can do is to shake its

security with occasional hints of his cherub scorn. The poem thus involuntarily conveys the depth of Emerson's antipathy to the community he chal-
lenged. Uriel's truth is allied to the inanimate forces of nature, and its
utterance, while it shakes society, transforms him also into something fey and
inhuman. In this poem, as elsewhere in his writings, we touch the chilling
core of Emerson's idealism and sense the presence there of something with
which no community is possible.

In a life lived so entirely in the mind as his, every serious engagement
with the outer world had long-continued repercussions, as he gradually
assimilated the implications of the brute event into the tissue of his thought.
His break with his Boston church was such a key event, and so to a lesser
extent was the *Address*. It forced him to see that society did not *want* to
renounce their opinions for the truth. In *The American Scholar* Emerson had
described a new Moses; 'Uriel' is the ironical allegory of such a Moses whose
people preferred the desert. After this time Emerson's image of the hero-
scholar, leading mankind to the promised land, steadily gave way to that of
the solitary observer, unregarded and unregarding of the multitude, quietly
faithful to his inspired glimpses of worlds not realized.

> Let theist, atheist, pantheist,
> Define and wrangle how they list,
> Fierce conserver, fierce destroyer,—
> But thou, joy-giver and enjoyer,
> Unknowing war, unknowing crime,
> Gentle Saadi, mind thy rhyme . . . .

The process thus assisted by the affair of the Divinity School *Address*
was carried on and brought to a conclusion by the wave of reforming
excitement that swept over certain elements in New England at the end of
the fourth and the beginning of the fifth decade of the nineteenth century. As
a phenomenon, Emerson welcomed and encouraged it. When impelled to
ask, 'Is the ideal society always to be only a dream, a song, a luxury of thought,
and never a step taken to realize the vision for living and indigent men
without misgivings within and wildest ridicule abroad?' he could point to the
reformer: 'I, for my part, am very well pleased to see the variety and velocity of
the movements that all over our broad land, in spots and corners, agitate
society. War, slavery, alcohol, animal food, domestic hired service, colleges,
creeds, and now at last money, also, have their spirited and unweariable
assailants, and must pass out of use or must learn a law.'

He acquired for a time a 'habitual feeling that the whole of our social
structure—State, School, Religion, Marriage, Trade, Science—has been
cut off from its root in the soul, and has only a superficial life, a "name to
live."' Reform became his name for whatever would allow him 'to restore for

myself these fruits to their stock, or to accept no church, school, state, or society which did not found itself in my own nature. . . . I should like to put all my practices back on their first thoughts, and do nothing for which I had not the whole world for my reason.'

Yet the gap between dream and fact remained. He never undertook the leap of faith and avoided the heroic life in practice. In his discussion of reform, we can perceive an underlying consciousness, increasing with time, that the whole enterprise is essentially romance. Thus, side by side with his deep sympathy with reform as a general idea, we find a progressive disillusionment with all actual reforms. Typical of his feeling toward concrete schemes of reform is his refusal to join the Brook Farm community.

This refusal is superficially surprising, because the root idea of that transcendental asylum was the most attractive of all reforms to Emerson, the one he called the Doctrine of the Farm: the scholar should not live by thought alone but should put himself into primary relations with the soil and nature by performing his part in the manual labor of the world. This sensible suggestion that the sedentary intellectual should spend some of his time outdoors and take adequate exercise meant much more to Emerson. Most of all, it seemed to him a means of approaching that *entirety* in his own life and his outer relations which was his deepest desire. The doctrine expressed an ideal of self-sufficiency through simplicity. A man should scale his needs down to the point where he could meet them by his own exertions. Such an ideal, of course, could never be completely realized, but steps could be taken to draw closer to it, each one of which would free one that much more from living for show and bring one that much closer to the holy and mysterious recesses of life. *Walden* is the logical outcome of this way of thinking, and Thoreau's 'Simplify, simplify' its slogan. But this was also an aim of Brook Farm—to simplify life and restore its primary relations with the soil. *Walden* and Brook Farm are alternative means for attaining the end that Emerson formulated for both when he wrote, 'The power which is at once spring and regulator in all efforts of reform is the conviction that there is an infinite worthiness in man, which will appear at the call of worth, and that all particular reforms are the removing of some impediment.'

But if the aim of reform for Emerson was independence, we can understand why he decided not to join the Brook Farmers, even though their aim was similar; for 'At the name of a society all my repulsions play, all my quills rise & sharpen.' 'I do not wish to remove from my present prison to a prison a little larger,' he wrote. 'I wish to break all prisons.' Ripley's project seemed a pretty circuitous route to the few, simple conditions he required. 'I have not yet conquered my own house. It irks and repents me. Shall I raise the siege of this hencoop, and march baffled away to a pretended siege of

Babylon?' The only reform that mattered to him, after all, was moral and personal.

His objection to Brook Farm, he found, applied to all cooperative schemes of reform; they were all external. 'The Reformers affirm the inward life, but they do not trust it, but use outward and vulgar means.' They were partial in their aims, exhausting their efforts on some contemptible village or dog-hutch; they banded themselves together in associations or philanthropic societies, relying on numbers instead of themselves. In coming closer to such reform he did not hear the call of worth, but found himself 'jostled, crowded, cramped, halved, quartered, or on all sides diminished of his proportion'; and he swung back, with some violence, to the sanctuary of the heart. 'I cannot find language of sufficient energy to convey my sense of the sacredness of private integrity.'

He thus found forced on him an open repudiation of his supposed obligation to act. True, 'These reforms are . . . our own light, and sight, and conscience; they only name the relation which subsists between us and the vicious institutions which they go to rectify.' Yet no one of them but was partial and superficial. Plainly then, such manipular attempts to realize the world of thought were premature. 'Many eager persons successively make an experiment in this way, and make themselves ridiculous. . . . Worse, I observe that in the history of mankind there is never a solitary example of success,—taking their own tests of success.' Then perforce he must consent to inaction. Henry Nash Smith points out that when, in his lecture on 'The Times,' Emerson divides the movement partly into the actors and the students, and rejects the former for the latter, he is formally repudiating the ideal of great action.

Yet the students are reformers too. Impressed, like the actors, with 'the contrast of the dwarfish Actual with the exorbitant 'Idea,' they see also that all practical effort to reduce this contrast is inadequate and are thus thrown back on beholding. 'It is not that men do not wish to act; they pine to be employed, but are paralyzed by the uncertainty what they should do.' One would suppose that such passive futility would earn Emerson's disapproval equally with the busy futility of the actors, and certainly he does not approve the students unreservedly. They do not show the natural firmness of a man, but a certain imbecility that is the result of their insoluble perplexities. Sicklied o'er with the pale cast of thought, their life is deprived of its natural spontaneity and joy and is oppressed with ennui and melancholy.

Yet Emerson values the students above the actors: 'Of the two, I own I like the speculators best.' The reason is, 'Their unbelief arises out of a greater Belief. . . .' Their aim and wish is to give up entirely to the spiritual principle, and therefore they abstain from low methods of changing society, realizing that all higher modes of living and action must proceed from a prior renovation of the actor. 'Their fault is that they have stopped at the intellectual perception; that their will is not yet inspired from the Fountain of Love.' 'But whose fault is this?' Emerson asks. At least they understand what and where is the spring of all power. The student is sustained, however, like the actor, by a sense of his potential greatness and of an imminent revolution in society. He will keep in training, trim his lamp and wait. 'A patience which is grand; a brave and cold neglect of the offices which prudence exacts, so it be done in a deep upper piety; a consent to solitude and inaction which proceed out of an unwillingness to violate character, is the century which makes the gem.'

Emerson returned to the students and characterized them at greater length in his lecture 'The Transcendentalist,' fourth in the same series on *The Times*. This lecture, by the fact of its title, has acquired a factitious authority, as though it were a definitive statement of what Emerson and his movement-party friends were about. It does indeed tell us much about its creator and about his times, but it must be read against some such background as I have tried to sketch in to be fully understood. In this case, he is clearly describing a *second choice*. Since the ideal of the scholar, who does live in the soul and lead men like a hero, has increasingly come to seem unrealizable, Emerson describes instead the closest practical substitute—a scholar on the waiting list, so to speak. He repeatedly makes it clear that his highest praise is reserved, as before, for strong spirits, for heroes. The transcendentalist is only the negative half of a man; he is an empty cup, but at least the cup is ready for filling.

The lack of spontaneity in the character of the transcendentalist soon disaffected Emerson with him also. Somehow his faith in greatness had led him into a blind alley. 'If we suddenly plant our foot and say,—I will neither eat nor drink nor wear nor touch any food or fabric which I do not know to be innocent, or deal with any person whose whole manner of life is not clear and rational, we shall stand still.' It is reasonable to rebel against one bad custom, as did the reformers, but the effort to uproot *all* custom from our life can end only in emptying it of everything except the paralyzing custom of saying No.

At this point we are ready to pay attention to the case of the Conservative, to whom Emerson devoted a lecture in the same series that included 'The Transcendentalist.' Though included, perhaps, as Burke seems to have been included in the series on *Biography*, for proper variety, he is portrayed with considerable sympathy. The conservative is one who respects facts—as Emerson was learning to do. His fault is that he has no faith; he also is a half-man. Yet his partial statement is within its limits indisputable and is something the reformer ignores at his peril.

That which is best about conservatism . . . is the Inevitable. . . . Here is the fact which men call Fate, and fate in dread degrees, fate behind fate, not to be disposed of by the consideration that the Conscience commands this or that, but necessitating the question whether the faculties of man will play him true in resisting the facts of universal experience?... We have all a certain intellection or presentiment of reform existing in the mind, which does not yet descend into the character, and those who throw themselves blindly on this lose themselves. Whatever they attempt in that direction, fails, and reacts suicidally on the actor himself. This is the penalty of having transcended nature. For the existing world is not a dream, and cannot with impunity be treated as a dream; neither is it a disease; but it is the ground on which you stand, it is the mother of whom you were born. Reform converses with possibilities, perchance with impossibilities; but here is sacred fact.

Though Emerson in the end still affirms his allegiance to the movement party, he treats the reformer in this lecture as a half-man, too. Each is an example of the exaggerating propensities of man, who cannot be a whole, but seizes on a half-truth and pursues it beyond all proportion. In the person of his conservative, a forerunner of his skeptic, Emerson takes a long step away from his earlier commitment to the movement party, toward a greater disengagement and a more balanced recognition of the permanent part played in life by both idea and fact. Other lectures of this pivotal course reflect the same step to a lesser degree.

Emerson's answer to a heroic declaration of Alcott's, some five years later, shortly after the latter, with his English friends Lane and Wright, and their 'twelve manuscript volumes of J.P. Greaves, and his head in a plaster cast,' had failed with their scheme for a 'Concordium' at Fruitlands, was by then his answer to every transcendental reformer, including the one in himself. 'Alcott thought he could find as good a ground for quarrel in the state tax as Socrates did in the edict of the Judges. Then I say, Be consistent. . . . Say boldly, "There is a sword sharp enough to cut sheer between flesh and spirit, and I will use it, and not any longer belong to this double-faced, equivocating, mixed, Jesuitical universe."

'. . . Your objection, then, to the State of Massachusetts is deceptive. Your true quarrel is with the state of Man.' Very neat, very well put, we can agree; but we may put to Emerson his own later question to Webster, *How came he there?* What else had the transcendentalist ever objected to than the state of Man? A new scepticism controls this comment on Alcott's anarchistic objection to the State which might well have disconcerted that good man, who had only to turn to Emerson's recently printed essay on 'Politics' to find objections to the states of Man and Massachusetts very similar to his own. But that essay was based on a lecture given in 1837, with additions from another of 1840, and since then Emerson had been visited by many second thoughts.

Emerson's farewell to action is finally as explicit as his earlier rejection of society, and for much the same reasons: his freedom was threatened. 'Do not ask me to your philanthropies, charities, and duties, as you term them;—mere circumstances, flakes of the snow-cloud, leaves of the trees;—I sit at home with the cause, grim or glad. I think I may never do anything that you shall call a deed again.' The conclusion of the essay 'Spiritual Laws,' in particular, is a rapid barrage of arguments against the name of action, most of them dating from the same year as the passage just quoted. '. . . why should we be cowed by the name of Action? 'T is a trick of the senses,—no more. We know that the ancestor of every action is a thought.' '. . . real action,' this essay argues, 'is in silent moments,' in the silent thought that revises our entire manner of life. He stated what he was getting at most plainly in 1845. 'The near-sighted people have much to say about action. But . . . It is by no means action which is the essential point, but some middle quality indifferent both to poet and to actor, and which we call Reality.'

He had already in at least one passage come to the same point from the opposite direction in *The American Scholar*, when disillusioned with the partiality of thought, as he is in 'Spiritual Laws' with that of action. '. . . when thoughts are no longer apprehended,' he then argued, '. . . [the scholar] has always the resource *to live*. . . . This is a total act. Thinking is a partial act. . . . Time shall teach him that the scholar loses no hour which the man lives.'

Against this background we can understand his increasing admiration for what he called Character. This 'elemental force,'—'a certain solidity of merit, . . . which is so essentially and manifestly virtue, that it is taken for granted that the right . . . step will be taken by it'—a combination of probity and practical competence in coöperation with, rather than in defiance of, the order of society—which in *The American Scholar* Emerson had found higher than intellect, became more and more his practical ideal, as his hope of a life of discovery and performance died out. His realization of the futility of reform correspondingly increased his valuation of this 'reserved force, which acts directly by presence and without means,' until, in his second series of essays, he went so far as to look to it for a 'victory to the senses' that would eclipse the 'great defeat' of Christ on the cross! But this attractive idea of action by magnetism does not solve his problem; it only lays bare the heart of it: How is such private quality bred?

Beneath the question of action lay a deeper problem, that of man's compound nature. This was the question that most seriously concerned the transcendentalists, beside which society's criticism of their inaction was superficial. '. . . the two lives, of the understanding and of the soul, which we lead, really show very little relation to each other; . . . one prevails now, all buzz and din; and the other prevails then, all infinitude and paradise.' 'The object of the man,' he wrote elsewhere, 'the aim of these moments [of silent thought], is to make daylight shine through him, to suffer the law to traverse his whole being without obstruction. . . . Now he is not homogeneous, but heterogeneous, and the ray does not traverse. . . .' Even if we drop the question of action, and seek only 'Reality,' the problem still remains, How is such wholeness to be won and kept? Is there any ground for hope 'that the moments will characterize the days'?

The means to this wholeness was what Emerson called Culture, a topic to which he devoted a lecture series in 1837–38. 'His own Culture,— the unfolding of his nature, is the chief end of man,' he told his audience. 'A divine impulse at the core of his being, impels him to this. The only motive at all commensurate with his force, is the ambition to discover *by exercising* his latent power. . . .' The single man, ideally the master of the world, is actually its pupil. No little part of Emerson's journals and other writings, particularly around this time, amount to an extended inventory of the educational facilities open to him.

Culture is a term that one associates more with his later thought than with the years of transcendental protest. He devoted an essay to it in *The Conduct of Life*; a Phi Beta Kappa address in 1867 at Harvard treated 'The Progress of Culture'; his essay on Goethe in *Representative Men* also discussed it. In these cases it signified chiefly all the influences that went to refine and redeem the raw egoism of the natural man. In the 1830's, however, when he had just picked up this 'Germanic term,' it meant rather the means that would release the wild nature of a man and redeem him from custom and tradition. 'Culture, in the high sense, does not consist in polishing or varnishing, but in so presenting the attractions of nature that the slumbering attributes of man may burst their iron sleep and rush, full-grown, into day.' It was a method of conversion, and its goal the kind of supernatural primitivism celebrated in the Divinity School *Address*, the awakening of the Soul. 'To coax and woo the strong Instinct to bestir itself and work its miracle is the end of all wise endeavor.'

By rights, Emerson felt, man should enter at a bound into his proper nature, annihilating his lower life by one blow of moral revolution. The bent spring, released, should snap upright by its own strength. But what were the means of release? The soul has various faculties, particularly the reason and the will; through which is its redemption to be achieved? Emerson did not know and at different times conceded primacy to each. The question to which he devoted much of his thought, especially in the decade or so after 1833, was that of the means of both moral and intellectual culture—the purification of the heart and the inspiration of the mind.

At the outset, he appears to have hoped for much from a course of ascetic self-discipline. Natural goodness was to be bred by a stern, high, stoical self-denial. 'I believe that virtue purges the eye, that the abstinent, meek, benevolent, industrious man is in a better state for the fine influences of the great universe to act upon him than the cold, idle, eating disputant.' So the paragraph in *Nature* containing the revelation that man is himself the creator in the finite concludes, 'This view, which admonishes me where the sources of wisdom and power lie, and points to virtue as to

> The golden key
> Which opes the palace of eternity,

carries upon its face the highest certificate of truth, because it animates me to create my own world through the purification of my soul.' The same preparatory asceticism is expounded in his address 'Literary Ethics,' where for discipline he recommends to the scholar solitude, labor, modesty and charity. '. . . we have need of a more rigorous scholastic rule; such an asceticism, I mean, as only the hardihood and devotion of the scholar himself can enforce. . . . Silence, seclusion, austerity, may pierce deep into the grandeur and secret of our being, and so diving, bring up out of secular darkness the sublimities of the moral constitution.' 'If [the scholar] have this twofold goodness,—the drill and the inspiration,—then he has health. . . .'

As it turned out, however, the drill and the inspiration had little relation to each other; health remained an unpredictable miracle. For this reason the theme of preparatory asceticism in time virtually dropped out of his thought; it simply did not work. The ethical life he knew was necessarily divided between moments of inspiration, and long intermediary times in which all his obedience to duty brought little visible fruit.

Duty he obeyed, nevertheless—for this was a primary obligation, whatever his state of grace. 'If we cannot at once rise to the sanctities of obedience and faith,' he wrote, 'let us at least resist our temptations. . . .' 'It is very hard to know what to do if you have great desires for benefitting mankind; but a very plain thing is your duty.' In the anomalous life of delay and waiting to which he was generally condemned, adrift in time and mortality, the one sea-anchor was the old elementary moral code he had learned in childhood. 'Play out the game,' he wrote his friends in later life. 'If the Gods have blundered, we will not.' 'We are thrown back on rectitude forever and ever, only rectitude,—to mend one; that is all we can do.'

Intellectual culture looked more promising. Here, he found, 'The means of culture is the related nature of man.' The same outside world from which culture was to wean the soul was also in all its parts a means to culture. '[Man] is so strangely related to every thing that he can go nowhere without meeting objects which solicit his senses, and yield him new meanings.' 'Let none wrong the truth,' he reminded himself, 'by too stiffly standing on the cold and proud doctrine of self-sufficiency.' '. . . nothing but God is self-dependent. Man is powerful only by the multitude of his affinities.' Since the NOT ME is, in the phrase from *The American Scholar*, a 'shadow of the soul, or *other me*,' man may confidently turn to it to find the means to awaken the 'me of me.'

The simplest way to distinguish between Emerson's rebellion against the outside world and his reliance on it for culture is to point out that in the former case he was thinking primarily of organized society, and in the latter primarily of nature. There is no question that nature could on occasion prompt the strong instinct to work its miracle. Several moments of sacred exhilaration are recorded in *Nature*, of which the 'transparent eyeball' passage is the most famous. Emerson's moments of gladness in nature, however, like Wordsworth's, diminished in number and intensity as he grew older. He soon came to see, also, that '. . . it is certain that the power to produce this delight does not reside in nature, but in man, or in a harmony of both.' Nature was at most 'a differential thermometer detecting the presence or absence of the divine spirit in man.' The illusion which he cherished in 1836 of a possible divine rapture to grow out of his wild poetic delight in nature had vanished by 1844. 'That bread which we ask of Nature is that she should entrance us, but amidst her beautiful or her grandest pictures I cannot escape the *second thought*. . . .'

But in the earlier period he entertained a more specific hope from nature which appears in the chapter of *Nature* on 'Language.' Nature was not merely a tonic to the spirit; she was significant of herself and spoke to the intelligence. Newly severed from the authority of the Bible, this reminiscent Puritan sought to read a new gospel from nature, God's perpetual revelation. 'Nature is a language, and every new fact that we learn is a new word; but rightly seen, taken all together, it is not merely a language, but the language put together into a most significant and universal book. I wish to learn the language, not that I may learn a new set of nouns and verbs, but that I may read the great book which is written in that tongue.'

For a brief while Emerson was attracted to Emanuel Swedenborg and his followers as interpreters of the language of nature. The influence of the Swedenborgians on his thought started with his reading of Sampson Reed's *The Growth of the Mind* in 1826 and reached its high point about ten years later. *Nature* contains numerous Swedenborgian echoes, more by a good margin than any subsequent writing of Emerson's. After that time he became increasingly conscious of Swedenborg's limitations—there is a distinct cooling off apparent between the paragraph on Swedenborg in *The American Scholar* and the essay on Swedenborg in *Representative Men*—at the same time that the New Church men in New England began publicly to repudiate him and the transcendentalism he represented.

What drew him was clearly the doctrine of correspondence. Sweden-borg developed this as a method of interpreting Scripture, but it was easily susceptible of a poetic extension, and that by warrant of the master: 'The whole natural world corresponds to the spiritual world, and not merely the natural world in general, but also every particular of it; and as a consequence every thing in the natural world that springs from the spiritual world is called a correspondent. . . . The animals of the earth correspond in general to affec-tion, mild and useful animals to good affections, fierce and useless ones to evil affections. In particular, cattle and their young correspond to the affections of the natural mind, sheep and lambs to the affections of the spiritual mind; while birds correspond, according to their species, to the intellectual things of the natural mind or the spiritual mind,' etc., etc. Emerson easily took the short step from this notion of a fixed natural symbolism to the conclusion that nature is not only a language but a book, that spiritual truths may be read directly from nature, by a purged mind, without the intervention of any other revelation. Hence, 'All things . . . preach to us.'

However congenial the thought of a mute gospel in nature to his truth-hungry mind, he quickly exhausted the Swedenborgians. Already in 1835 he was writing to Elizabeth Peabody, 'I sympathize with what you say of your aversion at being confined to Swedenborg's associations. . . .' The lite-ralism of Swedenborg became one of his main points of criticism in *Rep-resentative Men*. 'The slippery Proteus is not so easily caught. In nature, each individual symbol plays innumerable parts, as each particle of matter circu-lates in turn through every system. . . . Nature avenges herself speedily on the hard pedantry that would chain her waves. She is no literalist.' He soon dropped the notion that the meanings of natural objects could ever be fixed and written down. Yet a general sense that somewhere, beneath the surfaces of nature, lurked some great final meaning, if he could only get at it, continued to tease his reflections on nature. 'The love of Nature,—what is that but the presentiment of intelligence of it? Nature preparing to become a language to us.'

A more far-reaching attack on the meaning of nature was through natural science. Emerson shared the lively interest in the findings of science of his time, particularly in the emerging studies of geology and biology, but his spirit was hardly scientific. He read the ordinary fare available to the general reader of the day: J.F.W. Herschel, Cuvier, Humboldt, Playfair and later Lyell on geology, Kirby and Spence's *Entomology* and other such texts, various volumes in popular collections such as *The Library of Useful Knowl-edge, The American Library of Useful Knowledge*, Lardner's *The Cabinet Cyclo-paedia*, several of the Bridgewater treatises, not to speak of browsings in the *Transactions of the Royal Society* and other periodical literature. Scientists like

Galileo, Newton, Laplace, Lamarck, Linnaeus, Davy, Euler were high in his extensive list of great names.

What did he read this literature for? In the somewhat desultory years just after his return from Europe, when he did much such reading and lectured several times to groups of amateur students of science like himself, he more than once asked himself that question and finally confessed that he did not entirely know. '. . . all the reasons seem to me to fall far short of my faith upon the subject. Therefore, boldly press the cause as its own evidence; say that you love Nature, and would know her mysteries, and that you believe in your power by patient contemplation and docile experiment to learn them.' He read what the scientists had to say because he hoped to find in them some clue to nature's meanings.

Much of the writing on science that came to his hand was more or less apologetic in character, the Bridgewater treatises being an extreme example, anxious to protect science against the charge of atheism and encouraging a habit of sifting the scientific facts for evidences of divine contrivance. In this semipious atmosphere it was easy for Emerson to treat science, as he did, as a kind of embryonic revelation. His key thought on science was what he called, prompted by Coleridge, the 'humanity of science.' Nature was the 'externization' of something deep in man's consciousness; therefore man had somewhere within him the means of understanding all the phenomena of nature. True science was then as much a matter of extracting from oneself the Idea of the phenomena one knew as of collecting facts to be understood; find the true principles of unity in things, and the more or less of mere facts becomes unimportant. Since Goethe's scientific accomplishment, genetic and anti-Newtonian student of nature as he was, consisted largely in just such a disclosure of unifying ideas, he became something like Emerson's ideal scientist, one 'always watching for the glimmering of that pure, plastic Idea.'

Accordingly, Emerson was on the whole unsympathetic with the patient experimentation on which scientific achievement is based and pre-scribed instead a moral and spiritual reformation in the scientist. Scientists will never understand nature, he wrote in *Nature*, using Swedenborgian language, until they approach her in the fire of holiest affections, and not simply with the intellect. It was the duty of the naturalist, he wrote in an early lecture, to study in faith and in love; or, as he put it in 1840, 'science always goes abreast with the just elevation of the man. . . .'

With this view of science, it would appear that there was small hope of culture, in Emerson's sense, in the study of science, since the elevation culture was intended to bring about was necessary to make true science possible. And in point of fact he did not look to science much to coax and woo the great instinct; rather 'the greatest office of natural science [is] . . . to explain man to himself,' to help him to understand if not to heal his divided nature. The scientist, like the true orator, should be one 'who could reconcile your moral character and your natural history, who could explain your misfortunes, your fevers, your debts, your temperament, your habits of thought, your tastes, and in every explanation not sever you from the Whole, but unite you to it. . . .' In the rare moments of union with the Whole such questionings dropped away. Generally, however, as he put it, 'I have this latent omniscience coexistent with omnignorance.' Knowledge of the One did not explain the Many; 'The Idea according to which the Universe is made is wholly wanting to us. . . .' For this reason, we may suppose, the idea of evolution, throwing nature into the perspective of a new unifying idea, was able to catch his imagination in his later life. He accepted it uncritically as a conspicuous confirmation of his hope that science might 'uncover the living ligaments . . . which attach the dull men and things we converse with, to the splendor of the First Cause. . . .'

The Idea of nature Emerson desired, needless to say, was not forthcoming; the inspiration he sought from nature's influence was evanescent and illusory. Man could not immerse himself in the unconsciousness of nature, nor could he conquer her through consciousness, by achieving her explanation. He imaged his frustration in a series of mythological parallels. Nature was the Sphinx, asking her riddle of each passerby. She was Proteus, whose meanings changed as often as she was studied. Her lover was Tantalus, baffled by an apparent wealth of meaning that withdrew as often as he tried to seize it. Nature was an enchanted circle, which he was forbidden to enter. Like some creature of old romance, the 'universal dame' repeated her old challenge:

> Who telleth one of my meanings
> Is master of all I am.

But he knew that a hero with stronger magic than a mere sauntering poet could command would be needed to lift her spell. Nature served as a perpetual mute invitation to man to assume his rightful lordship but had no power to teach him to accept it. As he summed it up in a lecture, 'The co-presence of the living Soul is essential to all teaching.'

But this same fatal flaw held true of *all* the means of culture. In his lecture on 'The School,' for example, he spoke of persons and books as two of man's teachers. But these, which may be taken to sum up between them the cultural influences of man, as opposed to nature, had the same unpredictability. Emerson read books for scarcely any other reason than to provide himself with a stimulus to inspiration, 'for the lustres,' as he said, and was often successful. Yet books were, after all, but black marks on paper. They could live only with the life of the reader. 'As the proverb says, "He that would bring home the wealth of the Indies, must carry out the wealth of the Indies."

. . . When the mind is braced by labor and invention, the page of whatever book we read becomes luminous with manifold allusion.' Again, the soul illumines the book, not the book the soul.

Persons, the conversation of contemporaries, were a still more uncertain means. Emerson summed up the situation when he wrote in 'Friendship,' 'I do then with my friends as I do with my books.' Exactly—and as was true of books, a response to friends required 'the uprise of nature in us to the same degree it is in them.' All came back in the end to instinct, the primary teacher. 'Persons I labor at, and grope after, and experiment upon, make continual effort at sympathy, which sometimes is found and sometimes is missed; but I tire at last, and the fruit they bring to my intellect or affections is oft small and poor. But a thought has its own proper motion which it communicates to me, not borrows of me, and on its Pegasus back I override and overlook the world.'

The whole matter of the means of culture is summed up in one sentence in his journals: 'A day is a rich abyss of means, yet mute and void.' The poem Emerson wrote thirteen years later on this theme, 'Days,' testifies to his lasting regret at not achieving his morning wishes, but in its implied self-reproach is not representative of his by then settled acquiescence in the irremediable waywardness of the divine uprush of soul through which alone they could become reality.

Yet we would mistake his mood if we supposed that he ever finally despaired of culture. A day *was* a rich abyss of means. The daily anticipation, often rewarded, that the whole solid world might roll aside like a mist and show the living soul underneath, was ground for an ever-renewed hope, not despair. If we find that the days pass by and we are still the same, yet we can believe that the years teach much which the days never knew. As a ship advances by a succession of tacks, 'so in life our profession, our amusements, our errors even, give us with much parade, or with our own blushes, a little solid wisdom.' The upper world is always there, like the air we breathe, even when we are not aroused to awareness of it. How can it fail to affect us? 'Every moment instructs, and every object; for wisdom is infused into every form. It has been poured into us as blood; it convulsed us as pain; it slid into us as pleasure; it enveloped us in dull, melancholy days, or in days of cheerful labor; we did not guess its essence until after a long time.'

SACVAN BERCOVITCH

Emerson the Prophet: Romanticism, Puritanism, and Auto-American-Biography

America, . . . a vast unreal, intermediary thing. . . .
—D.H. LAWRENCE, *Letters*

*Being an American is not something to be inherited so much as something to
be achieved. . . . then, why are we so nervous? why do we so worry about
our identity?*
—PERRY MILLER, *Nature's Nation*

In *The Anxiety of Influence*, Harold
Bloom describes the British and American Romantics as the common heirs to
"a severely displaced Protestantism"; but "British poets swerve from their
precursors," he observes, "while American poets labor to 'complete' their
fathers." The contrast seems to me a compelling cultural as well as literary
insight. It directs us to Emerson as the central figure of the American
Renaissance; it recalls the strong prophetic strain in Emerson's thought; and
for my present purpose most importantly, it suggests that the long foreground
to Emerson the prophet is the legacy of the colonial Puritan fathers.

The Puritan emphasis on prophecy is well known. From the start, the
emigrants made the Book of Revelation a proof-text of the New England
Way. Their outlook followed the premises of Reformed millennialism, but

they went one step further. As visible saints on a social mission, they identified their progress with the progress of the church. European Protestants, from Luther through Foxe, were careful to distinguish between social and sacred identity. When they boasted of "national election" they used the concept metaphorically, to denote the provisional, latter-day conjunction of secular and redemptive history. The American Puritans changed metaphor to fact. They regarded their commonwealth, their locale, and their national convenant as being literally part of God's grand design. The New World and the remnant now arrived to redeem it were sacred as well as worldly facts. They represented the fulfillment of scriptural promises. In the settlers' formulaic phrase, they were types embossed upon the spiral of salvational time. History for them was prophecy postdated, and prophecy, history antedated. On these grounds, during the first decades, they fused personal and federal eschatology, the saint's preparation for heaven and the theocracy's march toward New Jerusalem. On these grounds, in defiance of exegetical convention, they recast the modern world as a setting for Armageddon: England as a second Babylon, ripe for the slaughter; America as the wilderness that was to blossom as the rose; all other peoples—in Asia, Africa, Europe, places still unknown or undiscovered—as spiritual dependencies, awaiting the completion of their errand. And on these grounds, toward the end of the century, the dwindling orthodoxy refused to abandon the fathers' ideal. In the face of an untoward present, they guaranteed the future by sustaining the rhetoric of the past. In effect, they rescued the venture by appropriating it to themselves. Interweaving autobiography and sacred history, they confirmed their role as prophets by asserting the communal purpose, and proved the continuity of purpose by the presence of their vision.

They compared themselves in this respect with the Old Testament seers; but again, their concept of an *American* mission impelled them toward a distinctive prophetic mode. Jeremiah derives his authority from tradition. The myth he represents is the commemorative expression of his race. His function as communal spokesman builds on the conflict between vision and fact; and accordingly, his outlook is dialectical, insistent on the irreconcilable dualism of what his people are and what they ought to be. The very need for prophecy, that is, arises out of an engagement with history and community; the very concept of fulfillment centers on the *problem* of the present. Even as he outlines the paradise to come, Jeremiah invokes the myth in terms of contradiction. He appeals to the past in order to call attention to the hiatus between fathers and sons. His representative stature, the authority both of his denunciations and of his predictions, is that of a tradition at odds with the course of history.

The prophetic outlook of the latter-day Puritan theocrats serves to obviate the contradiction. Cotton Mather earns his authority as communal spokesman not by his connection with any existent community, but by personal assertion. His myth is essentially projective and elite, the invention of expatriate idealists who declared themselves the party of the future, and then proceeded, in an astonishing act of will and imagination, to impose prophecy upon history. The first generations did not fully realize the potential of their rhetoric. Concerned as they were with building their city on a hill, they could not afford to disregard realities altogether. To some extent at least they had to confront the conflicts inherent in their venture. Mather's works show no such tension. His *Magnalia Christi Americana* seeks above all to confirm its author's representative stature. Mather intended it to be an epic history, and he referred constantly to earlier epics, especially those of Virgil and Milton. But Latium and Eden come to us from an irrevocable past. Like Jeremiah, Milton and Virgil use prophecy to suggest the inadequacies of the present. Mather locates his golden age in the future, and so conceives of America heuristically, as microcosm of the world-wide work of redemption and macrocosm of the redemptive work underway in its representative consciousness. Insofar as he berates his contemporaries for backsliding, he dissociates them from the country's "true history." Raising the process of fulfillment entirely into the realm of the imagination, he offers *himself*, the coherence of *his* vision, as the link between the promise and its realization.

Mather's method issues in a peculiarly self-contained concept of heroism. Traditionally, the epic hero culminates the myth-making process. Thus he serves to remind his imitators of their *incompleteness*; the transcendent model toward which they aspire accentuates their own limiting historical conditions. The *Magnalia*'s heroes, on the contrary, delineate the myth in process. Considered in context, they are successive harbingers of the Theopolis Americana at hand; each of them, in his distinctive historical situation, emerges as an emblem of destiny manifest. The retrospective *imitatio Christi* therefore opens into a developmental scheme, a sort of relay race toward eternity, where the participants are essentially the same (all one in Christ), while temporally they represent ascending stages of perfection. The sons, Mather tells us, improve upon the fathers, as the New Israel improves upon the Old, or "as a snowball, the *further* it rolls, the *bigger* it grows." To identify with (say) John Winthrop, "the American Nehemiah," is not merely to assume the characteristics of a life finished and justified. It is this too, but more largely it is to become part of a teleology. For Mather, the fathers are prophetic exemplars, and he a greater Nehemiah, who would define us, as Americans, in relation to the still-unfolding New World *magnalia*, somewhere midway between the theocratic garden of God and its consummation in the paradise to be regained. And wherever the midway point falls in that visionary "inter-Sabbatical line," the status of representative American designates a comprehensive social-divine selfhood that by definition surmounts the contradictions of secular time.

This concept of intermediate identity, in which self-perfection becomes synonymous with corporate progress, may be traced throughout the eighteenth and nineteenth centuries. In one form or another, it recurs in every form of national self-definition (the dream, the American mission, the redemptive West). It underlies the ambivalence toward the Puritans, as founding fathers *against* whom the sons measure their moral and political advance. It lends a special cast to American views of the "course of empire," of reform, technology, utopia, and the self-made man. It links Puritan chiliasm with Revivalist and Revolutionary post-millennialism. And (to return to my subject) it provides a clue to the character of Emerson's "severely displaced Protestantism." In a famous passage, Augustine describes theological displacement as the "*experimentum medietatis*," a "trial of the center," when the natural will overcomes the divine. The Puritans applied this concept to the false pilgrim's regress from Christ to the self; following Augustine, they found their main examples in Lucifer and Prometheus. The Romantics, we might say, redefined the *experimentum medietatis* as a victory of the soul. They undertook a Promethean journey that ascended *through* the Center of Indifference to an affirmation of the self as divinity incarnate. The development begins in England as early as the seventeenth century: with the Puritan "vulgar prophets" who arrogated the Godhead to themselves, with the Quaker notion of the inner light, with Milton's *De Doctrina Christiana* which announces that all believers are no less than Jesus sons of God. The line leads forward to the Romantics of our own time—to Carl Jung, for example, who warns us not to imitate Christ, since, properly seen, the self is God; or earlier, to Nietzsche, who advised man simply to forget God, love himself through self-generated grace, and thereby enact in himself the entire work of redemption.

So considered, the connection between Puritan and Romantic may be briefly stated. The Reformers, having unleashed the individual, doctrinally, through the principle of *sola fides*, the primacy of personal faith, found their defence against subjectivism in the principle of *sola scriptura*, the absolute authority of scripture. By that authority, they legislated the spiritual meaning of all facts—historical, experiential, natural, and above all the fact of the self. Every believer had to find his own way to God, but his success depended upon his capacity, by grace, to purge his inherent discrete identity and transform himself into an *exemplum fidei*, a christic emblem of the faith. He received the right to interpret, that is, by first interpreting himself in accordance with a shared biblical absolute. The Romantics displaced the entire structure simply by reversing the equation. They subsumed the concept of *exemplum fidei* under the principle of *sola fides*. Rendering subjectivism the touchstone of faith, they freed the individual to choose (or invent) his identity, and then to impose his own patterns upon experience, history, nature, Christ Himself.

In this context, it seems all but inevitable that the Romantic should be overwhelmed by the anxiety of influence. His imitation of Christ was a process of duplicating himself, fashioning emblems of faith in his own image—a deific creation *ex imaginatione* in which *caritas* depended on autonomy, and plenitude was narcissism extended to infinity. Accordingly, the precursor poet assumed the role formerly held by the tenacious natural self. The Puritan's dilemma was that the way from the self necessarily led through the self; history was part of the dialectic through which he had to overcome history. Sometimes the struggle became so severe that he could resolve it only by abandoning hope, or else (like the proto-Romantics just mentioned) by leaping, self and all, directly to Christ. For the Romantic, the way to the self led through the precursor poet. Only the strongest did not abandon either poetry or the self.

No Romantic voiced the need to persist more eloquently than Emerson did; and yet in public at least he subsumed anxiety in an assured external design. The influence he felt came, buoyantly, from national prospects. When he considered the advantages of experience, he spoke not only of the apoclapyse of the mind, but, more largely, of national destiny. With all Romantics, he shifted the center of inspiration from the Bible to nature. But like his forebears he conflated secular and sacred identity, rendering eschatology a function of teleology. The grand sentiment, he wrote, "which the geography of America inevitably inspires," proves that "the truly Human . . . exists for us, shines in on us unawares. . . . One thing is plain for all men of common sense and common conscience, that here, here in America, is the home of man." What makes this plain is not the men *in* America, but man *as* America, and America not as a state of mind but, specifically and uniquely, as the New World landscape, the Bible's *littera-allegoria* become American *natura-prophetica*. It is crucial to Emerson's great essay on nature that "Prospects," its final section, speaks directly to "the American . . . in his own country," that it presents its Orphic "prophecy" through the medium of a New England bard, and that its famous closing appeal, "Build therefore your own world," returns us to the essay's opening invocation to "new lands, new men, new thoughts." The European symbolist interpreted creation as part of his *Bildungsbiographie*, since he himself, in Carlyle's words, was the "Messias of Nature." Emerson's model of spiritual growth gathered meaning by its proleptic identification with the New World *telos*, of which the land itself was the prophecy—fact and promise entwined.

In short, the self Emerson sought was not only his but America's, or rather, in a unique blend of hermeneutics and symbolism, his as America's, and therefore America's as his. Erich Auerbach has noted that the *figura* differs from the symbol in that it refers us to an a priori historical design. "As we proceed from the thing to the thing signified," warns William Whitaker, the great Reformed exegete, "*we* bring no new sense, but only bring to light what was before concealed [by God] in the sign." The symbol, on the other hand, emerges through the direct interaction between perceiver and fact. "Every truly creative individual," writes Schelling, "must create his mythology for himself." Emerson's method is notable for its resistance to this distinction. The New World was for him a Puritan-Romantic text, simultaneously a discovered *figura* of redemptive history and a creation of the symbolic imagination. He undertook a *figural* trial of the center which, proceeding from the thing to the thing signified, fulfilled the self by merging it with the national myth. Insofar as he echoed the European Romantics, he may be said to have posited a double standard for selfhood, American and un-American. Un-Americans he analyzed in static terms, either as indices to the "genius of humanity" (pure intellects like Plato, who transcended time and place), or else as forces of secular history (public leaders like Napoleon, who embodied middle class greed). From this perspective, Emerson had no use for temporal distinctions. "History is a vanishing allegory, and repeats itself to tediousness, a thousand and a million times." Only when he turned to the New World did the past take shape and purpose. Those who "complain of the flatness of American life," he wrote, "have no perception of its destiny. They are not Americans." As a true American, he never wearied of repeating the familiar story—how the continent was "kept in reserve from the intellectual races until they should grow to it," how the Bay planters had undertaken a "holy errand into the wilderness," and how Boston in particular, Winthrop's city on a hill, was "appointed in the destinies of nations to lead . . . civilization."

Emerson's sources for this emergent allegory of history were the writings of the early colonists. He acknowledged them proudly, as a spiritual tribute. Constituting as they did "a bridge between the . . . Hebrew epoch, & our own," the Puritans, he declared, proved that "the Supreme Being exalts the history of this people." His son tells us that he "often spoke of a wish to write the story of Calvinism in New England," in order to commemorate the climactic "triumphs of humanity." Emerson's project is outlined in his essays from the 1830's through the Civil War. "The new is only the seed of the old," he wrote in 1841. "What is this abolition and non-resistance . . . but a continuation of Puritanism. . . ?" In 1863, after non-resistance had given way to armed conflict, he declared the country to be "in the midst of a great Revolution, still enacting the sentiment of the Puritans, and the dreams of young people thirty years ago." The sacred light that "brought the fathers hither" was guiding "the visible church of the existing generation" towards an unprecedented "harvest" of the spirit. It would be irrelevant, in this context, to point out that the visible American church of 1863 was *not* a fulfillment of the New England Way. Emerson was obviously speaking of fathers and sons not in any historical sense, but as aspects of the American idea as this made itself manifest in his thought. Like Mather's, his filiopietism is a self-celebrating summons to the future. "GOD WITH THE FATHERS, SO WITH US," he declares in his eulogy to Boston, and then adds: "Let us shame the fathers by superior virtue in the sons." As *figurae medietatis*, the sons labor to complete the fathers in a process of exodus, an organic exfoliation of personal and national divinity, whose essence is the Emersonian-American self.

Predictably, Emerson found the model of exodus in the Great Migration. His teleology requires, first, a clear sense of the past *as* the Old World. "Let the passion for America," he urges, "extract this tape-worm of Europe from the brains of our countrymen," and with it the stifling veneration of Europe's great men. "To us has been committed by Providence the higher and holier work of forming . . . true and entire men." All others, however high and holy, adumbrate the representative American who is "to prove what the human race can be"—the "exalted manhood" that has been decreed "The Fortune of the Republic." In 1833, after visiting Coleridge, Carlyle, and Wordsworth, Emerson recorded his sense of superiority to all of them and thanked God for bringing him to "the ship that steers westward." Milton may have been an obstacle to Coleridge's self-realization. Emerson thought that Milton—along with Homer, Virgil, Spenser, Swedenborg, Goethe—belonged to an outmoded "feudal school." "Not Shakespeare, not Plato . . . would do." They "call to us affectionately"—"But not all these, and all things else hear the trumpet, and must rush to judgment"; now, "America is a poem in our eyes."

The trumpet that Emerson heard required him—as the second major step in his teleology—to don the robes of a latter-day Nehemiah or John the Baptist. Over and again in his essays and journals, he heralds the New World messiah who will mirror "our incomparable materials." America's "urgent claims on her children . . . yet are all unanswered." "Where are the American writers" who are to solve "the great questions affecting our spiritual nature," where the philosophers and politicians who would adequately express this "country of . . . vast designs and expectations"? Emerson posed these challenges in his early and middle career. In 1868, at the age of sixty-five, after Whitman and Thoreau had in some measure at least answered his call—after

Lincoln, Daniel Webster (until 1850), and John Brown had each shown himself a "true representative of this continent," a blend of Revolutionary ardor with the "perfect Puritan faith"—even at sixty-five, Emerson was still seeking the spokesman for the "new era," and still reassuring his audiences that "he shall be found." Since "America is essentially great and *must* produce great men," he explained, "we shall yet have an American genius."

He expressed his faith most fully in "The American Scholar." He calls the essay "one more chapter" in a continuing "biography"—in effect, a prophetic biography of the American self as scholar. It is also, of course, an outline of Emerson's private aspirations. Indeed, several critics have argued that the Scholar is the protagonist of an unwritten *Prelude*. If so, the essay provides a sweeping contrast between American and European Romanticism. Wordsworth hopes to reconstitute in himself all that had been divided, and so must deal with the specifics of his personal and historical condition. Emerson can bypass such considerations because he bears witness to the rising glory of America. Insofar as he projects himself in his hero, he recasts Romantic autobiography into auto-American-biography, reveals himself as harbinger of the nation intended "by all prophecy, by all preparation . . . to fill the postponed expectation of the world." The myth of the primal One Man with which he begins is a Romantic commonplace. Emerson absorbs the One Man, as the "exponent of a vaster mind and will," into the Sun of Righteousness advancing across the continental dial. For the European Romantic, the Sun of Righteousness is his own conquering imagination; *Urzeit* and *Endzeit* embrace in self-discovery: "We behold as one," cries Los, Blake's archetypal poet, "As One Man all the Universal Family; and that One Man/ We call Jesus the Christ."

Blake's concept of Jesus points to the distinction I would make. It goes without saying that not all European Romantics asserted a comprehensive selfhood. Many believed they could achieve that only in infinite approximation; others were content to await some reintegrated and perfected exemplar of the new world of the mind. But as their very terms indicate, the ideal centered upon the self-determining, all-embracing *individual*. In these terms also, as Meyer Abrams has shown, the Romantics conceived of historical progression. They believed that humanity was circling "from the One back to the One," in a process of "self-education" that applied equally to mankind and to each "reflective" person. Despite their faith in the future, they were compelled by their commitment to the organic self to identify, as prophets, with the Jesus of the gospels, the model of the completed life. For all his commitment to the God within, Emerson's faith in America compelled him to find his model of organic selfhood in the coming Son of Man. He wished not to become Jesus the Christ but to fulfill Him. The Nazarene, according to "The Divinity School Address," serves us as one of many "noble provocations." He is part of a procession of "divine bards" that has prepared the way for a "new revelation," by a "newborn bard of the Spirit," through whom "America shall introduce a pure religion." From this vantage point Emerson summarized the history of modern theology: "Calvinism rushes to be Unitarianism, and Unitarianism rushes to be pure Theism"; the scriptures contain "immortal sentences; but they have no equal integrity; are fragmentary; are not shown in their order to the intellect. I look for the new Teacher."

The patriotic European Romantic looked in a different direction. The Germans based their mystique of the *Volksgeist* on popular epic and legend; their sense of destiny led them back to the origins of the race, to cultural antiquities. Emerson, like Mather, interpreted the national past through the double focus of prophecies accomplished and prophecies unfolding. In this respect he was perhaps closer to the English Romantics, who resurrected Milton's dream of national election (though they were far enough removed from their Puritan source to center their hopes on the French Revolution). But like Milton they distinguished, ultimately, between personal and national identity—christic and secular selfhood—and accordingly they reenacted the drama of political commitment, disillusionment, and retreat to the kingdom within. By 1837, when Emerson wrote "The American Scholar," their high argument was a revolution of *consciousness*. Blake's Albion symbolizes spiritual wholeness. The "Characters of the great Apocalypse," writes Wordsworth, are "types and symbols of Eternity." When Shelley has Young Atlantis speak the final chorus of *Hellas*—"The world's great age begins anew"—he is saying not that the United States will fulfill history, but that "Freedom belongs to Thought." As a prophetic company, these poets had no country. As English nature poets, their allegiance was to the countryside, the specifics of rural life and landscape, the regenerative cycle of the seasons. As citizens, their country, as Milton said after the Restoration, was wherever it is well with one.

Emerson sustained his faith not because the American Revolution was more successful than the French, but because his vision annihilated division. The rhetoric he inherited enabled him to dissolve the differences between history and self—as well as between the different functions of the self (civic, natural, prophetic)—and so to overcome political disenchantment by revealing himself the representative American. Significantly, he conceived his essays on nature, the scholar, and the new religious teacher at the height of what he termed the "emphatic and universal calamity" of the Jacksonian era. The 1828 election of Andrew Jackson was hailed as a spectacular triumph of the young democracy. His re-election in 1832 seemed to Emerson to undermine the very purpose of the Revolution; and the crash of 1837 convinced Emerson that society had "played out its last stake." But with the latter-day theocrats he found that his rhetoric blossomed in adversity. Confronted with a "barbaric" present, he reread the "whole past . . . in its infinite scope," and declared: "Let me begin anew!" His method of self-renewal consisted in investing the meaning of America in himself. God's angel is named freedom, he tells us in a review of the Great Migration. He pronounces his discoveries in thought in the same apocalyptic tone with which he has God say: "Lo! I uncover the land/ Which I hid of old time in the West." To the Romantic notion that "there is no history, only biography," Emerson added two crucial, and crucially related, stipulations: first, that "all biography is autobiography," and second, that "the American idea" concerns neither "caucuses nor congress, neither . . . presidents nor cabinet-ministers, nor . . . such as would make of America another Europe"; it belongs to "the purest minds" only, "and yet it is the only true" idea.

Emerson's conflation of the private with the national ideal characterizes the writings of most of the American Romantics, including the most belligerently anti-nationalistic among them. It is clear, for example, that Thoreau saw America as the golden West of the imagination. It is no less clear that, even at times of active disobedience, he identified the actual movement of the country with the redemptive story of mankind. And it is central to his meaning that we *not* choose between these disparate personal and historical commitments. Dante's new life leads him out of the world's dark forest; Teufelsdröckh's leads him back to the City of Man, but as an alien and a wanderer, circumambulating "the terraqueous Globe." *Sartor Resartus* insists that we distinguish the clothes from the soul, history from the kingdom, modern life from the Everlasting Yea. Thoreau insists upon his clothes, his locale, his life in the woods, as emblems of the American spirit. He does not walk anywhere, but *westward*. His "new country" mode—migrant, "manly," free-enterprising—evokes the frontier dream even as it mocks the Franklinesque Way to Wealth. Mather's Winthrop is an American who has made himself a cornerstone of the New World Jerusalem, and therefore part of the author's figural autobiography. *Walden* is the symbolic autobiography of the self as "the only true America." The bridge between these works is Emerson the prophet, who compensates for political failure by collapsing history, biography, and autobiography into "the American idea"—by creating himself, figurally, in the image of the New World, even as he internalizes the American experience, symbolically, as a Romantic journey of the soul.

One result of this outlook is the difference between the European and the American cult of genius. Perhaps the most misleading cliché in recent criticism is that our major literature through Emerson is antinomian. The Puritans, we recall, banished Anne Hutchinson because she set her private revelation above the public errand. The controversy foreshadows the fundamentally opposed meanings of greatness in Carlyle and Emerson. Carlyle's hero stands sufficient in himself, a titan born to master the multitude. He is the Frankenstein's monster of left-wing Protestantism, part of a latter-day antinomian brotherhood that includes Shaw's Superman and Ibsen's Master-builder; Nietzsche's Zarathustra, that "terrible teacher of the great contempt"; Byron's exiled saint, whose immortal mind "makes itself/ Requital for its good or evil thoughts." In contrast to all of these, Emerson posed the severely ethical code of the true American. European geniuses, he complained, "have an undisguised . . . contempt for common virtue standing on common principles." Accordingly, he reminded himself in his journals to "beware of Antinomianism," and declared in public that he had undertaken a battle against "mere antinomianism," in the interests of turning society towards the higher laws of chastity, simplicity, spiritual and intellectual awareness. "There was never a country in the world," he felt sure, "which could so easily exhibit this heroism as ours."

Of course, Emerson never denounced antinomianism with the old Puritan vehemence. Once or twice he spoke of it with a condescending admiration, as a "vein of folly" that helps the enthusiast reach "the people," and often enough we feel a powerful antinomian impulse in the absolutism of his claims. Nonetheless, his concept of greatness denies the tenets of antinomianism, in any meaningful sense of the term. More accurately, his teleology redefines his antinomian impulse, somewhat in the manner of Mather, as the revelation of the American Way. If Emerson's hero differs from the chauvinist by his Romantic self-reliance, he differs equally from the Romantic antinomian by his reliance on a national goal. He speaks not to the fit few, wherever they are, but to Young America. His natural habitat is not the sublime, anywhere, but the New World. "The land," writes Emerson, "is the appointed remedy for whatever is false and fantastic in our culture. The land, with its sanative influences, is to repair the errors of a scholastic and traditional education." This might be Nehemiah addressing his people in captivity, except that the land would then evoke the ancient claims of Israel. Or it might be Luther announcing the doctrine of *sola scriptura*, except that he would substitute the Bible for nature. Or again, it might be Wordsworth speaking of his home at Grasmere, except that he would apply its "sanative influences" to the kingdom within, as nourishment for the egotistical sublime.

Emerson combines all these themes and transmutes them in the image of America. His emphasis on nature sustains his myth of the new holy land; the influences he feels counteract (even as they complete) the traditions of the Old World; and the regeneration he promises pertains to a "truly Human" nation yet to be formed. "Greatness appeals to the future," he explains in "Self-Reliance" and other essays.

> It is [therefore] for want of self-culture that the superstition of Travelling, whose idols are Italy, England, Egypt, retains its fascination for all educated

Americans. The force of character is cumulative. All the foregone days of virtue work their health into this. They shed a united light on the advancing actor. The continent we inhabit is to be [our] physic and food; the native but hidden graces of the landscape [are] intruding a new element into the national mind. Without looking then to these extraordinary social influences which are now acting in precisely this direction, but only at what is inevitably doing around us, I think we must regard the land as the sanative influence, which promises to disclose new virtues for ages to come. Realize that this country, the last found, is the great charity of God to the human race. Accept the place the divine providence has found for you, the connection of events, transcendent destiny; and [become] guides, redeemers, and benefactors, obeying the Almighty effort.

Emerson's exhortation to greatness speaks directly to the paradox of a literature devoted at once to the exaltation of the individual and the search for a perfect community. Self-reliance builds upon both these extremes. It is the consummate expression of a culture which places an immense premium on independence while denouncing all forms of eccentricity and elitism. The denunciation, as Emerson indicates, is less a demand for conformity than a gesture against antinomianism. Anne Hutchinson's self-reliance, like Wordsworth's, Byron's, Carlyle's, and Nietzsche's, locates the divine center in the individual. The self-reliant American is by definition the national benefactor as guide and prophet. Or prophetess, in the case of Hester Prynne, Hawthorne's "living sermon" against the "haughty" and "carnal" Mrs. Hutchinson. To some extent, the "sermon" follows the homiletic tradition of the biblical Esther, exemplum of sorrow, duty, and love, and figura of the Virgin Mary ("Hester la tres amé/ Ke sauve la genz jugé"). But primarily Hawthorne's argument depends on his heroine's achieving the strength to make herself the American Esther. As the "A" she wears expands from "Adulteress" to "Angelic," its significance leads forward from the Puritan "Utopia" to that "brighter period" when the country will fulfill its "high and glorious destiny." More than any other aspect of the novel, it is Hester's intermediate identity that makes The Scarlet Letter an American romance. She is neither merely a doomed Romantic Dark Lady at her worst nor wholly a world-redeeming Romantic savior at her best, but a figura medietatis, like Phoebe and Hilda, Endicott and the Gray Champion, a "pledge that New England's sons [and daughters] will vindicate their ancestry."

The prophetic quality of American Romantic heroism expresses the furthest reach of Mather's daring strategy in the Magnalia. By comparison, the European great man, for all his superiority to the mass, is sadly restricted. His very self-reliance implies an adversary Other, not only the great precursor but everyone to whom he is superior, everything from which he is alienated—history, the common laws, the representative men and women that constitute social normality. The American self has no such limits. It advances a mode of personal identity intended to embrace both the individual and society, without allowing either for Romantic-antinomian hero-worship or for the claims of social pluralism. It offers a compensatory *replacement* for (rather than an alternative to) the ugly course of actual events. Hester herself is an inadequate example of this kind of heroism. Because she is part of a larger, complex, highly ironic design, the problems of history assume a weight equal to, if not greater than, the solace she offers. This, at any rate, is the implicit view of those who admire her as an antinomian, and insofar as Hawthorne shared their admiration he upheld the Old World convention, through *Antigone* to *Anna Karenina*, that the great soul reveals itself by confronting social realities and recognizing its limitations.

No doubt *The Scarlet Letter* owes much of its force to the tension between this tragic recognition and the optimism of its New World vision. My point is not to explore the tension, but to note the antithesis. Hester's Emersonian role as prophetess, if I may call it so, militates against the prospect of tragedy because it obliterates contradiction. According to F.O. Matthiessen, the earliest example of Emersonian compensation is the *dictum* that "God is promoted by the worst. Don't despise even the . . . Andrew Jacksons." We can hardly avoid seeing in this formula the strategy by which Emerson, in his seminal essays of the 1830's—sensing his solitude amidst a "wide and wild madness"—proclaimed himself the keeper of the dream. Not by accident his phrases echo those in the *Magnalia*'s General Introduction, where Mather announces that "whether New-England may *live* any where else or no, it must *live* in our History!" Emerson's essays set forth a doctrine of self-reliance, at a crucial post-Revolutionary moment, that lends a new symbolic scope to the Puritan outlook. Geoffrey Hartman has observed that Romantic selfhood took the triadic form of nature, self-consciousness, and imagination. Its issue was not only a victory of the imagination but alternately, and often simultaneously, the "visionary despair" of the "sole self." The Emersonian triad is American nature, the American self, and American destiny, a triple tautology designed to obviate the anxieties both of self-consciousness and of the recalcitrant world.

I am speaking here of the mythic self, of course. All evidence indicates that an enormous private anxiety underlies the affirmation. The Emersonian night of the soul rarely occurs in the open, and never involves the struggle with an external foe. Publicly, the dawn is forever radiant with hope, the enterprise "only at the cock-crowing and the morning star," and the protagonist always young and always "here" (even when he shakes his white locks at the runaway western sun). The struggle takes place in private, in journals, in notebooks, sometimes in letters and *marginalia*. "If I were to write an honest diary," Emerson confided, "what should I say? Alas, that life has shallowness, halfness." And again, more pointedly still: "If . . . the world is not a dualism, is not a bipolar Unity, but is *two*, is Me and It, then is there Alien, the Unknown, and all we have believed & chanted out of our deep instinctive hope is a pretty dream." Stephen Whicher has recorded Emerson's long effort to retain his belief, at the expense of shutting out the tragic vision, which is to say at the expense of self-acceptance. Against the felt dichotomy between Me and It, "the yawning gulf between the ambition of man and his power of performance," against the "double consciousness . . . of the Understanding & of the Soul" which he termed "the worst feature of our biography," Emerson chanted the prohetic self, a "dualism" emptied of two-ness, of the alien or the unknown—personal and national identity twined in the bipolar unity of auto-American-biography.

The reasons for the suppression of the private life are not far to seek. For Emerson, the evolution of mankind confirms the national mission. American history validates the individual dream, and the autobiographical *exemplum* serves as national prophecy. Granted this correspondence, his Romantic journey outward from subjective to universal stands opposed to the very concept of the incomplete sole self. The personal state, no less than the public, is destiny manifest. "My estimate of America," Emerson confessed, like my "estimate of my mental means and resources, is all or nothing." To despair in oneself is a symbolic gesture of equal magnitude to the affirmation of the dream. It is to declare oneself a *figura* of what we might call the negative apocalypse. The great example here is Melville's Pierre, whose private discovery of ambiguity reverses the national myth embodied in his colonial and Revolutionary sires. "Out of some past Egypt," the narrator begins, "we have come to this New Canaan, and from this New Canaan, we press on to some [ultimate] Circassia." Much later he acknowledges that the Circassia his hero represents is not the New World chiliad, but doomsday. Pierre's deepest despair follows upon the recognition of what for the European Romantic would be a triumphant antinomian epiphany—that the great man stands above the mass, since "all the world does never gregariously advance to Truth, but only here and there some of its individuals do; and by advancing, leave the rest behind." The amplest expression of his despair is Vivia, the protagonist of Pierre's unfinished auto-American-biography—and epitome of Pierre's titanic effort to cap the "fame-column" of his forebears—who emerges, near the novel's end, as the "American Enceladus," a "foreboding and prophetic" symbol of the void.

One of Pierre-Vivia's precursors is Vivenza, the American utopia described in *Mardi* as "a young Messiah," "promising as the morning." Another is the "Master Genius" Melville hailed in his essay on Hawthorne: the "literary Shiloh of America" who would demonstrate "the supremacy

. . . which prophetically awaits us." "We want no American Miltons," Melville declares here, directly after praising Hawthorne for his Calvinism; the very comparison insults any "true American author. . . . Call him an American, and have done; for you cannot say a nobler thing of him." Melville's career is a rapid growth toward this vision, and then a long falling away. *Redburn* and *White-Jacket* transform the journey of the soul into a voyage of the redeemer nation, "homeward-bound" for the millennium; their language is unmistakably Emersonian. The disillusionment that begins in *Mardi* reaches its nadir in *Pierre*, with its profound and savage critique of Transcendentalism. Thereafter the tone varies from Swiftian irony to the modern grotesque, but the original dynamic is transparent throughout, even in the mock-heroic voice of Israel Potter ("prophetically styled Israel by the good Puritans, his parents") who plays a diminished Revolutionary Ishmael to a series of parodic "true Americans"; even in the comic apocalypse of *The Confidence Man*—whose anti-hero, in one of his guises, is Emerson himself—or the bitter detachment of *Clarel*: "To Terminus build Fanes!/ Columbus ended earth's romance:/ No New World to mankind remains."

Emerson, too, heard the call of Terminus, "god of bounds," saying "No more!"—as did Thoreau and Whitman. If America is *not* "the Great Western Pioneer whom the nations follow," Thoreau wrote near the end of his life, then "to what end does the world go on . . . ?" It was a rhetorical question, of course; and an emendation in an early draft of *Walden* suggests the basis for his persisting optimism. "I could tell a pitiful story respecting myself," he had written, "with a sufficient list of failures, and flow as humbly as the very gutters." His revision, a direct echo of Emerson, became the motto for the entire work: "I do not propose to write an ode to dejection, but to brag as lustily as chanticleer in the morning, standing on his roost, if only to wake my neighbours up." Whitman's mode of compensation is perhaps best seen in his technique of avoidance. No Romantic autobiography, unless we classify "The American Scholar" in that genre, tells us so little about the author as does *Song of Myself*. "Apart from the pulling and hauling stands what I am," Whitman declares; but at the slightest danger of scrutiny he *flees, vanishes, slips away, eludes*, orders us (and presumably himself) to *stand back*. The self which Whitman does sign—which he anatomizes in epic catalogues—belongs to the "divine average," the christic-prophetic *I Am* as the New World: "America isolated yet embodying all, what is it finally, except myself?"

When Whitman deleted "myself" from the equation, when he left America on its own, he found it difficult to sustain his optimism. "The people's crudeness, vice, caprices," he admitted, might prove the United States "the most tremendous failure of time." He found it just as difficult to sustain his faith in himself when he deleted "divine" from the average he claimed to express. Considered merely as a poet, he feared, he might turn out

to be "the most lamentable of failures . . . in the known history of literature."
"All or nothing," Emerson had declared: Whitman, like his Master, found
the all in the divine American selfhood he celebrated throughout his career,
and never more confidently than during the corruption that followed the
Civil War. He denounced the "cancerous" Grant Administration with the
righteous fury of a Jeremiah, and, in the same prophetic breath, he salvaged
the national ideal by "assuming to himself," as he put it, "all the attributes of
his country," en masse. As the American New Man, "acme of things
accomplish'd, and . . . encloser of things to be," he could absorb the cheaters
and the cheated with equanimity. He has heard the cries of anguish, he tells
us, suffered the outrage—and, being "typical of it all," he has beheld also its
last result. Proclaiming his good news from atop the "towering selfhood" of
"America Herself," he charts the vistas which from eternity "the Almighty
had spread before this nation"—the democratic *magnalia Americana*, "daz-
zling as the sun," to which the present is a morning star. And for our assurance
he offers us songs of himself. In his representative life "past and present have
interchanged"; his quintessentially American poems give form to "the deepest basic elements and loftiest final meanings of history and man, on which all
the superstructures of the future are permanently to rest."

The superstructures were secured by Emerson. Their foundation was
laid in seventeenth-century Massachusetts. Undoubtedly, Mather would
have scorned the theology of the young visionary who, a century after his
death, took his post as minister of Boston's Second Church. Undoubtedly,
too, Whitman differed in important ways from Emerson, as did all the major
writers of the American Renaissance. To posit a common design is not to
simplify the differences—nor to imply that they are less significant than the
similarities—but on the contrary, to provide a context for discrimination.
What is remarkable, from this perspective, is that Emerson's great contemporaries all learned from him to turn the Romantic mode into a vehicle of
"the American idea." The qualities that made Emerson the most influential
thinker of the period were those which reveal him to be the crucial figure in
the continuity of the culture. His achievement lay above all in his synthesis of
abiding national themes. At the heart of that synthesis is Emerson the
prophet, who in himself vindicates the sons' long labor to complete the
fathers. If he succeeded no better than Mather in changing the course of
events, he had the prophet's triumph of perpetuating the ideal. And if the
facts contradict the teleology he affirmed, which makes the New England
Way a foreshadowing, *figura medietatis*, of Transcendentalism, nonetheless he
carried the Puritan errand to new heights of eloquence and vision, in a
Romantic assertion of the self that fused autobiography and history in the
evolving spiritual biography of America.

JAMES M. COX

R. W. Emerson:
The Circles of the Eye

Emerson is doubtless as visible as he has ever been in the University. Before the advent of American literature as a "subject," he may have enjoyed a wider reputation as a venerated presence in the society at large. Before the existence of that venerated presence there had been Emerson, a venerable presence himself, no longer brooding over Concord but dying in it after the Civil War; before that, there had been Emerson the lecturer, spending himself on lyceum circuit forays as an apostle of culture; and before the lecturer there had been the original Emerson, the preacher and writer who had, sixty years after the Declaration of Independence, set out to liberate the imagination of himself and his countrymen. It is surprising how quickly we are led back through these generations of Emerson as object of study through Emerson as genteel cultural presence through Emerson as Concord Sage through Emerson as cultural circuit rider to Emerson the Seer—the veritable eye of God and Self and Nature. How quickly, in other words, we are led back to the transparent eyeball through which Emerson originally declared his vision.

That metaphor—or was it a symbol?—was in its way everything for Emerson. It was as much, let us say, as Whitman's outsetting assertion

> I celebrate myself,
> And what I assume you shall assume
> For every atom belonging to me as good belongs to you

was to be for Whitman. Having imagined so much, Emerson must have felt

---

that everything was possible. Of course everything *wasn't* possible; if so much hadn't flowed from Emerson's outsetting announcement, the whole passage in *Nature* might be little more than a fine instance of a young idealist's whistling in the dark. Yet even if nothing had followed, surely, were we to encounter the passage among the papers of an unknown theological aspirant, we would hear the ring of prophetic assurance in this announcement of a symbolic identity. Indeed, when the passage in its earliest form takes shape in Emerson's journal (March 19, 1835), the eyeball metaphor is significantly absent:

> As I walked in the woods I felt what I often feel, that nothing can befall me in life, no calamity, no disgrace (leaving me my eyes) to which Nature will not offer a sweet consolation. Standing on the bare ground with my head bathed by the blithe air, and uplifted into the infinite space, I become happy in my universal relations. The name of the nearest friend sounds then foreign and accidental. I am the heir of uncontained beauty and power. And if then I walk with a companion, he should speak from his Reason to my Reason; that is, both from God. To be brothers, to be acquaintances, master or servant, is then a trifle too insignificant for remembrance. O, keep this humor, (which in your life-time may not come to you twice,) as the apple of your eye. Set a lamp before it in your memory which shall never be extinguished.

Harold Bloom believes that the fear that "the humor may never return creates the extraordinary image of the transparent eyeball, an image impatient with all possibility of loss, indeed less an image than a promise of perpetual repetition." This is good as far as it goes, but it doesn't go far enough. For the fact is that in the passage in *Nature*, the metaphoric eyeball *displaces* the fear—which is quite different from saying that it is created by the fear. Moreover, the fear in the original passage, far from being what we might call an anxious fear, is really a commonsensical fear, laced as it is to the logic of probability. The ringing proclamation of the self as eyeball is an eloquent conclusion, a poetic hyperbole, which serves as a concrete seal of the experience that has just been described. It is a conversion of the "I" into the Eye, of the Self into the Seer.

Ever since Christopher Cranch caricatured Emerson as a monstrous eyeball on two spindly legs, there has been no shortage of persons ready to bear witness to outlandishness in Emerson's original conception. Even Jonathan Bishop, who has written one of the finest books on Emerson, feels that the metaphor represents a lapse in style from the fine description of the "bare common" which initiates the passage. Yet just as Bloom seems to want the original fear to take a higher intensity than the journal passage warrants, Bishop wants the "realistic" or "concrete" Emerson to prevail over the oracular and transcendental prophet. In its immediate context—the context of *Nature*—and in the context of Emerson's whole career, the metaphor of

Emerson as transparent eyeball at once released and defined Emerson's act of imagination. If the metaphor did not cause Emerson to be what he was, it nonetheless reveals to us, in the light of what he turned out to be, *who* he was—and the passage in which it first appears is therefore worth concentrated attention:

> Nature is a setting that fits equally well a comic or a mourning piece. In good health, the air is a cordial of incredible virtue. Crossing a bare common, in snow puddles, at twilight, under a clouded sky, without having in my thoughts any occurrence of special good fortune, I have enjoyed a perfect exhilaration. I am glad to the brink of fear. In the woods, too, a man casts off his years, as the snake his slough, and at what period soever of life, is always a child. In the woods is perpetual youth. Within these plantations of God, a decorum and sanctity reign, a perennial festival is dressed, and the guest sees not how he should tire of them in a thousand years. In the woods, we return to reason and faith. There I feel that nothing can befall me in life,—no disgrace, no calamity (leaving me my eyes), which nature cannot repair. Standing on the bare ground,—my head bathed by the blithe air and uplifted into infinite space,—all mean egotism vanishes. I become a transparent eyeball; I am nothing; I see all; the currents of the Universal Being circulate through me; I am part or parcel of God. The name of the nearest friend sounds then foreign and accidental: to be brothers, to be acquaintances, master or servant, is then a trifle and a disturbance. I am the lover of uncontained and immortal beauty. In the wilderness, I find something more dear and connate than in streets or villages. In the tranquil landscape, and especially in the distant line of the horizon, man beholds somewhat as beautiful as his own nature.

In its immediate context, the context of the paragraph in which it appears, the metaphor is the climax of the description of the writer's perception of Nature—that section of Nature which is itself entitled "Nature"— and is thus the "nature" of *Nature*. In one sense, the metaphor is the symbolic transformation of the subject, the writer, into an identity equivalent to the state of being, a heightened gladness to the brink of fear, which has been experienced on the twilit bare common. As equivalent, it is a metaphor in the traditional sense. Or we might, following Bloom, call it an image. But in another sense, it is an *action*, a declaration of a change from being into seeing. The metaphor instantaneously transforms being into seeing; if it does not annihilate personal consciousness, it causes the personal experience to vanish by virtue of the expansion and uplift of the essential self into infinite space: "I am nothing. I see all." Moreover, there is a paradoxical relation between the eyeball and the infinite space it occupies. Since the eyeball is transparent and cannot be seen—is in effect an invisible organizing film presumably containing the universe, through which and in which the currents of the Universal Being circulate—it should be coextensive with the infinite universe. Yet the eyeball metaphor is nonetheless concrete, an assertion of infinite existence in a definite image. That paradox was not something Emerson sought to realize as an aspect of style— he particularly disliked that characteristic of Thoreau's writing. Rather, it was an expression of the essential relation between language and Nature. It was the inevitable and miraculous necessity of a true—that is, a poetic— language to assert the radical relationship between thought and thing. That is why Emerson did not, at his best, use metaphor decoratively and why, in this crucial instance, he did not say he became *like* a transparent eyeball. The transforming power of metaphor is, for Emerson, the active spiritualizing power of language—it is the God acting as language—and Emerson's be- coming a transparent eyeball is his master metaphor. This transformation is a fatally idealizing process in which mean egotism becomes nothing, whereupon

> nothing can befall me in life. . . . The name of the nearest friend sounds then foreign and accidental: to be brothers, to be acquaintances, master or servant, is then a trifle and a disturbance.

Yet for all the idealizing in Emerson's act of vision, the metaphor keeps the vision from being totally subjective. It is subjective in the sense that the consciousness in the form of the eyeball in effect contains everything. Still, there *is* the metaphor, which carries Emerson outside himself. The mean ego has vanished in order for Nature to exist. To be sure, it is impossible to tell whether Eye or Nature comes first. In the sequence of the entire passage, Nature precedes the eye, though it is clear that, by becoming part or parcel of God, the Eye sees Nature—as if God passed through the Eye to create Nature. All three entities—God, Man, and Nature—clearly interpenetrate each other, and Emerson's logic throughout the essay wants to place them in an equal relationship. That is why both the argument and direction of the entire essay bend to embrace that equality; it is also why the initial eyeball metaphor is the instantaneous enactment of the whole idea of Nature. The metaphor is, after all, the image of the imagination seeing nature, and the essay is not only the elaboration but the result of that vision.

While Emerson's logic is equalizing, or attempting to equalize, God and Man and Nature, at the same time his rhetorical bias, his inheritance of traditional religious language, and his transformation via transcendence all combine to form a current of relentless idealization of Nature. Thus Emer- son's movement in the essay is from the "low" commodity of Nature up through aesthetic to moral and intellectual beauty, through language, through discipline and on to idealism. These terms constitute the very ladder of his aspirational vision. Yet however much Emerson's impulse is to idealize Nature, he has to reject idealism because it would degrade Nature into phenomena and thereby deny the existence of the very entity he has set out to redeem; it would, as he says late in the essay, "leave me in the splendid labyrinth of my perceptions to wander without end."

For that reason, Emerson moves from idealism to the realm of spirit, the active principle of idealism—what we might call thought in motion—which sends up and illuminates the Universe. Spirit is, of course, God—the Supreme Being which, according to Emerson, "puts forth Nature through Us." But Nature is, by virtue of the passage through us, like the human body, an inferior incarnation of God, a projection of God in the unconscious. Spirit is the impulse which organizes and gives direction and purpose to Nature; its equivalent in style is the imperative, hortatory, moral tone which characterizes Emerson's prose, inspiring him to radical metaphor but also constantly threatening to weaken the power in Nature which he seeks.

For Nature, that which the transparent eyeball at once sees and contains, must be, like the eye which sees it, radically there. And like the eye which sees it, the limits of nature are infinite; indeed, despite the solitary pastoral setting in which Emerson sees it, Nature really can include society. Though the solitude has the benignant aspects bestowed upon it by the equally benignant and idealized Nature, there is outside the perimeter of the eye the negative world of the vanished ego—the world which Emerson can, as the mood moves him, cast outside or inside nature. It is the world of talent rather than genius, convention rather than originality, the past rather than the present, the church rather than God, institutions rather than men—in a word, it is society rather than the essential self in Nature. It forms the negative but highly necessary background which affords Emerson an instantaneous perceptual dialectic, enabling him to pour positive energy into his charmed field of vision and thus dramatize the original power so necessary to keep the idealizing impulse invigorated.

So what we have in *Nature* is a declaration of independence not so much from society as in society—for it is society which surrounds Emerson. After all, it is a *bare common* from which Emerson soars into his new identity. Moreover, the bare common was not present in the journal entry. To be sure, Emerson allows himself free passage from bare common to Nature's woods in his movement toward his ultimate assertion. Even so, he clearly has that bare common much in mind when he says, at the very threshold of translating himself into a visionary, "Standing on the bare ground . . . all mean egotism vanishes."

Thus, in his first essay, however much Emerson sought to define Nature, he meant to possess the ground from which he could see society. This twilight walker is occupying the space at the center of the village, not to reject the village, not to reform it, as much as to envision it in the fullest sense of the word. For all the infinite space which Emerson occupies with his metaphor, he is still on that bare common, and his whole aim, located as he is at the center of society, is to free himself to become the center—to possess the *common* nature possessed by the village and make it something more than bare. The possession is not of course in terms of legal, material ownership—the village and town already own it materially—but in terms of a vision which will discover the force of Nature which exists not only on the bare common but also in the heart of the sleeping society. By being the veritable pupil of Nature, Emerson will be the true teacher of society. The bare common is therefore the crucial ground on which Emerson stands; to realize it is to recover the full meaning of Emerson's decision, at the outset of *Nature*, "to use the word [nature] in both senses;—in its common and in its philosophical import." The *common* sense of Nature is, as Emerson says, those essences unchanged by man, whereas all those constructions of man—houses, roads, canals, towns—fall under the heading of Art. By deliberately refusing to deny this common sense of Nature, even though it would *exclude* the bare common from the realm of the natural and place it in the realm of the artistic and social, Emerson means to subject the common sense of Nature as well as the bare common to full re-vision.

The whole argument of Emerson's first essay is thus rooted in the instantaneous act of the metaphor which precedes the argument. Jonathan Bishop in discussing Emerson's style wisely observes that Emerson knew that a man's metaphors mean what they say. Surely this one, as much as any Emerson ever imagined, bears witness to that observation. The initial metaphor foretells the conclusion of *Nature* in which Emerson says

> The problem of restoring to the world original and eternal beauty is solved by the redemption of the soul. The ruin or blank that we see in nature is in our own eye. The axis of vision is not coincident with the axis of things, and so they appear not transparent but opaque.

And he goes on to say that once we have integrated spirit and matter into their original unity then we will look at the world with new eyes. He even evokes his Orphic Poet to proclaim in the last sentences of *Nature*:

> As when the summer comes from the south the snow banks melt and the face of the earth becomes green before it, so shall the advancing spirit create its ornaments along its path, and carry with it the beauty it visits and the song which enchants it; it shall draw beautiful faces, warm hearts, wise discourse, and heroic acts, around its way, until Evil is no more seen. The kingdom of man over nature, which cometh not with observation—a dominion such as now is beyond his dream of God,—he shall enter without more wonder than the blind man feels who is gradually restored to perfect sight.

Though the poetic utterance gives us once again the metaphor of vision, it is nonetheless flaccid. The "as when . . . so shall" construction is far from the swift, spirited oracular language of the essay. Of course Emerson could say—really does say—that it is not himself but his Orphic Poet speaking, but that is an insufficient defense. If the Poet is Bronson Alcott, then why choose Alcott, if he can do no better than this? Besides, it isn't Alcott; it is Emerson, run beyond his true ending into weak vision and weak language. Here is indeed vapidity, and it occurs the moment Emerson enters a "heavenly" realm in which there is not the sharp resistance of those opaque things. In such a realm, Emerson is in the resistless air of spirit, and the world of Nature is always at the threshold of becoming a weakly poeticized prospect rather than a strongly imagined figure of spirit.

If we take Emerson, standing on the bare common, become an eye at the natural center of society to see and thereby recreate it, we have the essential Emerson—the Emerson of *Nature* imagined by himself at the outset of his career as the fixed center of the existent universe. He had his essential thought, as Kenneth Cameron has shown; he had a style to match his vision, a style in which metaphor (itself the visible presence, in language, of thought in the act of becoming image) at once preceded and made possible his argument; and he had his role, that of teacher and preacher to the townsmen he would instruct and exhort; finally he had his form, the essay, which through his eye was an experiment in vision—an urgent perception intent upon disclosing the unity of man and nature. Since Emerson was a writer, not an artist, his seeing perforce had to be saying. What Emerson sought in style was a rhythm and a decisiveness which would equal the perception he was proclaiming. Discursive argument was largely closed to him, for his initial position put him out of linear logic, a point Sherman Paul decisively made twenty years ago; his poetic, symbolic, or metaphoric identity—call it what we will—kept his language constantly charged with affect; his denial of time, in favor of circular repetition, drove him toward compression and epigrammatic execution of thought and away from expansion, discursiveness, exposition, or narrative, which he felt were enslaved to clarity, the mere light of the understanding.

His vision sought to pierce through the surface of Nature and Man and literally review the traditional terms, the essential generalizations which form the permanent structure of man in society. The very titles of his successive series of essays display his central concerns: History, Self-Reliance, Compensation, Spiritual Laws, Love, Friendship, Prudence, Heroism, the Over-Soul, Circles, Intellect, The Poet, Experience, Character, Manners, Gifts, Nature (not the original essay but a subsequent and quite subordinate attempt on the term), Politics, and Nominalist and Realist.

These are what I choose to call the Circles of the Eye. It is no more an accident that the one geometric form to which Emerson devotes an essay is the circle than that that essay should begin with the following sentences:

> The eye is the first circle; the horizon which it forms is the second; and throughout nature this primary figure is repeated without end. It is the highest emblem in the cipher of the world.

There is the Emersonian style at its finest—a strong, unqualified assertion, followed by another and yet another. The second two assertions are in one sense restatements of the first one, though they are just as clearly consequences of it. And the third is at once declarative and metaphoric. That word *cipher* does a world of work. For the cipher is of course a zero, an empty arithmetic circle which, placed at the right of, or following a number, increases its value tenfold. And it is also a coding, a symbolic reading, which discovers meaning. The sentences, sufficiently independent to be epigrammatic, create a momentary but decisive gap between each other, which the eye and ear of the reader and listener bridge with a responsive intellectual leap of energy. Moreover, the metaphoric third sentence is not illustrative, but equivalent, as if it were inevitably called forth. In a fine way, the metaphor is buried, or rooted in the very sense of the passage. It is, in other words, a third and final circle of the primary eye. How quickly all this is done, and how completely. Begin an essay this way, and how can you fail?

Well, you can fail even so, and Emerson sometimes does fail, though certainly not in this essay. It is one of his best—short, fierce, and utterly complete. The "I" of the author is fully converted into the reading eye of the reader. Emerson does not see for us but sees through, by means of us. The connections we have to make to discover the full sequence are by no means free association; they are the fated spatial silences between the sentences, instinct with implicit energy—dots, we might say, which when connected form the circle of the essay. Emerson ends on the following note:

> The one thing which we seek with insatiable desire is to forget ourselves, to be surprised out of our propriety, to lose our sempiternal memory and to do something without knowing how or why; in short to draw a new circle. Nothing great was ever achieved without enthusiasm. The way of life is wonderful; it is by abandonment. The great moments of history are the facilities of performance through the strength of ideas, as the works of genius and religion. "A man," said Oliver Cromwell, "never rises so high as when he knows not whither he is going." Dreams and drunkenness, the use of opium and alcohol are the semblance and counterfeit of this oracular genius, and hence their dangerous attraction for men. For the like reason they ask the aid of wild passions, as in gaming and war, to ape in some manner these flames and generosities of the heart.

I have not quoted the passage for the presence of a final circle in it, though it is good to see Emerson strongly return to his primary figure. Nor is it quoted for possessing the utterly typical absolute assertion: "Nothing great was ever achieved without enthusiasm." That is an example of the Emersonian sentiment of assurance executed as epigram; yet for all its absoluteness, it is nonetheless the expression of a mood, and Emerson has already said in this very essay that "our moods do not believe in each other." Emerson knows quite well outside the circle of this essay that something great might be achieved without enthusiasm. But that would be another circle—possibly the circle of Prudence, or Wealth, or Manners, or Politics.

No, not for these is the passage exquisite, but for the rare, and in its movement, the daring ending—the abrupt illumination of Cromwell's somewhat grandiose utterance in terms of drunkenness, opium, and alcohol. Here is a swift and pungent explanation of rankly sensual behavior under the aegis of the idealized statement. The abruptness, which is to say the instantaneous decision, of the move sends life and meaning in both directions. For Cromwell's statement depicts a stage of drunkenness—a not knowing where one is going—just as the state of actual drunkenness is also some effort to get out of oneself. Such a fine blunt move seems to me a genuine realization of Emerson's contention at the outset of the passage that "we seek with an insatiable desire . . . to be surprised out of our propriety." The sudden juxtaposition of the two activities; the sequence, which is to say the direction, from high to low; and the relationship, so much of which is left implicit or silent in the momentary space between the sentences—all combine to charge the field.

These sentences of Emerson are like atoms; they are striving to be worlds of their own; they bear out again and again in the action of their form his endless plea for the present to prevail over the past, and are thus repeatedly executing his central theme, just as their self-containment repeats his central figure. The high mind—even the high-mindedness—of Emerson is always present, even dominant; it is the resonance of his tone. But its swift reach into the so-called material and instinctual world is richly audacious. These descents of the spirit are as fraught with ecstasy as any ascent Emerson could make. They not only promise but recover a wildness of spirit. Such conversions of spirit to Nature are the perceptions of the transparent eye.

The Emersonian sentence, charged with its atomic independent impulse—he once referred to his sentences as infinitely repellent particles—is the analogue for the essay which struggles to contain it. For the essays are the larger self-contained circles which stand by themselves, yet are bound to each other by the larger silent spaces between them. In a way they are all repetitions of *Nature*, for Emerson is an alarmingly repetitive writer. And these silent spaces between the essays are the vanished mean ego—the first-person pronoun of Emerson—which has become the charged space wherein we connect or leap the gap from essay to essay. We might even say

that the vanished mean ego, the *biography* of Emerson, which has literally
dissolved into the spaces between the intense intuitional moments of vision
which literally are the essays, is admonished into silence by the voice of
vision, the sayings of the seer. After all, Emerson's essays are self-directions as
much as they are directions to an audience. No, not quite as much, for the
hortatory tone of the preacher attempting to lift us out of ourselves represents
a balance of admonition flowing outward in the form of address.

    This vision of the essays as circles of the central eye is of course
nothing but a metaphor—yet I mean for it to have consequences.

    First of all, the repeated conversion of the "I" into the Eye cannot be
taken lightly. There is enormous psychological cost in such an idealizing
process. If the "I" and all the personalities which existed around Emerson in
time and place—his parents, his brothers, his wives, his children—are not
annihilated, they are threatened with consumption by the vision. There is a
sense in which Emerson literally feeds off the death of those around him.
Before he wrote *Nature* he had already lost two brothers and a first wife, all
victims of tuberculosis, and he himself hovered at the threshold of consumption during his early life. Breath, which is our literal physical experience of
the spirit of life, was thus crucial, even desperate, to Emerson; hence the
astonishing literal force in his use of the verbs *inspire, transpire, conspire,
expire, aspire.* There is, for example, a felt relation between his bursts of
inspiration and the death of his first wife. If he does not exult in her death,
there is nonetheless an influx of energy consequent on her passing—an
imaginative energy boldly evident in the journal. Her spiritualization, which
Emerson's traditional religious attitude embraces, makes her a part of the air
he breathes. And the clear despair which he records on the loss of his brother
Charles is but a prelude to the strong assertion of *Nature.* Getting out of the
"I," the personal pronoun, and getting over the deaths of loved ones is no
tired or traditional "spiritual" vision for Emerson precisely because it is a
literal breathing in, or inspiration, of the death of life.

    Moreover, there is in Emerson's bold assertions of self-confidence a
threat to everyone around him. In the face of prior disasters and griefs, even if
we grant that his second marriage and the birth of a son may have given him
needed assurance for launching himself as a writer, Emerson's assertion of an
idealized metaphoric self which, short of blindness, would be impervious to
any evil, has about it a ferocious element of provocation. If Margaret Fuller
had proclaimed her acceptance of the Universe, Emerson had both stared and
dared it to its face. Implicit in his contention that no evil can befall him in his
form of transparent eyeball is a challenge to the Universe to do what it will,
since he can see by himself. How glad we should be that he at least had the
grace and wit and common sense to exempt his eyes, both of them, from his

all but absolute act of pride! Looking at the statement from another point of view, we could say that if we had been little Waldo and had been precocious enough, we would have wished to say before we were five years old, "Father, *why* did you say such a thing?" For if Emerson was austerely coming out of evil, he was at the same time asking for more. It would be the fuel for his flame. How have pride and not be stricken? And no amount of transforming pride into obedience can quite charm Emerson's circle unless rude Nature and violent spirit are surging within it. Otherwise, it will be just a charming circle in the form of a decorative metaphor.

There is thus, I think, in Emerson's fine sentences early in *Nature*, an implicit sentence of death for little Waldo. And indeed, can we, looking at Emerson's life, wish that Waldo had lived? Can we really imagine he would have grown up to be a flaming independent imagination? Emerson's other children hardly fared well. There was Ellen Tucker Emerson, named for the dead first wife as if she were to be an admonition to Lydia (who had herself suffered a renaming as Lydian to get her out of the unfortunate New England vernacular pronunciation), who took care of the Concord Sage in his declining years. There was Edith Emerson, whose husband, W.H. Forbes, helped Emerson with his finances and securities. And finally there was Edward Waldo Emerson, inheritor of the sickly Emersonian constitution who couldn't go to the Civil War—was indeed actively denied his wish to go by his concerned parents—and who was left to edit Mr. Emerson's journals. He did creditable work, I think we could say, but every line of his prose affirms his role as undertaker of the body of Emerson's work. Whatever vengeance was in the children lay in building a sepulchre of the father. The true children of Emerson were elsewhere. Born of the seeds of language, Thoreau and Whitman, Emily Dickinson and Robert Frost (and Frank Lloyd Wright and Charles Ives too), were wild, recalcitrant embodiments of the Emersonian spirit, flaming by the ponds and in the cities, villages, and fields of the republic.

I am not higgling about Emerson's failure to be a good parent—whoso would higgle, let him dare to have children and know what it is to possess them. I simply wish to welcome the fate which was in Emerson's freedom, the death in his life. Already in *Nature* he had said at the end of the section on discipline (which precedes the section on idealism):

> When much intercourse with a friend has supplied us with a standard of excellence, and has increased our respect for the resources of God who thus sends a real person to outgo our ideal; when he has, moreover, become an object of thought, and whilst his character retains all its unconscious effect, is converted in the mind into solid and sweet wisdom,—it is a sign to us that his office is closing, and he is commonly withdrawn from our sight in a short time.

Biographically considered, that passage clearly refers to Charles, who had just died. But it just as clearly looks forward to the passage in "Experience," which deals with the death of Waldo. Logically considered, the passage unremittingly defines the terms of the transparent eyeball. Seeing a friend is at once a conversion of life into thought, a *taking* of life. And if such seeing is to continue, more life is going to have to be taken. To be sure, in the sweet dialectic of transcendence, thought has preceded life anyway and can be declared as the more intense conception and conclusion of life. Yet Emerson's prose is never as sweet as it may look. He himself wanted bite and sting and decision in prose.

This vision of Emerson's Eye in relation to his personal life may seem appalling, yet I think much of the writing on Emerson discloses attitudes which could well be considered expressions of precisely this vision held *unconsciously*. There is, for example, a distinct wish expressed by critics of Emerson that his personal life should have been more of a trial of his ideas than it actually was. Thus there is even a downright resentment about his "success," his too serene middle years. Similarly, there is, on the part of those who praise Emerson, a slight lament that he lost something of his early fire when his house became warm and comfortable.

All of which brings me to the second consequence of seeing Emerson's essays as the circles of his Eye. For all the change which Emerson celebrated—remember that the currents of the Universal Being are constantly circulating through the transparent eyeball—the Eye is just as constantly fixed. Though Emerson can look on the faces of Nature, the tyrannous Unity must assert itself and be asserted again and again. I do not see Emerson as "developing" or "progressing" or "declining." Of course he declined into old age; of course he finally lost his energy (he had always maintained that he had never been given enough to begin with); but he lived long enough as a writer to make it necessary for those who posit a decline to bury him prematurely in order to confirm their vision.

Nor do those who see Emerson as somehow discovering more reality than he first bargained for fare much better. If the one party tends to see Emerson as a revolutionary who slumped into society, the second tends to see him as an emerging Realist whose initial dream was superseded by experience. Stephen Whicher, who regretted a bit too much the absence of evil in Emerson, wishes to rescue the later Emerson, the Emerson who faced the hate of his earlier freedom. Jonathan Bishop, on the other hand, finds the early Emerson sounding the bolder note and receding through the crises of Waldo's death into the practical world of *The Conduct of Life*. And now Quentin Anderson appears to applaud Bishop's evaluation of the early Emerson as the more revolutionary, but to assert that the revolution was a mistake. Anderson has seen the student riots, the Vietnam War, the imperial American expansion into Asia, and, implicitly as well as explicitly relating this recent history to the Emersonian imagination, he deplores the imperial Emersonian self, which he sees as what he calls a "coming out of culture."

There is no doubt that the early Emerson is central; Emerson was in effect all there at the beginning and all that he was to do was implicit in the metaphoric identity he proclaimed for himself. Of course he had experience; of course he saw things in life which he could not quite have foreseen at the outset. But visions of Emerson's career in terms of crises and turning points, in ups and downs, in directions from revolution to compromise or from idealism to realism have their own distortion. That there was entropy of energy I am delighted to acknowledge, but never the kind of entropy which could not produce the old flame from the slow decay.

Indeed, locating Emerson's revolutionary power in his early years causes Anderson to distort the image of the outsetting Emerson. Emerson never was so revolutionary as Anderson wishes to have him. He had from the very beginning a deeply conservative quality. He was right on that bare common in the center of village culture. It was the eccentric Thoreau who occupied the ground at the edge of the village. If Emerson had revolted against the church, it was nonetheless a one-man revolt which Emerson never wanted vulgarized into a movement. Thus he was not asking the divinity students to leave the church but to be themselves within it and thereby renew it. Emerson is always aware that society exists; he very much wants it to exist; he has no real doubt that it will continue to exist; he is very much aware that the very isolate position he assumes in relation to it is just that—in *relation* to it, and therefore in a deep way, deep enough to be rooted in instinctual consciousness, dependent upon society as an entity all but equal to whatever self he can ever assert.

It is true that he is always determined to affirm the self over society, but the affirmation always has the ring of exhortation. The appeal in Emerson's imperatives is a recognition that the balance of power is on society's side and must always be proclaimed for the self precisely because it has been so fatally surrendered. There is from the beginning a margin of safety on the bare common which has somehow been secured by law and is therefore a sanctuary, a new church to move into. Thus Emerson is calling to us to rely on ourselves out of a profound recognition that we will not and have not; the ringing of his bell is a reminder of what we could but will probably never be. What keeps Emerson strongly present beneath the ringing of that bell is his solid grasp of the fate—the persistent and repeated form—of society. By getting out of history, Emerson wants to see the external stability of change almost as much as he wants to accomplish the change of getting out. The self he proclaims has about it no small measure of tradition; it is a recovery as well as a departure.

Emerson's very language embraces the traditional aspect of speech. He does not want a new language so much as he wants a renewal of the existing language. He loves proverbs and is delighted to see new experience conform to the traditional, proverbial, common wisdom. If he earnestly desires to lodge his own proverbs in the language, he nonetheless knows that he has chosen the proverb and the epigram as the desired form into which to cast himself. That is an inextricable aspect of his aphoristic and oracular style. For all his ringing insistence that man is innocent instead of originally sinful, Emerson wants the innocent self to be a conscience—a new conscience to be sure, but withal a conscience. Hence the admonitory aspect of his essays. Emerson's blessed encouragement is, as everyone knows who reads him, both accompanied by and charged with admonition. His uplift is not without squelch. Consciousness is forever at the threshold of becoming conscience. The teacher is always about to be the preacher; the lecture or the essay is never far from being the sermon. The Emersonian sentence is sufficiently instinct with judgment to carry conviction.

Emerson's whole drive toward unity, toward circularity, illustrates this conservative element in his imagination. For the circle, however much it may be impelled to expand, is seeking both to include and to contain all of experience rather than to reject and destroy it. The two eyes which become one in transparent sight integrate rather than divide the field of vision. The very fact that vision is Emerson's metaphor of thought makes him know the aspect of illusion which dwells in the realm of what he would call reality. If it is inevitable that he should have written an essay on circles it is equally inevitable that he should have written one on illusions. What is great about Emerson is his willingness to expose and thereby anticipate the illusoriness of his own thought. The bullet-like force of his self-relying sentences always threatens to put the reality of the preceding sentence in jeopardy.

There is a deep impulse in Emerson to declare everything as an illusion—everything. The question which then stands up to this hard Yankee pressure is "What is the most powerful illusion?" The answer is, I think, the central self, that transparent eye of consciousness. Yet because even it is ultimate vision it has an element of illusion in it—which is far different from saying that it is necessarily unreal or illusory. Surely Emerson's repeated and memorable admonition to *trust* the self betrays in its very terminology the appeal at the heart of the imperative. The appeal is for every man to believe in and assent to those momentary flashes in experience when issues appear clear, when emotion is translated into adequate action, when thought seems the very double of the body. The motion of the body is, when it moves instinctively beneath the sway of mind, the double of the will and is our primary experience of Nature instinct with thought.

This illusion of a central self is so persistent that Emerson is willing to risk all on its being a reality. And so the central self is the anchor of essays so apparently disparate as "Self-Reliance," "Experience," and "Fate." "Self-Reliance" is a buoyant call to trust those intuitional moments when perception—which for Emerson is instantaneous thought—yields total presence, blotting out the image of the self in relation to society (which is conformity) and the image of the self in relation to past experience (which is consistency). "Experience," on the other hand, instead of exhorting to self-trust, rushes headlong through the categories of perception, which Emerson denominates Illusion, Temperament, Succession, Surface, Surprise, Reality, and Subjectiveness. These are the lords of life, the very illusions by means of which man creates his existence. Indeed *experience* is, as Emerson sees it in what seems to me the most exhilarating of all his essays, the swift exposure of these dominant categories of perception—what we rely on as our ideas of life—as illusions. These forms of perception are the means by which we temporarily fix Nature only to see it burst into another life. Without the fix, the *idea* of Nature or Life, we cannot see it, yet the moment form gives our vision identity, Nature dances into life again. There is nothing left at the last—after the successive disillusions—but the sanity of the self which creates the illusory lords of life. Thus, if "Self-Reliance" was a ringing exhortation to trust the self, "Experience" turns out to disclose that, after the last disillusion of experience, there is nothing else to rely on *but* the self, of which Emerson bravely says: "We must hold hard to this poverty, however scandalous, and by more repeated self-recoveries, after the sallies of action, possess our axis more firmly." That axis is surely the volatile line relating Experience to Self-Reliance, and the two essays are really its poles. If the one is positive and the other negative, they are the alternations of a single current of energy. And surely "Fate," far from being a change in Emerson's central philosophy, is a change in perspective. Once Fate is seen—and Emerson burns with all his original energy as he sees it—then Self-Reliance is once more possible. For the man who can humbly accept his destiny can even recklessly obey his impulses.

To believe in the self enables a person to see society more than it makes him wish to reject or even reform it. Every person must see it by and for himself; otherwise he merely joins a movement and is engulfed by a party of society. And the seeing is likely to be as brief as it is sure—as brief as a sentence or an essay. The solitary intensity of vision predicates a stubborn, conservative, persistent society which will perennially occupy the interstices between the moments of intuition.

Is Emerson then a conservative? Not on my life. After all the admonition, the exhortation, the relentless and even fearful idealization, there is a buoyant hope in Emerson—and buoyant not because it is hope but because it is shown by Emerson to be a state of mind which practically exists in every waking day—as near as the air we breathe. Of course Emerson can be weak and distant—not merely in his late years but in his early ones too. He is, as John Jay Chapman astutely remarked, weak on the fine arts. His overwhelming belief in language prevented him from being able to see visually. Seeing is really always saying in Emerson; perception is always thought. And if Emerson is not weak on love, he is certainly hard on it. Because he sees every self as a circle, two selves can touch at only one point. The more intense the point of contact, the more appetency and hunger which must be aroused at other points along the vast perimeters of the two selves. Thus after all is given to love and particularly when all is given, the self can and must come into its own. Such a view goes hard with romance, with narrative, with the novel. And though Emerson could write on the Comic (how pleasantly surprising that he made the attempt) he hasn't much of a sense of humor. He has no patience with anyone who giggles, and says so in a way to chill the playful heart. He can, after a long session of reading him, seem to have enough moral seriousness about him to make a reader, or this one at least, embrace Mark Twain's contention that the Moral Sense makes us the lowest rather than the highest creatures in God's Kingdom of Nature.

Yet count over his weaknesses as we will—count them over with savage delight—Emerson still sees us, really makes us possible. He was, after all, a prophet, not in predicting the future but in making it happen. He called for a scholar and there was Thoreau. He called for a poet and there was Whitman. Reading Emerson at his best is always a reminder as well as a recognition that I am. I do not know his work well enough. I have not read it all. I have not devoted myself long enough or hard enough to the task of understanding him. But there he is to tell me that there are better things to do than to read him, that I have read enough of him, that I am as good as he is, that I too, at this instant, shall prevail. And all in a voice at once exacting and exhilarating, a voice which, when heard, is proof as well as prompting of my inmost character. Here is no coming out of culture, but a making culture possible.

DAVID PORTER

The Muse Has a Deeper Secret

The death of young Waldo was only the most tragic of all the experiences that were absorbed by Emerson's aesthetic concentration. The poems assimilated experience to the introspective life of his poetic imagination. No matter what the ostensible subject—a walk in the countryside, a snowstorm, a camping trip, a commemorative verse, even the death of a son—the deep determining subject remained constant. But the great writers, as Proust's narrator explains somewhere, have never written more than a single work, expressing rather through diverse transformations the unique ardor by which they are animated. This observation in no way denies the useful groupings of the poems which Emerson scholars have made according to such categories as the domestic poems (say "Threnody"), political ("Ode to W.H. Channing"), descriptive ("May-Day"), or philosophical ("Brahma"). Firkins argued that "the number of *species* in Emerson's verse is large in proportion to the number of poems. He is always doing something not quite like other people and not quite like himself." Others have enumerated the poetic genres at some length. But within the poems exists a structural sameness that organizes the apparent distinctions at the surface.

Detecting Emerson's brooding search for ways to allow the unimpeded outlet of the poetic imagination is quite different from concluding, as readers have, that Emerson's poems are mostly distilled philosophy. They are, in fact, transformings of a persistent inner imperative that lodged below the level of Emerson's conscious aim. Jonathan Bishop's observation on Emerson's preoccupation with the process of the Soul is on the mark exactly: "The metamorphosis of circumstances into consciousness is the consummation of the

Soul's great act. The trajectory of that act is sketched in a hundred remarks."
The fixation was stronger than that: it was single, intense, distracting. This is
why, as Arnold implied when he said the reader of "The Titmouse" never
quite arrives at learning what the bird in the poem actually did for the man,
many poems are so curiously indecisive. Labeling the poems "philosophical"
seems to have been a way of getting at this indeterminate quality that is
marked in poems like "The Sphinx" and "The Problem." They are surely not
philosophical in the way Wordsworth's poems are, turning identifiable issues
in explicit development; they are as inconclusive in statement as they are
earnest in tone.

Emerson's poems took their mode from his world of stratified values
and of stratified mind. The structure of the mind became the structure of the
poems. The basic binarism was mapped out in the poem "Merlin": nature
comes in ascending pairs, a kind of moral double helix through which the
mind rises, and in this doubled world, "like the dancers' ordered band,
thoughts come also hand in hand." Emerson's twoness comprised for him a
symmetry that produced balance, replication, and joy, and thus "The animals
are sick with love / Lovesick with rhyme." Furthermore, because the doubles
reproduce themselves, they are immortal, they repeat truth, keep it "undecayed," triumph over time, and establish the Universal harmony. Like the
Platonists, in whose system justice resides in the stable order beneath Truth
and Love, Emerson plots that same abstract virtue in the symmetrical structure of nature. "Justice is the rhyme of things," he says in "Merlin."

It was a dynamic order in which the things that rhymed were not
nearly so important as the rhyming itself. Emerson's younger contemporary,
Matthew Arnold, sought to fix a multitudinous world, to establish for things,
as Richard Ohmann has put it, "the fixity of being properly named" and not
"to let concepts, actions, properties, or groups of people drift in a limbo of
namelessness." Emerson's aim was to keep dissolving those constraining
definitions, to break down barriers and life-denying rituals, to rediscover
one's manifold being in the universal circuit, and to yield oneself to the
perfect whole. It is a powerful vision whose central light was Emerson's
conception of the poetic imagination in the act of conversion. This was the
enormously beneficent process of savage nature itself. In art, he believed, a
comparable radical transforming primitivism was needed. In "The American
Scholar," which, together with "Poetry and Imagination," forms the central
document in the radical poetics of Emerson, we read this: "Not out of those
on whom systems of education have exhausted their culture, comes the
helpful giant to destroy the old or to build the new, but out of unhandselled
savage nature; out of terrible Druids and Berserkers come at last Alfred and
Shakespeare" (W, I, 99–100).

That helpful giant is Emerson's wonderfully muscular embodiment of the imagination, filled with power to convert, to liberate, to build the new out of the old, to reject all systems of established religions, able indeed to convert the world. He is the heroic figure of the artist's imagination, and he secretly inhabits almost every poem. Some poems relinquish their own power because they serve the giant and not their particular selves. Others, like "Merlin" and "The Snow-Storm," take on a powerful aesthetic significance.

This covert allegory explains in part why the world has so little reality in Emerson's poems. It is a bright rhyming world a long way from Charles Olson's "In cold hell, in thicket." What the poems lose in worldliness, however, they gain as an artist's concern with the working of creative energy. The discussion that follows is a new look at Emerson's poems as they distractedly circle again and again the three basic aspects of the poet's imagination: how it is structured, how it operates, and what its goal is.

In "Threnody" two levels of mind frame the dialogue of the poem and provide the poles between which the abrupt confrontation takes place. One way to identify these poles is by their Platonic designations of Being and Becoming. The father-mourner is the consciousness directly involved in the experience, actively mourning the death of the son. He confronts the loss and suffers the torments. Yet he fails to see the tragedy in its larger reconciling aspect, which is the function of the "deep Heart." This second consciousness perceives the significance of the death and offers the reconciliation for the mourner. The dramatic basis of the poem and the stage on which the performance takes place come directly from Emerson's idea of the low and high steps of the poetic imagination. As we have seen, the genetic action of "Threnody" is not the death itself but the negotiation of these levels of the imagination that lead to elevation, understanding, and resolution.

Emerson identified these layers in many ways, always maintaining the distinction that the experiencing stage of the imagination was the lower, the resolving level the higher. In "Poetry and Imagination" he saw them reflected in the separation of science and art. "The solid men," he says, "complain that the idealist leaves out the fundamental facts; the poet complains that the solid men leave out the sky. To every plant there are two powers; one shoots down as rootlet, and one upward as tree. You must have eyes of science to see in the seed its nodes; you must have the vivacity of the poet to perceive in the thought its futurities" (W, VIII, 71). In attempting to analyze precisely how contemporary events are transformed to thought, Emerson had earlier employed a similar vertical division, resorting finally to the orchard metaphor:

> The actions and events of our childhood and youth are now matters of calmest observation. They lie like fair pictures in the air. Not so with our recent actions,—with the business which we now have in hand. On this we

are quite unable to speculate. Our affections as yet circulate through it. We no more feel or know it than we feel the feet, or the hand, or the brain of our body. The new deed is yet a part of life,—remains for a time immersed in our unconscious life. In some contemplative hour it detaches itself from the life like a ripe fruit, to become a thought of the mind. Instantly it is raised, transfigured; the corruptible has put on incorruption. Henceforth it is an object of beauty, however base its origin and neighborhood.

(W, I, 96)

This process of transformation, both moral and aesthetic as the quotation indicates, habitually informs Emerson's poetry. The separation of functions between the lower experiencing consciousness and the higher perceiving consciousness marks the distinction Emerson defined variously as that between talent and genius, fancy and the imagination, Understanding and Reason. It is the very armature and substance of the poem "The Problem." The speaker's cherished deep truth and creative act rise not from "a vain or shallow thought" but rather issue from fundamental and terrifying sources:

> Out from the heart of nature rolled
> The burdens of the Bible old;
> The litanies of nations came,
> Like the volcano's tongue of flame,
> Up from the burning core below.

Part of the "problem" is that the churchman's cowl signifies a deep consort with primal laws that no one would casually presume to possess. That sort of genius is not acquired simply by choice of the clerical profession. Emerson abhorred that presumption, and the argument of the poem, very much like that in "Threnody" (note the similar humbling rhetorical questions: "Know'st thou what wove yon woodbird's nest / . . . Or how the fish out-built her shell[?]"), divides between the lesser powers of mere preaching and the powers of genius, whose love and terror create wonders equal to Nature's.

Ambivalent as the poem is, despite its decisive opening and closing lines, it argues finally the speaker's desire to be an original *maker* and not simply a *transmitter*. It is an artist's poem, for inside its somewhat indeterminate exterior, the poem celebrates beauty and not religion.

"Give All to Love" contains a similar divided structure, based on the same model of the imagination. The poem also proceeds from the lower power to the higher. In the beginning, it cheerfully promotes the human proclivity to give all to love and to the things of the day, ascending in experience with them:

> Obey thy heart;
> Friends, kindred, days,
> Estate, good-fame,

> Plans, credit and the Muse,—
> Nothing refuse.

By its end, abruptly, in that slackening of intention we have seen, the poem urges freedom from those lower claims:

> Keep thee to-day,
> To-morrow, forever.
> Free as an Arab
> Of thy beloved.

The two-staged experience comes directly to the surface in the final lines where the choice between an earthly love and the ideal is made clear:

> Though thou loved her as thyself,
> As a self of purer clay,
> Though her parting dims the day,
> Stealing grace from all alive;
> Heartily know,
> When half-gods go,
> The gods arrive.

Once again Emerson draws the distinction between a half-perception and the full ideal one. The half-gods, corrupted and partial by definition, are kin to those Plato describes in the *Apology* as the demi-gods who are the illegitimate sons of the gods sired on nymphs or mortals. Here they are embodiments of that familiar Emersonian choice between the half-sight focused on means and the full perception open to truth. Of George Herbert's idea of man as microcosm ("Man is one world, and hath / Another to attend him"), Emerson says in *Nature*: "The perception of this class of truths makes the attraction which draws men to science, but the end is lost sight of in attention to the means. In view of this half-sight of science, we accept the sentence of Plato, that 'poetry comes nearer to vital truth than history' " (*W*, I, 69). In Emerson's aesthetic equation, that half-sight of science equals poetic talent as opposed to genius, literary convention as opposed to prophetic content. The hierarchy thus had its personifications not only in the father-mourner as opposed to the deep Heart, but also the work-a-day preacher as opposed to the genius in possession of the word, the sensuous mortal pursuing the half-god of profane love as opposed to the idealist in quest of the gods themselves. The intention of each poem is thus linear, often abruptly so, proceeding from a first state of confusion, ignorance, or paralysis (sometimes all three) to a state of clarity, revelation, and liberation.

This basic structural model provides the armature in almost all of Emerson's poetry. In "Each and All," it is the speaker of simple talent or fancy who "aggregates" experiences, collecting a sparrow and seashells without discerning the plan of "the perfect whole" from which they are organically inseparable. Here again, the speaker starts out misled into thinking he can possess things as he pleases; he soon discovers that removed from their place in the great circuit, they become, like the shells, "poor, unsightly, noisome things." Through a slow, deliberate version of the eyeball experience, the speaker's consciousness finally rises so that he "sees" the larger beauty. Again we confront Emerson's world as it was limited to experiences that could be used to demonstrate the two levels of the imagination. But there was an opening in Emerson's scheme that will be important to us later and is appropriately to be noted here. The philosophical assumption of an organic universe had extremely significant ramifications in Emerson's developing aesthetics of poetic form. He says in a journal entry of May 16, 1834: "I learned that Composition was more important than the beauty of individual forms to effect" (*JMN*, IV, 291). The poem "Each and All" enacts this credo by an allegory of what was essentially an aesthetic tenet of Emerson's, perhaps the most important and most "modern" one, the need for more aggregate and fully receptive forms.

"Brahma" is a late example of his structural obsession. Despite its moebius-loop view of the universe where all things turn on their opposites—it is the insight of genius that Brahma possesses—the poem rests on that familiar ladder of the ascending consciousness. At its conclusion, the half-perception is associated with "heaven" and a partial way of seeing. Brahma in effect says at the end, "Turn your back on single systems of thought exemplified by the idea of heaven and be liberated into the realm of total perceptions with me." The sweep toward revelation and thus at least a theoretical liberation from confinement is both a formal and philosophical paradigm here, as in other Emerson poems. Brahma urges a full and knowing receptiveness to this world below. It is the lower order of mind that thinks it can slay or be slain; the higher order sits where all the contraries converge. We hear in the poem another not so simple version of the deep Heart in "Threnody"; we stand at the burning core in "The Problem"; we face the gods in "Give All to Love."

The overheard Poet in that most inconclusive of all of Emerson's published poems, "The Sphinx," gives us a gloss on the higher sight of Brahma:

> "To vision profounder,
>   Man's spirit must dive;
> His aye-rolling orb
>   At no goal will arrive;
> The heavens that now draw him
>   With sweetness untold,
> Once found,—for new heavens
>   He spurneth the old."

By that marvelous etherializing process of conversion that Emerson never ceased portraying, the drowsy Sphinx finally "melts," "silvers," "spires," "flowers," "flows" into nature's forms. From a stony mystery she becomes the airy spiritual truth of nature, a not unfamiliar progression in the poetry of Emerson. Again he has moved along the trajectory from ignorance to revelation. "The Sphinx" is a paradigm itself of Emerson's conception of the poetic function. For this reason if for no other, Emerson was justified in placing it at the beginning of his first volume of poems in 1846.

But Emerson's contemporaries found the poem impenetrable, as most readers have since. Ambiguous, apparently contradictory in viewpoint, it did not provide a welcome entry to his other poems, and later editors moved it back from the head position. Edward Emerson said it "cut off, in the very portal, readers who would have found good and joyful words for themselves, had not her riddle been beyond their powers" (W, IX, 403). The poem's vexing ambiguity comes largely because it is unclear whether or not the Poet solves the Sphinx's riddle. The Poet seems to defeat the Sphinx ("Dull Sphinx, Jove keep thy five wits") and to be defeated (the Sphinx replies: "Thou art the unanswered question ... And each answer is a lie."). Yet encompassing the two-level structures of the supernatural riddler and the human riddle-solver, joyful nature and melancholy man, is a primary consciousness. This all-seeing maker of the poem contains the dull Sphinx's opacity as well as its protean dynamism, the picture of oafish man as well as the cheerful poet's confident reply. That primary speaker, part Emerson and part an idealization, knows both the Poet's craving for universal principles and the Sphinx's knowledge of infinite forms and transformations. It is this speaker, then, who sees the truth that nature is incessant change and has no single identifiable center such as Love, as the overheard Poet says. And it is this super Emersonian speaker presumably who was intended to preside over the poems in the book. "The Sphinx" was the essential statement and act of all the other poems that accompanied it. In it, Emerson's speaker is the Central Poet outside his two-tiered system for once, living fully in the world, serene in its flux, beyond grasping after absolutes.

The drama between the grasping but ignorant low mind and the enduring, all-perceiving imagination or high mind is played out later in "Hamatreya" by the farmers on the one hand and the earth on the other. Emerson, we recall, said near the conclusion of "Poetry and Imagination" that "Men are facts as well as persons, and the involuntary part of their life is so much as to fill the mind and leave them no countenance to say aught of what is so trivial as their selfish thinking and doing" (W, VIII, 75). In the poem this "trivial doing" is the vain regard of the farmers soon to die. The facticity of their lives is established at the beginning with drumming directness (and no little humor) as their names form a list exactly parallel to the "things" of their toil:

> Bulkeley, Hunt, Willard, Hosmer, Meriam, Flint,
> Possessed the land which rendered to their toil
> Hay, corn, roots, hemp, flax, apples, wool, and wood.

In Emerson's equation men are the facts while the Earth (yet another disembodied voice out of the deep) stands for the larger and finally absorbing truth. In a further parallel, the aggregating lower mind is mirrored in the farmers' vain and possessive beliefs, while the Imagination has knowledge like the enduring Earth's:

> "They called me theirs,
> Who so controlled me;
> Yet every one
> Wished to stay, and is gone,
> How am I theirs,
> If they cannot hold me,
> But I hold them?"

To the extent that Emerson conceived of men as convertible elements in an eternal scheme, they were indeed facts. Both Alcott and Parker remarked that he thought of men as ideas, but Emerson's conception was always a part of a higher humanism. When he saw individual men, like the farmers in "Hamatreya," blinded by their vanity, Emerson's moral wrath could explode. Sampson Reed, his early guide, when he displayed his own kind of vanity in dogmatic narrowness, Emerson condemned in outrage in the poem "S.R.," calling him "Sleek deacon of the New Jerusalem" and "A blind man's blind man" (*VP*, 358). In aesthetic terms, all these men are failed poets, captives of their fancies, unable to liberate themselves from petty vanities and ascend to the higher imagination.

The rural man in nature displayed for Emerson the clear sight of the imagination, while the grasping city man among the money-mad crowd collected wealth but not sane contentedness. The citydweller in "Woodnotes II" does not see beyond his acquisitions. The forester has acquired qualities of the supernatural Sphinx:

> Whoso walks in solitude
> And inhabiteth the wood,
> Choosing light, wave, rock and bird,
> Before the money-loving herd,
> Into that forester shall pass,
> From these companions, power and grace.
> Clean shall he be, without, within,
> From the old adhering sin,
> All ill dissolving in the light
> Of his triumphant piercing sight:
> Not vain, sour, nor frivolous;
> Not mad, athirst, nor garrulous.

The seemingly blessed possessor in "Guy" is another version of factual man mistaking his material abundance for the higher power he lacks. Prosperous but not quite an example of "the balanced soul in harmony with nature," as Edward Emerson describes him in a note on the poem, Guy is rather another vain fact in an allegory of the lower mind. Emerson is careful in the poem to have us distinguish between fancy and genius. Guy's enormous vanity is established at the outset:

> Mortal mixed of middle clay,
> Attempered to the night and day,
> Interchangeable with things,
> Needs no amulets nor rings.
> Guy possessed the talisman
> That all things from him began.

He prospers in all he does, and it appears he has "caught Nature in his snares." In his vanity he supposes, like the farmers of "Hamatreya," that "fortune was his guard and lover." Indeed, he thinks himself (lovely parody of the eyeball) concentric with the universe:

> In strange junctures, felt, with awe,
> His own symmetry with law.

He believes he shares God's genius:

> It seemed his Genius discreet
> Worked on the Maker's own receipt.

But his end, one infers from the repeated overstatements, will be that of Polycrates, who suffered a cruel death despite his unbroken good fortune. Mere possessiveness and smug satisfaction with the lower virtues are not to be confused with the higher humbling power to see the larger plan. The swelled pride is wonderfully punctured by the Byronic rhyme at the end where Guy's values converge on the single word: "Belonged to wind and world the toil / And venture, and to Guy the oil."

The model of mind was the stage for Emerson's actors, and he directs them in the poems with varying degrees of obviousness. The allegory determined the characters he chose and comprised the shadowy significance of the subjects he presented. The philosophy behind this divided model of the imagination as it perceived a convertible world had more significance for the artist, however, than simply the matters of vain possession and spiritual insight. The two levels of mind were the basis for an aesthetics that was part of the allegory.

Characteristically, the aesthetic suppositions take protean forms, and if we follow his principal ones we will end up seeing in Emerson's cherished snowstorm, of all places, the acting out of a forceful poetics. The way to this disclosure begins with Emerson's idea of the function of a college and his image of a fire. Colleges, he said in "The American Scholar," "only highly serve us when they aim not to drill, but to create; when they gather from far every ray of various genius to their hospitable halls, and by the concentrated fires, set the hearts of their youth on flame" (W, I, 93). He describes the ideal college not as a simple aggregating fancy but, like genius, as a distiller and transformer of those aggregated elements to inspiring flame. Only a little leap from this analogy is necessary to see the aesthetic meaning of the famous humble-bee. Emerson calls the bee "rover of the underwoods" and describes him as gatherer of all nature's sweetnesses, who by leaving the chaff and taking the wheat (in the poet's strained metaphor) transforms the gatherings to honey. The bee is his own self-reliant generator of heat ("Thou animated torrid-zone!"), the center of his society ("Joy of thy dominion!"), and perceiver of the ideal ("Yellow-breeched philosopher!"). There is a classical origin of course for these metaphorical associations of the bee, but in Emerson the figure embodies his constant vision of the transforming power of the imagination as it operates on the aggregations of the fancy.

In the aesthetic application of this model, we understand that genius transforms the gathered experiences into art. By way of the bee, we see also the naturalness of this transforming process; its wider analogy is the workings of nature, and these are visible most dramatically in Emerson's snowstorm. That equating of artistic creation with some form of great power appears repeatedly in the prose. In "The American Scholar" Emerson identified "the helpful giant" with the primitive force of the unschooled and natural. Only a transfer of metaphor is needed to make the snowstorm. Or it can be reached by the architecture metaphor with which the snowstorm ends. Emerson, in "The Poet," says of the poet that he "does not wait for the hero or the sage, but, as they act and think primarily, so he writes primarily what will and must be spoken, reckoning the others, though primaries also, yet, in respect to him, secondaries and servants; as sitters or models in the studio of a painter, or as assistants who bring building-materials to an architect" (W, III, 7-8). Overlapping, merging, the analogues crowd forth—college, bumblebee, giant, painter-artist, and architect. They are the gatherers and transformers, the honey-makers and the builders, all those who make a new construction out of their gathered materials. The fury of this creation and its identification with nature come in a passage of prose on the great poets. All the emblems converge. "Every good poem that I know," says Emerson in "Poetry and Imagination," "I recall by its rhythm also [as well as its rhyme]. Rhyme is a pretty good measure of the latitude and opulence of a writer. If unskilful, he is at once detected by the poverty of his chimes . . . Now try Spenser, Marlowe, Chapman, and see how wide they fly for weapons, and how rich and lavish their profusion. In their rhythm is no manufacture, but a vortex or musical tornado, which, falling on words and the experience of a learned mind, whirls these materials into the same grand order as planets and moons obey, and seasons, and monsoons" (W, VIII, 49-50). Here is that habitual movement from flux and chaos to the orderly, from the changeable to the systematic or monumental. That conversion of the mind and the correlative binary view of nature's own processes are ultimately founded in the basic elements that structured Emerson's thought: movement and stasis, chaos and order, the passing and the permanent. The writer, says Emerson in "Poetry and Imagination," "needs a frolic health . . . he must be at the top of his condition. In that prosperity he is sometimes caught up into a perception of . . . funds of power hitherto utterly unknown to him, whereby he can transfer his visions to mortal canvas, or reduce them into iambic or trochaic, into lyric or heroic rhyme. These successes are not less admirable and astonishing to the poet than they are to his audience" (W, VIII, 40). We have now in aggregate all of the primary analogies that structure the snowstorm poem, and, whereas earlier we were concerned with discovering the Emersonian linear arrangement and deliverance scheme of the poem, here it stands forth also as a concentrated poetics. While students may search the meteorological records of Concord for the early 1830s in search of an actual snowstorm source, we can satisfy ourselves that the much more demanding subject was Emerson the Artist's, and that was the idealized storm of poetic creation to which he yearned to submit. The poem is about a snowstorm and it is a program for poetry. It is worth quoting in its entirety:

> Announced by all the trumpets of the sky,
> Arrives the snow, and, driving o'er the fields,
> Seems nowhere to alight: the whited air
> Hides hills and woods, the river, and the heaven,
> And veils the farm-house at the garden's end.
> The sled and traveller stopped, the courier's feet
> Delayed, all friends shut out, the housemates sit
> Around the radiant fireplace, enclosed
> In a tumultuous privacy of storm.
>
>   Come see the north wind's masonry.
> Out of an unseen quarry evermore
> Furnished with tile, the fierce artificer
> Curves his white bastions with projected roof
> Round every windward stake, or tree, or door.
> Speeding, the myriad-handed, his wild work
> So fanciful, so savage, nought cares he
> For number or proportion. Mockingly,
> On coop or kennel he hangs Parian wreaths;
> A swan-like form invests the hidden thorn;

> Fills up the farmer's lane from wall to wall,
> Maugre the farmer's sighs; and at the gate
> A tapering turret overtops the work.
> And when his hours are numbered, and the world
> Is all his own, retiring, as he were not,
> Leaves, when the sun appears, astonished Art
> To mimic in slow structures, stone by stone,
> Built in an age, the mad wind's night-work,
> The frolic architecture of the snow.

Emerson's superb oxymorons—"tumultuous privacy," "fierce artificer," "so fanciful, so savage," "astonished Art," "slow structures," and "frolic architecture"—combine in a severely compacted way his idealized contraries of free imagination and ordered art. What seems chaotic, the storm, in the final perception is ordered, still, graceful, a part of nature itself in the way the Pyramids, St. Peter's, and the Parthenon are in the poem "The Problem." There is more: those freely formed contours of the snow sculpture rest upon but at the same time *obliterate* the rigid supporting forms beneath:

> So fanciful, so savage, nought cares he
> For number or proportion. Mockingly,
> On coop or kennel he hangs Parian wreaths;
> A swan-like form invests the hidden thorn;
> Fills up the farmer's lane from wall to wall.

The aesthetic principle behind the metaphor of the storm is central to Emerson's move toward more open compositional forms. He admonished writers not so much to await inspiration (this is a superficial view of Emerson's hardheaded methods) as to allow language strings, like snow, to fall into mimetic shapes: "Shun manufacture or the introducing an artificial arrangement in your thoughts, it will surely crack and come to nothing, but let alone tinkering and wait for the natural arrangement of your treasures." In the light of the poetics within the poem, we see as much an *aesthetic* sense in the famous thorn passage as a moral one. Emerson's moral stance was one with his aesthetics: poetry rightly shows the beautiful and ideal, and they in turn are moral because the humdrum and base are raised to the spiritual level. The moral and the aesthetic were to Emerson inseparable, as were the forces both of nature and human genius. As in "The Problem," it was an artist's philosophical system that had at its center not a moral point but the sensuous ideal of Beauty.

One final association and I shall be done with this line of exposition. When Emerson says in the essay "The Poet" that he sees nowhere among his contemporaries the poet of America, that is, the *genius* of the country, we understand now that he is calling for that great converting consciousness figured in the poetic snowstorm and in the great creative act of the helpful giant. The poet is to transform, like the bee, like the architect, like the storm itself, the vast and varied materials of the country into an aesthetic and visionary whole. That deep impulse to transform America to its noblest essence—at the same time to see it as an aesthetic whole—is Emerson's meaning when he says "America is a poem in our eyes." "We have yet had," he said, "no genius in America, with tyrannous eye, which knew the value of our incomparable materials" (W, III, 37). What Emerson missed in the poets of past ages, as he contemplated the kind of ideal imagination needed to convert the diverse nation to its ideal, were the basic qualities that emerge in "The Snow-Storm": the epic-sized transforming imagination with language equal to the task. "If I have not found that excellent combination of gifts in my countrymen which I seek," Emerson said, "neither could I aid myself to fix the idea of the poet by reading now and then in Chalmer's collection of five centuries of English poets. These are wits more than poets, though there have been poets among them. But when we adhere to the ideal of the poet, we have our difficulties even with Milton and Homer. Milton is too literary, and Homer too literal and historical" (W, III, 38). Emerson glimpsed that ideal poet in himself, animated as he was by a vision of what was possible. He had already freed himself from the literal by his constant process of transforming to the essence; he sought in theory a way to free himself also from the literary past that had no voice for his age. In the poems is the tirelessly worked ground of that theme.

    The seer-genius stage of the imagination found expression in Emerson's structural drama through a dissociated voice, in a curious but habitual separation from his poet-speaker. We took account earlier of the admonitory voice of the deep Heart in "Threnody" which catechizes the mourning father and argues the way to consolation for the death of the son. That strategy of the wise counter-voice has deep roots in Emerson's poetry. In his journal for 1845 he saw his own poetic role as that of a reporter of this voice of natural wisdom: "I will sing aloud and free / From the heart of the world" (JMN, IX, 168). Much earlier, in "The American Scholar," he considered this transmitting of the heart's voice to be one of the principal functions of the scholar: "Whatsoever oracles the human heart, in all emergencies, in all solemn hours, has uttered as its commentary on the world of actions,—these he [Man Thinking] shall receive and impart" (W, I, 102). The schema of the separated poetic consciousness appears almost everywhere in the poetry. The dissociated voice, which is the expression of that schema, sounds conspicuously in "Hamatreya" (fancy speaks in the person of the farmers, the earth is the imagination), "Monadnoc" (the mountain speaks), "Woodnotes II" (the pinetree speaks), "To Ellen at the South" (flowers), "Hermione" (the dying Arab and Nature), "Celestial Love III" (God), "Saadi" (fakirs and the muse), "Dirge" (the bird), "May-Day" (old man), "Freedom" (spirit), "Boston

Hymn" (God), "Voluntaries" (Destiny), "Boston" (the mountain, Boston, King George), "Solution" (the muse), "The Titmouse" (bird), "Seashore" (the sea), "Song of Nature" (nature), "Terminus" (the god Terminus), "The Poet" (the mighty). Even so selective a list indicates the fixity of Emerson's preoccupation.

Confronting a voice out of the heart of things was not uncommon in the work of Emerson's contemporaries, but it was less programmatic. The enchanting paradigm of the encounter occurs in the "Spring" section of *Walden*, where Thoreau finds himself present at Creation. The railroad bank thaws, flows into primal forms, and thereby speaks to Thoreau the language of the earth's original plan. "No wonder that the earth expresses itself outwardly in leaves, it so labors with the idea inwardly." Inwardly the earth speaks liquid words; outwardly they are leaves and wing feathers. Wet *love* becomes dry *leaf*. Thoreau's literal-mindedness was, characteristically, total. There are comparable meetings in Emily Dickinson, the essential text being "Further in Summer than the Birds," where the voice is the cricket nation's in a canticle of death. A similar encounter takes place in Frederick Tuckerman's great poem "The Cricket." In a rapt moment, the poet feels himself on the verge of conversing in the secret language of nature, drawn toward its mystery, and tempted finally to die into it (the dissolution that Yvor Winters called moral failure). In a later day, it is this direct encounter, as we have seen, that Robert Frost's solitary characters seek in the woods, even cry out for as in "The Most of It" but, with the exception of the mower in "The Tuft of Flowers," never accomplish. Because revelation, the eyeball experience, does not really come, Frost's is a poetry of aborted communion. A contemporary version of the instinctual heart-actor—predatory, brooding, bereft of light, yet stubborn, unkillable, wily, surviving—is Ted Hughes's crow.

Merlin is the lately-at-court figure in whom Emerson's own emblematic deep Heart, the technique of the separated voice, and his idea of the poet come together. The identification is most fully apparent if the poem "Merlin" is held alongside Emerson's extended remarks in "Poetry and Imagination." Emerson quotes in the essay as a high and memorable experience the section in *Morte d'Arthur* when Merlin speaks for the last time to Gawain from his enchanted prison in the forest. "Whilst I served King Arthur, I was well known by you and by other barons, but because I have left the court, I am known no longer, and put in forgetfulness, which I ought not to be if faith reigned in the world." The similarity to Emerson's leaving the ministry and his later ostracism because of the lecture to the divinity students is striking. Merlin continues: "you will never see me more, and that grieves me, but I cannot remedy it, and when you shall have departed from this place, I shall nevermore speak to you nor to any other person, save only my mistress;

for never other person will be able to discover this place for anything which may befall; neither shall I ever go out from hence, for in the world there is no such strong tower as this wherein I am confined; and it is neither of wood, nor of iron, nor of stone, but of air" (W, VIII, 61). This voice literally imprisoned in the heart of nature is Emerson's exemplary voice. He described that particular passage from *Morte d'Arthur* as the "height which attracts more than other parts, and is best remembered" (W, VIII, 60). It is concerned with the voice Emerson believed poets should strive to hear and to transmit. Aspects of it rise again and again from other poems, most fervently in "Threnody," very pointedly in "The Problem," where the seer inside nature is the very figure the speaker cannot presume to be, even though he might wear the cowl that signifies it. The humbling voice issues from the center of all the circles: "Out from the heart of nature rolled / The burdens of the Bible old." But it also sounds in the forest, like Merlin's, to the lover's ear:

> The word by seers or sibyls told,
> In groves of oak, or fanes of gold,
> Still floats upon the morning wind,
> Still whispers to the willing mind.

Emerson sought that willing mind in the poem and in himself and elaborately projected it as Man Thinking. The poet of willing mind will earn his freedom and learn his craft from that voice of knowing nature. Merlin, then, is the exemplary poet, and in the Merlin poem Emerson stresses liberation from constraints of form, calls for artful thunder, and specifies the goal: "Great is the art, / Great be the manners, of the bard." Merlin is the authentic voice, Guy's is delusive, for despite all his pride of nature's cooperation, Guy gets only the oil. Merlin's

> blows are strokes of fate,
> Chiming with the forest tone,
> When boughs buffet boughs in the wood;
> Chiming with the gasp and moan
> Of the ice-imprisoned flood.

No simple meddling wit can stand with the angels, but rather only the propitious mind.

> There are open hours
> When the God's will sallies free,
> And the dull idiot might see
> The flowing fortunes of a thousand years.

Emerson also knew the blind moments. He experienced the failure of nature's language and the blockage of the poetic imagination when communication is shut down. The ambivalence cuts into the lines of "Merlin" which follow immediately and end the positive first section:

> Sudden, at unawares,
> Self-moved, fly-to-the-doors,
> Nor sword of angels could reveal
> What they conceal.

Edward Emerson accurately described Merlin as typifying for Emerson "the haughty, free and liberating poet, working the magic of thought through the charm of Art" (W, IX, 440). Merlin says the primal word because he is unencumbered by the courtly restraints of artifice. In Emerson's early journal version of the poem, the poet is admonished to reject the devices of the merely talented poets—"gentle touches," the tinklings of a guitar, telling "a pretty tale" only to "pretty people in a nice saloon," all false creations "borrowed from their expectation" (JMN, IX, 167-168). There are, instead, qualities of the self-reliant, manly figure in Emerson's poet. He described that unfettered myth-phallic figure in the powerful essay "Experience": "The great and crescive self, rooted in absolute nature, supplants all relative existence and ruins the kingdom of mortal friendship and love" (W, III, 77).

Among Emerson's constructs of the poetic imagination, the central one is Merlin. All those dissociated voices speaking out of his poems are versions of that central poet.

The figures crowd Emerson's verse. In "Threnody" alone, as we saw, there are three: young Waldo as the budding poet dead before his time, the desperate father as the failed poet-seer, and the deep Heart as the thunder-poet out of the volcano.

The variety of forms this allegory takes attests to the obsessiveness of the poet's role in Emerson's thought. He could be quite literal-minded in pointing out likenesses. Some of the psychological faddists of his time— people he believed capable of controlling other individuals because they possessed an absolute "natural" power—share, perhaps debased a bit, the ways of the poet. Among examples of "the action of man upon nature with his entire force,—with reason as well as understanding" Emerson includes "Animal Magnetism" and "the miracles of enthusiasm" as reported by Swedenborg, Hohenloke, and the Shakers. These, says Emerson, are examples of "Reason's momentary grasp of the sceptre; the exertions of a power which exists not in time or space, but an instantaneous in-streaming causing power" (W, I, 73).

Emerson's literal-mindedness in this respect is unique. It was his attempt to make his insights available to the common man, *to make the poet's revelation a democratic enterprise.* This distinguishes him in a fundamental way from the willfully alienated poet-seers of the Romantic temper. The convention of isolation was a concomitant of the higher vision with its sight of revelation. Frank Kermode defines the direct correlation between "these two beliefs—in the Image as a radiant truth out of space and time, and in the necessary isolation or estrangement of men who can perceive it." Not so with Emerson. He refused to promote the fanciful isolation of the seer-poet but rather, as he says in "Merlin," strove to open the doors, making the vision available to all who would attempt it. In so doing, he staked out the fundamental American variant to the central Romantic myth.

Carl Strauch calls Emerson's poet figures masks: "Uriel, Merlin, Saadi, these are poetic masks for the attributes and functions of the poet as Emerson saw them. Uriel is an archetypal emblem of the rebellious intellect, Merlin typifies power, and Saadi represents the cheerful acceptance of isolation until the propitious moment has arrived for the poet to deliver his message." Beyond these, however, and enclosing them all is the basic figure of the perceiving imagination. The variety of versions indicates how obsessive this theoretical subject was for Emerson. Uriel, for example, who possessed a "look that solved the sphere" and who is able to declare "Line in nature is not found" and "Evil will bless, and ice will burn," acts as much the role of a conscious eyeball as a resigned minister or the rebellious deliverer of the Divinity School address. Each role contributes to his conception of the liberated and liberating poet, which is to say that while the free and imaginative man took many forms in Emerson, he was never distinct from the poet, whether Man Thinking or angel rebelling.

One inevitably sees "Brahma" as a version of the poet. Here again is Emerson on the eye: "The eye is the best of artists. By the mutual action of its structure and of the laws of light, perspective is produced, which integrates every mass of objects, of what character soever, into a well colored and shaded globe, so that where the particular objects are mean and unaffecting, the landscape which they compose is round and symmetrical" (W, I, 15). Condensed here is every basic element of Emerson's structural poetics: the converting imagination as the eyeball, its structure integral with nature, its highly selective and transforming power over reality, the consequent reduction of reality to a symmetrical moral equation. The prose contains the aesthetic and the moral geometry of the poem "Brahma," with the Oriental consciousness as the transforming center of the poem. It is Emerson's basic model of the world as seen through a shaping eyeball that merges the moral and aesthetic imagination and inevitably abstracts reality to a scheme inseparable from that vision. Brahma is one of Emerson's ultimate poets and, not surprisingly, the poem for all its economy and control presents the moral and aesthetic problem of his poetry. The final line, in that habitual Emersonian movement, dismisses the half-god of a human belief ("turn thy back on heaven") for the whole but abstract purity of the ideal vision.

There are yet other poet figures. The poet in "The Sphinx," overheard by the yet more complete mind of the poet's maker, literally converts the beast from ugliness to beauty, from mystery to intelligibility, liberating mankind as befits the poet Emerson described as a liberating god. The Sphinx is ponderous fact; the poet transforms it into bright Truth. In a similar plot, though less dramatic, the protagonists in "The Rhodora" and "Each and All" who are failed poets as the poems begin, come, through the auspices of nature, to their own revelation of the natural symmetry of the world's beauty and the imagination ("Rhodora": "The self-same Power that brought me there brought you"), and a fresh recognition that the higher unity includes man ("Each and All": "Beauty through my senses stole; / I yielded myself to the perfect whole.")

Nonhuman actors embody types of the artist, as we saw in "The Snow-Storm." Another actor is the humble-bee. As he transforms the materials of his foraging, he plays the part of the imagination. The same qualities of intellectual nomadism, in characteristic Emerson fashion, circulate in all his actors. The "forest seer" in "Woodnotes I," while justifiably identified as Thoreau in literal readings of the poem (see Edward Emerson's note, W, IX, 420), is very much the poet as a personified bee! The terms are identical:

> It seemed that Nature could not raise
> A plant in any secret place . . .
> But he would come in the very hour
> It opened in its virgin bower . . .
> It seemed as if the breezes brought him,
> It seemed as if the sparrows taught him;
> As if by secret sight he knew
> Where, in far fields, the orchis grew . . .
> What others did at distance hear,
> And guessed within the thicket's gloom,
> Was shown to this philosopher,
> And at his bidding seemed to come.

"In poetry," Emerson says, "we say we require the miracle. The bee flies among the flowers, and gets mint and marjoram, and generates a new product, which is not mint and marjoram, but honey . . . and the poet listens to conversation and beholds all objects in Nature, to give back, not them, but a new and transcendent whole" (W, VIII, 16-17). There is a further loop in this skein of concern with the poet and the imagination. Emerson says in the essay "The Poet" that the Ancients remind us that poets speak "not with intellect alone but with the intellect inebriated by nectar" (W, III, 27). In the Emersonian aesthetic, the nectar is visionary. Having come round by way of snowstorm, Brahma, and bee, we recognize how deep-drawing is the concern in the poem "Bacchus" with the poetic enterprise. A colossal ballast of aesthetic rumination feeds the urgent imperatives of the poet-speaker:

> Give me of the true . . .
> Wine of wine,
> Blood of the world,
> Form of forms, and mould of statures,
> That I intoxicated,
> And by the draught assimilated,
> May float at pleasure through all natures;
> The bird-language rightly spell,
> And that which roses say so well.

A circuit closes between this poem and the Sphinx poem that Emerson had placed at the head of the 1846 edition:

> I thank the joyful juice
> For all I know,—
> Winds of remembering
> Of the ancient being blow,
> And seeming-solid walls of use
> Open and flow.

"Imagination intoxicates the poet," Emerson tells us (W, III, 30), and the poet in turn, by his clarifying symbols, intoxicates and therefore liberates men. The poetic act centers in the plenitude of the single imagination, self-intoxicating. This is the aesthetic equivalent in his poetics of what Emerson called in social and moral contexts the self-reliant man.

We are not done with versions of the poet. The pinetree in "Wood-notes II" admonishes the poet-listener in a long discourse marked by some of Emerson's most egregious rhymes and meters:

> "Come learn with me the fatal song
> Which knits the world in music strong,—
> Come lift thine eyes to lofty rhymes . . .
> I, that to-day am a pine,
> Yesterday was a bundle of grass.
> He [God, the eternal Pan] is free and libertine,
> Pouring of his power the wine
> To every age, to every race;
> Unto every race and age
> He emptieth the beverage;
> Unto each, and unto all,
> Maker and original."

God, Bacchus, humble-bee, forest seer, Uriel, Brahma, pinetree: all are versions of the poet and types of the imagination just as Bulkeley, Hunt, and Willard, Guy, the mourning father, the hiker in the snowy woods (and many more both early and late) are figures of the merely acquisitive or perceiving sense. Ideas of the aesthetic transaction were so crucial to Emerson's imagination that even the rifles that fire the shot in "Concord Hymn," as we shall discover, inescapably figure as yet another version of the imagination. We shall reach that disclosure by leaving off now the examples of structures of the imagination in the poems to see how Emerson's conception of the *process* of the poetic alembic lies equally deep and formative in the poetry.

Wordsworth said that objects should be reported not as they are but as they seem, and it is the seeming that is literally reported. In Emerson's poetry, the process of conversion is reported, the apparent subjects being thus quite interchangeable. The poems, no matter what objects occupy their vision, enact the process of the beholding and coenergizing mind as it transforms reality on the way from the nerve ends to the mind in that now familiar train of conversion from sensation to experience to thought.

This transfer of energy inevitably rests on the pairs that stand behind the spirals that Emerson's figurative thought favored. These different structural metaphors are related. His circles and spirals are the connecting motions of the mind as it plays over the fundamental dialectic, which takes the form of horizontal and vertical dualities. The horizontal doubleness embraces the reassuring paired structure of nature that everywhere manifests the universal symmetry. Emerson located himself pleasurably in that cosmic rhyme. As he put it in a marvelous lexical playback: "The animals are sick with love, / Lovesick with rhyme." The vertical duality consists in the Platonic division of experience into lower shadows of Becoming and the higher light of Being. Across this grid of two dimensions Emerson conceived the imagination playing its constant act of conversion. In the poems, the conversion arcs again and again.

The more complicated motions of conversion I traced in several poems: facts transformed to principle in "The Snow-Storm," "Humble-bee," "Each and All," "Rhodora." Its outline rationalizes the otherwise awkward and even fractured progress of "Threnody," a major display of the powerful structural set of Emerson's aesthetic beliefs. A revealing occasion occurs in "Each and All," where the conversion seems made with little conviction, almost as a gratuitous assertion. It is in fact the structure of Emerson's poetics right on the surface, with no shadowing allegory. Instead, in a kind of eyeball instance, there is an abrupt transfer of fact into thought at the end of the poem. The revelation arrives out of the blue with no explanation of how the "facts" fly together in the viewer's mind to make the instructive principle.

> I said, "I covet truth;
> Beauty is unripe childhood's cheat;
> I leave it behind with the games of youth:"—

As I spoke, beneath my feet
The ground-pine curled its pretty wreath,
Running over the club-moss burrs;
I inhaled the violet's breath;
Around me stood the oaks and firs;
Pine-cones and acorns lay on the ground;
Over me soared the eternal sky,
Full of light and of deity;
Again I saw, again I heard,
The rolling river, the morning bird;—
Beauty through my senses stole;
I yielded myself to the perfect whole.

We can see in this apparently random list of natural things the familiar Platonic structure of the high and low: the ground-pine beneath the towering trees; the fallen acorns beneath the soaring and eternal sky. In what seems a casual but is surely a deliberate symmetry are what Emerson called the visual rhymes of nature. Out of the details of this picture, the cosmic coherence is more or less taken on trust. The viewer in the poem, at the outset a poet lacking imagination and possessing a fragmenting scientific mind, wins through despite himself to a final ideal vision. Because the process is so mechanically delivered here, "Each and All" discloses the assumptions in the deeper part of Emerson's consciousness. There is almost no surface enactment of the process of conversion. In a revealing prose passage, Emerson came no closer to explaining that buried transfer: "It is easier to read Sanscrit, to decipher the arrow-head character, than to interpret . . . familiar sights. It is even much to name them. Thus Thomson's 'Seasons' and the best parts of many old and many new poets are simply enumerations by a person who felt the beauty of the common sights and sounds, without any attempt to draw a moral or affix a meaning" (W, VIII, 22-23).

The most fully drawn conversion unfolds in "The Snow-Storm." It is a process that reaches back to the mythopoeic confrontation in "The Sphinx," the individual deciphering the code of his existence. Poem after poem, as it enacts the conversion, points to the centrality of this movement in Emerson's mind. In "Berrying" the occasion is virtually identical to that in "Each and All," revealing now as well its links to other poems, like "The Titmouse":

"May be true what I had heard,—
Earth's a howling wilderness,
Truculent with fraud and force,"
Said I, strolling through the pastures,
And along the river-side.
Caught among the blackberry vines,
Feeding on the Ethiops sweet,

> Pleasant fancies overtook me.
> I said, "What influence me preferred,
> Elect, to dreams thus beautiful?"
> The vines replied, "And didst thou deem
> No wisdom from our berries went?"

The poem "Étienne de la Boéce," based on a friendship of Montaigne's, is a rare and stunning example where the process obsessive to Emerson the artist dominated even the treatment of this historical relationship. Once again the goal of the poem is to disclose the essential value of the experience, which for the Montaigne-Emerson figure is the divine spark that makes a "resistant" manhood, not simply a shadow of Boéce but his equal in inspiration. We recognize how much like Brahma is that miraculously transforming soul Emerson ascribes to Montaigne:

> if I could,
> In severe or cordial mood,
> Lead you rightly to my altar,
> Where the wisest Muses falter,
> And worship that world-warming spark
> Which dazzles me in midnight dark,
> Equalizing small and large,
> While the soul it doth surcharge,
> Till the poor is wealthy grown,
> And the hermit never alone,—
> The traveller and the road seem one
> With the errand to be done,—
> That were a man's and lover's part,
> That were Freedom's whitest chart.

The same converting process exists as a plaintive fixation of the artist who speaks in "Blight." The poem begins with what is now familiar to us as the act of drawing the visionary out of the factual. Again, the syntax is demanding because completion is deliberately suspended:

> Give me truths;
> For I am weary of the surfaces,
> And die of inanition. If I knew
> Only the herbs and simples of the wood,
> Rue, cinquefoil, gill, vervain and agrimony,
> Blue-vetch and trillium, hawkweed, sassafras,
> Milkweeds and murky brakes, quaint pipes and sundew,
> And rare and virtuous roots, which in these woods
> Draw untold juices from the common earth,
> Untold, unknown, and I could surely spell
> Their fragrance, and their chemistry apply
> By sweet affinities to human flesh,

> Driving the foe and stablishing the friend,—
> O, that were much, and I could be a part
> Of the round day, related to the sun
> And planted world, and full executor
> Of their imperfect functions.

Here is the characteristic recognition once more of the deep forces that generate the green outer world's language. It was the way Emerson sought the significance of the life around him, and it was the way of his poems.

The conversion act is imminent in "Days." He described the scholar as "watching days and months sometimes for a few facts" (W, 1, 101). His speaker in "May-Day" saw hidden in the spring days the gods themselves:

> I saw them mask their awful glance
> Sidewise meek in gossamer lids . . .
> It was as if the eternal gods,
> Tired of their starry periods,
> Hid their majesty in cloth
> Woven of tulips and painted moth.

The man in his pleached garden is one more Emersonian poet waiting for the revelation. The association is suggested by an 1843 journal entry: "Somebody . . . saw in a dream a host of angels descending with salvers of glory in their hands. On asking one of them for whom those were intended, he answered, 'for Shaikh Saadi of Shiraz, who has written a stanza of poetry that has met the approbation of God Almighty'" (W, IX, 447-448). The same archetypal visitation constitutes the central metaphor in the early poem "The Day's Ration." As in "Days," the awaiting consciousness, the mind's chalice, cannot take the inflow:

> To-day, when friends approach, and every hour
> Brings book, or starbright scroll of genius,
> The little cup will hold not a bead more,
> And all the costly liquor runs to waste.

A specific emphasis in "Days" is worth noting: the imagination confronts not only visionary moments but actual days. Emerson, as his journals show, was acutely aware of the facts of his own days, from political and economic to intellectual, and he searched them with the poet's transfiguring imagination for their essential truth. He urged the same on every poet. The pleached garden of his poem was already implicit in a passage from the essay "The Poet" seven years earlier: "I look in vain for the poet whom I describe. We do not with sufficient plainness or sufficient profoundness address ourselves to life, nor dare we chaunt our own times and social circumstance. If we filled the day with bravery, we should not shrink from celebrating it. Time and nature yield us many gifts" (W, III, 37). I shall have more to say about Emerson's occasional depiction of the poet as a reluctant converter, for this passivity is one of the crucial aspects of the deeply idealistic structure of the imagination. For the present, we can see that "Days" provides the quintessential converting situation undisguised. The poem has no diversionary subject—a walk, a bereavement, a characterization—but like "The Sphinx" deals directly with a conspicuous allegory of the imagination confronting reality. The conversion fails, and we are surprised by Emerson's explicit depiction of the defeat:

> I, in my pleached garden, watched the pomp,
> Forgot my morning wishes, hastily
> Took a few herbs and apples, and the Day
> Turned and departed silent. I, too late,
> Under her solemn fillet saw the scorn.

"Days" takes account of untranslatable realities rarely brought into Emerson's poetry. Here is an occasion when experience presents itself but is not taken up, as if it were unintelligible to the poet-viewer. This is a lurking nightmare in Emerson that readers often miss. The balletic imagery of "Days" does not penetrate to the depth we glimpsed in "Threnody," but the desperation over a whole reality that goes unperceived and unconverted is as genuine.

Successful conversion takes place almost everywhere else in Emerson's poetry. The opening of second sight into the compensatory plan of nature manages to occur. As each poem makes its drama out of that process, each then is a variation of the transparent-eyeball experience at the visionary heart of *Nature*. The eyeball conversion is the accelerated ideal. The others in the individual poems, though they may be extended out in time for dramatic purposes, are in fact deliberately slackened examples of that one ecstatic act of the poetic imagination.

Seen in its full coherence, the eyeball process defines the aesthetics of Emerson's moral beliefs by establishing the emblematic equation between the physical eye and the poetic imagination. It is the single, homely metaphor in which the Platonic terms Emerson adopted for himself converge in an instant dependence of form upon soul. Once we see the centrality of this crucial image, we recognize how it ramifies into other analogies. The pleached garden of "Days," in which the poet stands passively and enclosed, is itself a sort of enlarged eyeball and the two figures in turn make a metaphor for the receiving consciousness. In the allegory of "Days," that consciousness confronts reality in the form of maidens. Exotic, their appearance distracts the fancy of the waiting man, and the encounter fails of revelation. What did *not* happen is the poem's subject, and we find it described in "Poetry and Imagination": "The test of the poet is the power to take the passing day, with its news, its cares, its fears, as he shares them, and hold it up to a divine reason, till he sees it to have a purpose and beauty, and to be related to astronomy and history and the eternal order of the world" (*W, VIII, 35*).

These are inescapable consequences, both for Emerson's view of reality and for his perception of contemporary culture, in this idea of the poetic imagination and its relation to reality. He called the eye the best of artists, integrating groups of things so that where particular objects are mean and unaffecting, the landscape they compose is round and symmetrical. That vision of balanced wholeness composes the "each" and the "all"; the individual reality, of whatever form or moral state, is part of the whole, being swept up in a final aesthetic incorporation. Particulars are sacrificed to the demands of the symmetrical, dramatic, and moral whole. The perceiving eye registers a world whose moral and cultural disparities, whose tragic possibilities, and whose grey ambiguities and indefiniteness disappear in the aesthetic compass and balance. The overviewing eye has no vision capable of rendering the finer lines of reality. If the world we live in is the words we use, then the world Emerson's poetry saw is the poetry that Emerson wrote. The vision sacrificed the possible subjective life of individual poems to the underlying structure of a harmonizing aesthetic theory.

Emerson returned again and again in the poems to the image of monumentality. It seems a repudiation of the dynamism in the essay "Circles," for instance, and in the circular poems "Brahma" and "Uriel," where perceptual motion pushes out from concentrated centers of self-knowledge to the edges of dispersal. That yielding to the perfect whole is the plot of many familiar outward-flowing passages from the poems, but the little-noticed monument image, briefly noted earlier, came out of the poetics and determined the focus of some of the poems. The monument stands against the flux, providing stasis amid the onwardness and outwardness of Emerson's contrary images. It is an integral part of the mind's converting process even though it seems a compromise of Emerson's concept of natural organicism. It most certainly is a departure from the biological figure upon which Coleridge depended in discussing art. There is a strong sense of deliberate craftsmanship in Emerson's view of the artist. A monument stands at the end of "Threnody," an objective parallel to the consolation of the deep Heart as it unfolds the larger purpose in which the boy's death is made intelligible as well as blessed.

The snowstorm poem follows the metaphor of architecture, the graceful forms taking shape by the savage and chaotic labors of the storm. The oxymoron "frolic architecture" captures that instantaneous creation of stasis from movement, order from chaos, and beauty from savagery. The contradictory joining of "fierce" and "artificer" holds the paradox of wild genius issuing in graceful form. In "The Problem" the most noble expression of genius takes the form of buildings: the Parthenon, the Pyramids, St. Peter's, and England's abbeys. "Out of Thought's interior sphere / These wonders rose to upper air." Buildings, then, are emblems of inspired genius. In Emerson's ordering system, as in Pythagoras', the fixed is associated with the preferred (bright, straight, male) and with eternal values (the good, the one). The realm of shifting values and Becoming (many, female, moving) is associated with flux. But Emerson, like Swedenborg, could sit without terror in the midst of flux, among the "hated waves." The poem "Illusions" speaks of "the endless imbroglio" of this universe where "no anchorage is." But the vision leads Emerson not to existential terror, but rather to the durable confidence that Arnold admired.

> first shalt thou know,
> That in the wild turmoil,
> Horsed on the Proteus,
> Thou ridest to power,
> And to endurance.

Monumentality has two principal associations for Emerson, and they merge in the figure of the poet. The first association is philosophical, that monumentality is a way of standing in the world. The second association is aesthetic, that monumentality is a way of conceiving art in its relationship to that world. Philosophically, the monumental is principled firmness. In "Ode: Inscribed to W.H. Channing," for example, whoever does not stand fast to principle is on the side of ignorance, slavery, and chaos. In Emerson's bitter closing parable, the Muse is the solid mooring point when the victors divide and "Half for freedom strike and stand." The positive philosophical association is emphatic in "Monadnoc" where the poet-speaker proclaims the virtues of the mountain:

> Man in these crags a fastness find
> To fight pollution of the mind;
> In the wide thaw and ooze of wrong,
> Adhere like this foundation strong,
> The insanity of towns to stem
> With simpleness for strategem.

This is a virtuous monumentality to set beside Robert Frost's definition of poetry as a momentary stay against confusion. It is Platonic Being set against Becoming. The man who sees the immutable and can make the permanent symbol of it is the poet. Emerson says in the essay "The Poet": "He is the poet and shall draw us with love and terror, who sees through the flowing vest the firm nature, and can declare it" (W, III, 37). Swedenborg, as I noted earlier, was one of Emerson's early heroes who fulfilled that role: "Swedenborg, of all men in the recent ages, stands eminently for the translator of nature into thought . . . Before him the metamorphosis continually plays" (W, III, 35).

To Emerson, the thought that is taken from the flowing metamorphosis was the artifact itself, and that is the aesthetics of his monumentality. Thought put into language—poem, essay, lecture—was a fixed entity, a verbal monument. There was no doubt the biblical association: "The word unto the prophet spoken / Was writ on tables yet unbroken." In "Uriel," with spirited humor, Emerson parodied the lesser documents of order, the "Laws of form, and metre first," even the calendar of months and days, which the vain young gods discuss. It is Uriel who "solves the sphere" with his higher knowledge ("Line in nature is not found"), and immediately Fate's balance beam gives way and heaven slides to confusion.

In the poem "To Ellen," the lives of the two lovers are intelligible only as they are recorded on a page:

> And Ellen, when the graybeard years
>   Have brought us to life's evening hour,
> And all the crowded Past appears
>   A tiny scene of sun and shower,
> Then, if I read the page aright
>   Where Hope, the soothsayer, reads our lot,
> Thyself shalt own the page was bright,
>   Well that we loved, woe had we not.

Emerson's neoclassical predilection for attaching general values to monuments, seeing life over the shoulder as exemplum, strait-jacketed his poetry. The fixity at the end of "The Snow-Storm," despite the summoning of savage genius and colossal artistic energy, makes the closing exclusionary, cold, and inanimate. Whitman managed a more difficult unity by inclusion. His reality was not abstracted into monuments but, by a new linguistic drift and sweep, caught up not only the contradictions but the wayward drama of experience taking form.

Emerson's impulse toward liberation in his philosophy, in his life, and in his art equaled his need for monuments. Structure and constraint, the "virtue of self-trust," appear in the middle essays "Montaigne" and "Experience" as necessary modes for life, just as the young Emerson acknowledged the utility of custom, as here in the early poem "Grace":

> How much, preventing God, how much I owe
> To the defences thou has round me set;
> Example, custom, fear, occasion slow.

But Emerson's compulsion toward liberation in the name of imaginative exploration and deep-diving moral and aesthetic discovery, the discovery of self, was the dynamo of his existence. It sounded in his poems at times with exultant tones. More often it was a plaintive undertheme in which the artist considered the ideal ability to feel fully and to give fully in his art.

Liberation paired in Emerson's mind with power, as if the imagination, once freed from material vanities, could possess the resources of nature itself. The circulation of nature's forces concentrated and replenished the sources of imaginative energy. The poet, Emerson wrote, "is capable of a new energy . . . by abandonment to the nature of things" (W, III, 26). In "The American Scholar," he saw no dissipation of this energy once tapped: "There is never a beginning, there is never an end, to the inexplicable continuity of this web of God, but always circular power returning into itself" (W, I, 85). Once gathered by the poetic imagination, ideally transformed into poetry, this concentrated power liberates mankind. Readers of poetry, he said, are like persons who come out of a cave or cellar into the open air. It was a new way of seeing that comes when men are freed, as Gertrude Stein was to say about Picasso's revolution, from the habit of knowing what they are looking at. Emerson's dilemma, then, was not in the theory of goals, but in the creation of a language that could grasp the energies of liberation.

In the geology of his poems this liberation from closed forms recurs as the principal but sometimes buried meaning. In "Brahma," as I pointed out earlier, the admonition "turn thy back on heaven" is less a rejection of Christian doctrine than a summons to the higher imagination to turn away from single forms of seeing. "Form is imprisonment and heaven itself a decoy," he wrote in his journal a decade earlier (JMN, IX, 322). And before that, in the essay "The Poet," he said: "Every thought is also a prison; every heaven is also a prison (W, III, 33). The admonition in "Brahma" is echoed earlier still in "The Sphinx" as the Poet describes man's instinctual restlessness:

> The heavens that now draw him
> With sweetness untold
> Once found,—for new heavens
> He spurneth the old.

"The Sphinx" was a bold credo of the poet's liberating crusade. By a parable, because to be explicit about the poet as the converter of the world was absurdly heady, the poem set out the goal of the poet, the goal of Emerson's book of poems, the goal of Emerson the artist. Other poems, extending out to the limits of Emerson's poetic canon, by one plot or another follow the same impulse. In "Bacchus" it takes the form of intoxication; in "Give All to Love" it is transacted in the exchange of half-gods for the gods. Each was a reenactment of the archetypal release from the cave into the sun. As in "Threnody" and all the others, that linear arrangement of dramatic action led in the same direction. With such assumptions so dominant in Emerson's vision, it is not surprising that in poems like "Rhodora" and "Each and All" the revelation arrives presumptuously. The archetype is more integral in the structure of "Uriel" and "The Snow-Storm." Rarely, however, was that mental chain that leads to revelation broken or distorted.

Emerson, to our great relief, took account of the contrary workings of fate and the preposterous optimism of his poet's credo. In "Nemesis," following the rhetorical question "Will a woman's fan the oceans smooth?" we find the counterclaim:

> In spite of Virtue and the Muse,
> Nemesis will have her dues,
> And all our struggles and our toils
> Tighter wind the giant coils.

This dire aspect Harold Bloom emphasizes in plotting the dark-bright dialectic in Emerson's world. But though Emerson came to grips with the negation of his idealist philosophy, the set of his deepest beliefs assumed a powerful converting imagination whose function in turn necessarily assumed the free state into which art was to liberate all men.

Emerson's poetic theory was so powerful a generator of his poems that it molded to its own shape even the geographical and historical facts of the Concord battle that opened the Revolutionary War. The landscape, the action, and the actors he selected for the ceremonial poem "Concord Hymn" were an artist's choice. It was an unlikely vehicle for a theory of poetry, but there was no material that could withstand alteration in the deep set of Emerson's mind.

Most famous of all American works of the artistic mind, "Concord Hymn" took its shape and hidden concerns from the poetics. Emerson wrote the poem in 1837 when he was thirty-four for the dedication of the Revolutionary battle monument raised at Concord on July Fourth of that year. The citizens of Concord sang the poem's sixteen lines to the tune of the familiar hymn "Old Hundred." There were prayers and an address by a congressman. The local paper said the hymn spoke for itself, exciting "ideas of originality" and "poetic genius." Emerson himself was absent from the ceremony, visiting his in-laws in Plymouth and trying to get over a cold.

This year was the watershed of Emerson's life. On April 21, 1837, he wrote in his journal his own declaration of independence from guilt over his choice of writing as a profession. Like the Massachusetts industrialists, Emerson surmised, the writer did not depend on the weather. He could stop his own "morbid sympathy" for the farmers every time New England temperatures fell. "Climate touches not my own work," he concluded. "Where they have the sun, let them plant; we who have it not, will drive our pens." He declared with elation, "I am gay as a canary bird with this new knowledge." And then he announced: "I will write and so teach my countrymen their office" (*JMN*, V, 301).

While Emerson prepared his hymn, his great address "The American Scholar" was also taking form in his journal. He had been invited on June 22, at short notice, to be a substitute speaker and deliver the Phi Beta Kappa address at Harvard College on August 31. That speech, as Holmes said, was America's intellectual Declaration of Independence. The audacity of it still shocks us if we look at the proposition Emerson makes. The work of the native scholar was to be nothing less than "the conversion of the world." Emerson's purpose, he announced at the beginning, was to awaken "the sluggard intellect of this continent," and to free it from subservience to the Old World. "We will walk on our own feet; we will work with our own hands," he declared. "It is for you," he charged the young men at Cambridge, "to dare all."

At this high-running time of his life, Emerson's journal is filled with the urgent language from which he eventually extracted passages for more than three dozen essays and lectures. His personal life was equally crowded. Among his many activities, he finished delivering a series of lectures in Boston on the philosophy of history, planted thirty-one fruit trees near his house, corresponded with Thomas Carlyle in London, took lessons in German pronunciation from the formidable Margaret Fuller, and resisted his brother's entreaties to put some of the inheritance from his deceased first wife into a real-estate venture on Staten Island.

He records his alarm at the condition of the country. The times are bleak with fear of economic collapse. Men are breaking, and there is a run on banks in Boston and New York. The Exchange in New Orleans is burned. Emerson grieves for "the desponding hearts of the people in these black times." Yet "Concord Hymn" with its soaring affirmation never swerved from Emerson's first concern, freedom from stifling conventions. Here is the complete poem:

> By the rude bridge that arched the flood,
>   Their flag to April's breeze unfurled,
> Here once the embattled farmers stood
>   And fired the shot heard round the world.
>
> The foe long since in silence slept;
>   Alike the conqueror silent sleeps;
> And Time the ruined bridge has swept
>   Down the dark stream which seaward creeps.
>
> On this green bank, by this soft stream,
>   We set to-day a votive stone;
> That memory may their deed redeem,
>   When, like our sires, our sons are gone.
>
> Spirit, that made those heroes dare
>   To die, and leave their children free,

> Bid Time and Nature gently spare
> The shaft we raise to them and thee.

"Concord Hymn" is an Emersonian conversion poem. The several binary pairings mirror the same pattern in his other poems. "Justice is the rhyme of things" he said in "Merlin," which keeps "truth undecayed." Those paired elements—in setting, actors, action, and time—are visible in "Concord Hymn": the river and the land, the soft stream and the stone shaft, the conqueror and the foe, the deed and the memory, sires and their sons, the battlefield and the wide round world, the stream and the sea, the heroes and their children, Time and Nature (the *rude* bridge becomes in line seven a *ruined* bridge), then and now. The close interior rhyme of bridge *swept* and votive stone *set* focuses, perhaps without Emerson's conscious design, his basic opposition of what is in motion and what holds fast. Symbolically, every pair divides in Pythagorean fashion along Emerson's line between the transient and the permanent.

The conversion process goes on everywhere. The flux of battle becomes the stasis of the monument, the fact becomes the ideal of freedom, matter becomes spirit, the stream finds its way to the world-coiling sea, and Concord's battle becomes the world's battlecry. The arching conversion is the death and transsubstantiation of the original actors who, like Bulkeley, Hunt, and Willard of "Hamatreya," pass into dust and are held by the abiding earth. Foe and conqueror alike have become one. The high truth has been revealed in the Concord fight. Every element participates in the elaborate process.

Because it is under the dictate of that deep structure, the shot heard round the world sets up a veritable hum of resonances from other poems. The shot is an audible variant of "that world-warming spark / Which dazzles me in midnight dark, / Equalizing small and large" from the poem "Étienne de la Boéce." Twenty years to the day after the monument ceremony, Emerson picked up the analogy in the recently laid Atlantic cable, commemorated in his "Ode: Sung in the Town Hall, Concord, July 4, 1857." Cannons boom from town to town in that poem, but the cable is to carry the earth-circling song:

> henceforth there shall be no chain,
> Save underneath the sea
> The wires shall murmur through the main
> Sweet songs of liberty.

Emerson himself got word of the cable hookup in America while he was on the camping trip to the Adirondacks in 1858. He reports in his poetic account that two campers return with news of

> the wire-cable laid beneath the sea,
> And landed on our coast, and pulsating
> With ductile fire.

"We have a few moments in the longest life," he then declares, "Of such delight and wonder as there grew." Electricity was now schooled to spell "with guided tongue man's messages / Shot through the weltering pit of the salt sea." These echoing lines transmit a single idea and share visual forms and symbolic associations, for the trajectory of the bullet and the path of the cable make actual arcs that become conceptual circles that travel around the world.

Uriel, a poet figure, sees a world whose apparently straight lines bend into the closing arcs that structure the universe. His voice has the effect of a shot, and the result parallels the Emersonian revelatory "shudder of joy":

> As Uriel spoke with piercing eye,
> A shudder ran around the sky.

Stephen Whicher suggested the relationship of this shooting figure to Emerson's poetics. Referring to the essay "Circles" and to "Uriel" he wrote: "Both speak for Emerson's pride in the explosive properties of his thought, and his ill-concealed delight at the thought of the havoc he could wreak—if people were once to listen to him."

Emerson's prose repeatedly links poets and soldiers. He conceived his self-reliant man as an embattled defender at the parapets. He says in the lecture series he began in Boston in 1836, entitled "The Philosophy of History," "Society must come again under the yoke of the base and selfish, but the individual heart faithful to itself is fenced with a sacred palisado not to be traversed or approached unto, and is free forevermore" (EL, II, 186). To his mind the thundering affectiveness of the poet was a manly virtue to be preferred to the character of Bryant's poems, Greenough's sculpture, and Dr. Channing's preaching. Of these he said: "They are all *feminine* or receptive and not masculine or creative" (JMN, V, 195). He idealized the devastating power possible in public address, whose form he described in his journal as "a panharmonicon,—every note on the longest gamut, from the explosion of cannon to the tinkle of a guitar. Let us try if Folly, Custom, Convention and Phlegm cannot hear our sharp artillery" (JMN, VII, 265). The orator feels the discharge the same as the soldier: "The least effect of the oration is on the orator. Yet it is something; a faint recoil; a kicking of the gun" (JMN, V, 362). To re-establish Adam in the garden, to recover our power and mission as divine beings, he says elsewhere, we "must fire . . . the artillery of sympathy and emotion" against "the mechanical powers and the mechanical philosophy of this time" (JMN, VII, 271).

The poets are liberating gods. The Concord minutemen are liberating poets. At the heart of the identification is the chief element in Emerson's concept of the poetic imagination: power and the ability to convert the present act into the ideal vision it contains. Emerson's passage in "Poetry and Imagination" now rings with added resonance: the poet "reads in the word or action of the man its yet untold results. His inspiration is power to carry out and complete the metamorphosis" (*W*, VIII, 39). The crucial passage describing conversion in "The American Scholar" reveals how he identified Man Thinking, poet in action, and soldier with his musket: the world "came into him life; it went out from him truth. It came to him short-lived actions; it went out from him immortal thoughts. It came to him business; it went from him poetry. It was dead fact; now, it is quick thought" (*W*, I, 87). The shot at Concord is like a poem of freedom, the riflemen are figures of the imagination. What came to them as lead musketballs went from them as the force that would convert the world. It was a marvelous allegory of the brave belief in "Poetry and the Imagination," that poetry could trigger the conversion of the world: "Is not poetry the little chamber in the brain where is generated the explosive force which, by gentle shocks, sets in action the intellectual world?" (*W*, VIII, 64).

New power is the good which the soul seeks, Emerson announced. It was the gigantic duty of his poet. As Emerson inevitably associated the farmer-rifleman with the American poets, he called upon them to overthrow the foes of literary freedom. In the Concord battle poem not only are Minutemen firing on British Redcoats, but, I unabashedly propose, rebel American poets are shooting down the stiff, ornamented troops of poetic tradition.

That breakthrough into freedom is the principal quality by which we know the open-form poetry we call modern. William Carlos Williams carried the rebellion forward. In the mid-twentieth century he is the great hater of blockages. *Paterson* (1946-1958), his splendid, sprawling poem of release, sings of

> —a dark flame,
> a wind, a flood—counter to all staleness.

Two marvelously subversive lines in *Paterson* sum up the American aesthetic that began with the revolutionary ferment in Emerson's stirring hymn:

> beauty is
> a defiance of authority.

Oliver Wendell Holmes said that the poem's "one conspicuous line— 'And fired the shot heard round the world'—must not take to itself all the praise deserved by this perfect little poem." The syntax of that most famous American line, however, holds emblematically the trajectory of the poetics. So powerful is the conversion structure of Emerson's poetic forms that inevitably his syntax duplicates that structure. In "Threnody," the paradox at the end of the poem sets out a compact linguistic model of the conversion toward which the poem works. "Lost in God, in Godhead found" holds syntactically the movement from material dissolution to spiritual fulfillment and from the mistaken idea of "loss" to the spiritual revelation of discovery. In "Concord Hymn," the famous line compacts the Emersonian conversion process, its syntax acting out the basic movement of the conversion. The "plot" of this crucial line proceeds precisely from the fact to the truth. The actual line, with the one preceding it, has undergone fairly complicated transformations to achieve this. The deep content structure would look something like this: (Someone) embattle(d) the farmers. The farmers (stood) here once. The farmers fire(d) the shot. (Someone) (heard) round the world the shot. But because Emerson conceived the process of conversion always as from fact to truth, from the act to its significance, he wrote what he did. Its order is exact as the flowing of the stream to the sea, another linear and transmutive image in the poem. As the shot becomes the idea of freedom, the syntax manifests the movement from act to idea, from the farmers to the world, from the smaller to the larger, from the small musket ball to the great globe itself.

The poem's larger transaction (from adversity to triumph, from the embattled to the redemptive) parallels in an extraordinarily close way the structure of "The Snow-Storm." Both poems move from frantic activity to stasis and from confusion and paralysis to liberation. The monument of "Concord Hymn" is a model for that aspect of Emerson's poetics in which the poet extracts the lasting from the transient, making art the votive stone of experience. The poet "sees through the flowing vest the firm nature, and can declare it" (W, III, 37). The shaft fills the now familiar objective of Emerson's poetics by its upward idealizing sign toward the Platonic realm. The activity in "Concord Hymn" is quintessentially Emersonian, as the generalized citizen-speaker gathers his crucial elements from the horizontal landscape for the purpose of building the vertical shaft of significance. It is the literal setting-up of the moral coordinates from a journal entry of the same year: "Pride, and Thrift, and Expediency, who jeered and chirped and were so well pleased with themselves, and made merry with the dream, as they termed it, of Philosophy and Love,—behold they are all flat, and here is the Soul erect and unconquered still" (JMN, V, 332). Sherman Paul discerned the basic structural alignments in Emerson's moral space: "The paradoxes and polarity of his thought reflect [the] struggle to inform the life of the horizontal with the quality of the vertical, and by means of the horizontal to raise himself into the erect position." Whereas Whitman's poems pushed out to preserve the full process of experience, Emerson's monument poems carved closely to preserve the meaning. In the hymn, the shaft is the artifact, literally the truth of the matter.

The poem, with all its associations, is an intricate model of the poetics. The two Emersonian forces, one outward toward fluid dissipation and the other inward toward concentration and fixity, work simultaneously. The obsessive design of the poem, its surface faultlessly crafted as a communal tribute for a public ceremony, is fundamentally that of a poet commemorating the poetic enterprise. Ralph Rusk said of "Concord Hymn" that "Though it was to become a part of the American tradition and deserved immortality," the poem "offered Emerson no pattern for his future verse" (Rusk, 274). Quite to the contrary, the poem reflects in every element—its structure, players, images, syntax, its *idea*—the poetics that presided over Emerson's craft. The poem's deepest springs, as we have seen, fed his other aesthetic pronouncements. It would be remarkable, in fact, if this were not so, for the poem was composed at a highly charged time when Emerson's theoretical energies and sense of mission were beaming out in every direction. Within a year and a few days he was to deliver both "The American Scholar" address, his credo on the artist's imagination, and the Divinity School address, his explosive call to liberation from the old forms. When those Concord worthies sang the hymn for their dead heroes, they were also singing of Emerson's hopes for a new poetry. A remarkable occasion indeed. But knowing that Emerson's poetics was the dynamo that energized all he did, we also know it could not have been otherwise.

HAROLD BLOOM

Emerson: The American Religion

I start from a warning of Lichtenberg's:

> As soon as a man begins to see everything, he generally expresses himself
> obscurely—begins to speak with the tongues of angels.

But Lichtenberg also wrote, "The itch of a great prince gave us long
sleeves." The lengthened shadow of our American culture is Emerson's, and
Emerson indeed saw everything in everything, and spoke with the tongue of a
daemon. His truest achievement was to invent the American religion, and
my reverie intends a spiraling out from his center in order to track the
circumferences of that religion in a broad selection of those who emanated
out from him, directly and evasively, celebratory of or in negation to his
Gnosis. Starting from Emerson we came to where we are, and from that
impasse, which he prophesied, we will go by a path that most likely he marked
out also. The mind of Emerson is the mind of America, for worse and for
glory, and the central concern of that mind was the American religion, which
most memorably was named "self-reliance."

Of this religion, I begin by noting that it is *self*-reliance as opposed to
God-reliance, though Emerson thought the two were the same. I will emphasize this proper interpretation by calling the doctrine "*self*-reliance," in
distinction from Emerson's essay *Self-Reliance*. "Reliance" is not of the essence, but the Emersonian *self* is: "To talk of reliance is a poor external way of
speaking. Speak rather of that which relies because it works and is." What
"works and is" is the stranger god, or even alien god, within. Within? Deeper
than the *psyche* is the *pneuma*, the spark, the uncreated self, distinct from the
soul that God (or Demiurge) created. *Self*-reliance, in Emerson as in Meister
Eckhart or in Valentinus the Gnostic, is the religion that celebrates and

---

reveres what in the self is before the Creation, a whatness which from the perspective of religious orthodoxy can only be the primal Abyss.

In September 1866, when he was sixty-three, and burned out by his prophetic exultation during the Civil War, Emerson brooded in his Journals on the return of the primal Abyss, which he had named Necessity, and which his descendant Stevens was to hail as "fatal Ananke the common god." Earlier in 1866, pondering Hegel, Emerson had set down, with a certain irony, his awareness of the European vision of the end of speculation:

> Hegel seems to say, Look, I have sat long gazing at the all but imperceptible transitions of thought to thought, until I have seen with eyes the true boundary. . . . I know that all observation will justify me, and to the future metaphysician I say, that he may measure the power of his perception by the degree of his accord with mine. This is the twilight of the gods, predicted in the Scandinavian mythology.

A few months later, this irony at another's apocalyptic egocentricity was transcended by a post-apocalyptic or Gnostic realization:

> There may be two or three or four steps, according to the genius of each, but for every seeing soul there are two absorbing facts,—I and the Abyss.

This grand outflaring of negative theology is a major text, however gnomic, of the American religion, Emersonianism, which [I have attempted] to identify, to describe, to celebrate, to join. I am not happy with the accounts of Emersonianism available to me. Of the religions native to the United States, Emersonianism or our literary religion remains the most diffuse and diffused, yet the only faith of spiritual significance, still of prophetic force for our future. An excursus upon the religions starting in America is necessary before I quest into the wavering interiors of the American religion proper. Sydney Ahlstrom in his definitive A Religious History of the American People (1972) recognizes "that Emerson is in fact the theologian of something we may almost term 'the American religion.'" Who were or could have been Emerson's rivals? Of religious geniuses our evening-land has been strangely unproductive, when our place in Western history is fully considered. We have had one great systematic theologian, in Jonathan Edwards, and something close to a second such figure in Horace Bushnell. But we have only the one seer, Emerson, and the essentially literary traditions that he fostered.

The founders of American heresies that have endured are quite plentiful, yet our major historians of American religion—Ahlstrom, W. W. Sweet, H. R. Niebuhr, M. E. Marty, S. E. Mead, C. E. Olmstead, among others—tend to agree that only a handful are of central importance. These would include Ellen Harmon White of the Seventh Day Adventists, Joseph

Smith of the Mormons, Alexander Campbell of the Disciples of Christ, Mary Baker Eddy of Christian Science, and Charles Taze Russell of Jehovah's Witnesses. To read any or all of these is a difficult experience, for the founder's texts lack the power that the doctrines clearly are able to manifest. There is, thankfully, no Emersonian church, yet there are certain currents of Harmonial American religion that dubiously assert their descent from the visionary of *Nature* and the *Essays*. Aside from Mrs. Eddy, who seized on poor Bronson Alcott for an endorsement after the subtle Emerson had evaded her, the "health and harmony" Positive Thinkers notably include Ralph Waldo Trine, author of *In Tune with the Infinite* (1897), and his spiritual descendants Harry Emerson Fosdick and Norman Vincent Peale. We can add to this pseudo-Emersonian jumble the various Aquarian theosophies that continue to proliferate in America a decade after the sixties ebbed out. I cite all these sects and schisms because all of them have failed the true Emersonian test for the American religion, which I will state as my own dogma: *it cannot become the American religion until it first is canonized as American literature.* Though this explicit dogma is mine, it was the genius of Emerson implicitly to have established such a principle among us.

II

What in the nineteenth and twentieth centuries *is* religious writing? What can it be? Which of these passages, setting their polemics aside, is better described as religious writing?

> People say to me, that it is but a dream to suppose that Christianity should regain the organic power in human society which once it possessed. I cannot help that; I never said it could. I am not a politician; I am proposing no measures, but exposing a fallacy, and resisting a pretence. Let Benthamism reign, if men dare no aspirations; but do not tell them to be romantic, and then solace them with glory; do not attempt by philosophy what was once done by religion. The ascendancy of Faith may be impracticable, but the reign of Knowledge is incomprehensible. . . .

> . . . He that has done nothing has known nothing. Vain is it to sit scheming and plausibly discoursing: up and be doing! If thy knowledge be real, put it forth from thee: grapple with real Nature; try thy theories there, and see how they hold out. *Do* one thing, for the first time in thy life do a thing; a new light will rise to thee on the doing of all things whatsoever. . . .

I have taken these passages randomly enough; they lay near by. The distinguished first extract is both truly religious and wonderfully written, but the second is religious writing. Newman, in the first, from *The Tamworth*

Reading Room (1841), knows both the truth and his own mind, and the relation between the two. Carlyle, in the second, from *Corn-Law Rhymes* (1832), knows only his own knowing, and sets that above both Newman's contraries, religion and philosophy. *Corn-Law Rhymes* became a precursor text for Emerson because he could recognize what had to be religious writing for the nineteenth century, and to that recognition, which alone would not have sufficed, Emerson added the American difference, which Carlyle could not ever understand. Subtle as this difference is, another intertextual juxtaposition can help reveal it:

> "But it is with man's Soul as it was with Nature: the beginning of Creation is—Light. Till the eye have vision, the whole members are in bonds. Divine moment, when over the tempest-tossed Soul, as once over the wild-weltering Chaos, it is spoken: Let there be Light! Ever to the greatest that has felt such moment, is it not miraculous and God-announcing; even as, under simpler figures, to the simplest and least. The mad primeval Discord is hushed; the rudely-jumbled conflicting elements bind themselves into separate Firmaments: deep silent rock-foundations are built beneath; and the skyey vault with its everlasting Luminaries above: instead of a dark wasteful Chaos, we have a blooming, fertile, heaven-encompassed World."

> "Nature is not fixed but fluid, Spirit alters, molds, makes it. The immobility or bruteness of nature is the absence of spirit; to pure spirit it is fluid, it is volatile, it is obedient. Every spirit builds itself a house, and beyond its house a world, and beyond its world a heaven. Know then that the world exists for you. For you is the phenomenon perfect. What we are, that only can we see. . . . Build therefore your own world. As fast as you conform your life to the pure idea in your mind, that will unfold its great proportions. . . . The kingdom of man over nature, which cometh not with observation,—a dominion such as now is beyond his dream of God,—he shall enter without more wonder than the blind man feels who is gradually, restored to perfect sight."

This juxtaposition is central, because the passages are. The first rhapsode is Carlyle's Teufelsdröckh uttering his Everlasting Yea in *Sartor Resartus*; the second is Emerson's Orphic poet chanting the conclusion of *Nature*. Carlyle's seeing soul triumphs over the Abyss, until he can say to himself: "Be no longer a Chaos, but a World, or even Worldkin. Produce! Produce!" The Abyss is bondage, the production is freedom, somehow still "in God's name!" Emerson, despite his supposed discipleship to Carlyle in *Nature*, has his seeing soul proclaim a world so metamorphic and beyond natural metamorphosis that its status is radically *prior* to that of the existent universe. For the earth is only part of the blind man's "dream of God." Carlyle's imagination remains orthodox, and rejects Chaos. Emerson's seeing, beyond observation, is more theosophical than Germanic Transcendental. The freedom to imagine "the pure idea in your mind" is the heretical absolute freedom of the Gnostic who identified his mind's purest idea with the original Abyss. American freedom, in the context of Emerson's American religion, indeed might be called "Abyss-radiance."

I return to the question of what, in the nineteenth century, makes writing *religious*. Having set Carlyle in the midst, between Newman and Emerson, I cite next the step in religious writing beyond even Emerson:

> . . . we have an interval, and then our place knows us no more. Some spend this interval in listlessness, some in high passions, the wisest, at least among "the children of this world," in art and song. For our one chance lies in expanding that interval, in getting as many pulsations as possible into the given time. . . .

Pater, concluding *The Renaissance*, plays audaciously against Luke 16:8, where "the children of this world are in their generation wiser than the children of light." Literalizing the Gospel's irony, Pater insinuates that in his generation the children of this world are the only children of light. Light expands our fiction of duration, our interval or place in art, by a concealed allusion to the Blakean trope that also fascinated Yeats; the pulsation of an artery in which the poet's work is done. Pater sinuously murmurs his credo, which elsewhere in *The Renaissance* is truly intimated to be "a strange rival religion" opposed to warring orthodoxies, fit for "those who are neither for Jehovah nor for His enemies."

To name Emerson and Pater as truly "religious writers" is to call into question very nearly everything that phrase usually implies. More interestingly, this naming also questions that mode of displacement. M.H. Abrams analyzes in his strong study *Natural Supernaturalism:* "not . . . the deletion and replacement of religious ideas but rather the assimilation and reinterpretation of religious ideas." I believe that the following remarks of Abrams touch their limit precisely where Carlyle and Emerson part, on the American difference, and also where Carlyle and Ruskin part from Pater and what comes after. The story Abrams tells has been questioned by Hillis Miller, from a Nietzschean linguistic or Deconstructive perspective, so that Miller dissents from Abrams exactly where Nietzsche himself chose to attack Carlyle (which I cite below). But there is a more ancient perspective to turn against Abrams's patterns-of-displacement, an argument as to whether poetry did not inform religion before religion ever instructed poetry. And beyond this argument, there is the Gnostic critique of creation-theories both Hebraic and Platonic, a critique that relies always upon the awesome trope of the primal Abyss.

Abrams states his "displacement" thesis in a rhetoric of continuity:

> Much of what distinguishes writers I call "Romantic" derives from the fact

that they undertook, whatever their religious creed or lack of creed, to save traditional concepts, schemes, and values which had been based on the relation of the Creator to his creature and creation, but to reformulate them within the prevailing two-term system of subject and object, ego and non-ego, the human mind or consciousness and its transactions with nature. Despite their displacement from a supernatural to a natural frame of reference, however, the ancient problems, terminology, and ways of thinking about human nature and history survived, as the implicit distinctions and categories through which even radically secular writers saw themselves and their world. . . .

Such "displacement" is a rather benign process, as though the incarnation of the Poetic Character and the Incarnation proper could be assimilated to one another, or the former serve as the reinterpretation of the latter. But what if poetry as such is always a counter-theology, or Gentile Mythus, as Vico believed? Abrams, not unlike Matthew Arnold, reads religion as abiding in poetry, as though the poem were a saving remnant. But perhaps the saving remnant *of poetry* is the only force of what we call theology? And what can theology be except what Geoffrey Hartman anxiously terms it: "a vast, intricate domain of psychopoetic events," another litany of evasions? Poems are the original lies-against-time, as the Gnostics understood when they turned their dialectics to revisionary interpretations not only of the Bible and Plato, but of Homer as well. Gnosticism was the inaugural and most powerful of Deconstructions because it undid all genealogies, scrambled all hierarchies, allegorized every microcosm/macrocosm relation, and rejected every representation of divinity as non-referential.

Carlyle, though he gave Abrams both the scheme of displacement and the title-phrase of "natural supernaturalism," seems to me less and less self-deceived as he progressed onwards in life and work, which I think accounts for his always growing fury. Here I follow Nietzsche, in the twelfth "Skirmish" of *Twilight of the Idols* where he leaves us not much of the supposedly exemplary life of Carlyle:

> . . . this unconscious and involuntary farce, this heroic-moralistic interpretation of dyspeptic states. Carlyle: a man of strong words and attitudes, a rhetor from *need*, constantly lured by the craving for a strong faith and the feeling of his incapacity for it (in this respect, a typical romantic!). The craving for a strong faith is no proof of a strong faith, but quite the contrary. If one has such a faith, then one can afford the beautiful luxury of skepticism; one is sure enough, firm enough, has ties enough for that. Carlyle drugs something in himself with the fortissimo of his veneration of men of strong faith and with his rage against the less simple minded: he *requires* noise. A constant passionate dishonesty against himself—that is his *proprium*; in this respect he is and remains interesting. Of course, in England he is admired precisely for his honesty. Well, that is English; and in view of the

fact that the English are the people of consummate cant, it is even as it should be, and not only comprehensible. At bottom, Carlyle is an English atheist who makes it a point of honor not to be one.

It seems merely just to observe, following Nietzsche's formidable wit, that Carlyle contrived to be a religious writer without being a religious man. His clear sense of the signs and characteristics of the times taught him that the authentic nineteenth-century writer had to be religious *qua* writer. The burden, as Carlyle knew, was not so much godlessness as belatedness, which compels a turn to Carlyle (and Emerson) on history.

III

Carlyle, with grim cheerfulness, tells us that history is an unreadable text, indeed a "complex manuscript, covered over with formless inextricably-entangled unknown characters,—nay, which is a Palimpsest, and had once prophetic writing, still dimly legible there. . . ." We can see emerging in this dark observation the basis for *The French Revolution*, and even for *Past and Present*. But that was Carlyle *On History* in 1830, just before the advent of Diogenes Teufelsdröckh, the author of *On History Again* in 1833, where the unreadable is read as Autobiography repressed by all Mankind: "a like unconscious talent of remembering and of forgetting again does the work here." The great instance of this hyperbolic or Sublime repression is surely Goethe, whose superb self-confidence breathes fiercely in his couplet cited by Carlyle as the first epigraph to *Sartor Resartus*:

Mein Vermächtnis, wie herrlich weit und breit!
Die Zeit ist mein Vermächtnis, mein Acker ist die Zeit.

Goethe's splendid, wide and broad inheritance is time itself, the seed-field that has the glory of having grown Goethe! But then, Goethe had no precursors in his own language, or none at least that could make him anxious. Carlyle trumpets his German inheritance: Goethe, Schiller, Fichte, Novalis, Kant, Schelling. His English inheritance was more troublesome to him, and the vehemence of his portrait of Coleridge reveals an unresolved relationship. This unacknowledged debt to Coleridge, with its too-conscious swerve away from Coleridge and into decisiveness and overt courage, pain accepted and work deified, may be the hidden basis for the paradoxes of Carlyle on time, at once resented with a Gnostic passion and worshipped as the seed-bed of a Goethean greatness made possible for the self. It is a liberation to know the American difference again when the reader turns from Carlyle's two essays on history to *History*, placed first of the *Essays* (1841) of Emerson:

This human mind wrote history, and this must read it. The Sphinx must solve her own riddle. If the whole of history is in one man, it is all to be explained from individual experience. . . .

. . . Property also holds of the soul, covers great spiritual facts, and instinctively we at first hold to it with swords and laws and wide and complex combinations. The obscure consciousness of this fact is the light of all our day, the claim of claims; the plea for education, for justice, for charity; the foundation of friendship and love and of the heroism and grandeur which belong to acts of self-reliance. It is remarkable that involuntarily we always read as superior beings. . . .

. . . . The student is to read history actively and not passively; to esteem his own life the text, and books the commentary. . . .

So much then for Carlyle on history; so much indeed for history. The text is not interpretable? But there is no text! There is only your own life, and the Wordsworthian light of all our day turns out to be: self-reliance. Emerson, in describing an 1847 quarrel with Carlyle in London, gave a vivid sense of his enforcing the American difference, somewhat at the expense of a friendship that was never the same again:

Carlyle . . . had grown impatient of opposition, especially when talking of Cromwell. I differed from him . . . in his estimate of Cromwell's character, and he rose like a great Norse giant from his chair—and, drawing a line with his finger across the table, said, with terrible fierceness: "Then, sir, there is a line of separation between you and me as wide as that, and as deep as the pit."

Hardly a hyperbole, the reader will reflect, when he reads what two years later Carlyle printed as *The Nigger Question*. This remarkable performance doubtless was aimed against "Christian Philanthropy" and related hypocrisies, but the abominable greatness of the tract stems from its undeniable madness. The astonished reader discovers not fascism, but a terrible sexual hysteria rising up from poor Carlyle, as the repressed returns in the extraordinary trope of black pumpkin-eating:

. . . far over the sea, we have a few black persons rendered extremely "free" indeed. . . . Sitting yonder with their beautiful muzzles up to the ears in pumpkins, imbibing sweet pulps and juices; the grinder and incisor teeth ready for ever new work, and the pumpkins cheap as grass in those rich climates: while the sugar-crops rot round them uncut, because labour cannot be hired, so cheap are the pumpkins. . . .

. . . and beautiful Blacks sitting there up to the ears in pumpkins, and doleful Whites sitting here without potatoes to eat. . . .

. . . The fortunate Black man, very swiftly does he settle *his* account with supply and demand:—not so swiftly the less fortunate white man of those tropical locations. A bad case, his, just now. He himself cannot work; and his black neighbor, rich in pumpkin, is in no haste to help him. Sunk to the ears in pumpkin, imbibing saccharine juices, and much at his ease in the

Creation, he can listen to the less fortunate white man's "demand" and take his own time in supplying it. . . .

> . . . An idle White gentleman is not pleasant to me: though I confess the real work for him is not easy to find, in these our epochs; and perhaps he is seeking, poor soul, and may find at last. But what say you to an idle Black gentleman, with his rum-bottle in his hand (for a little additional pumpkin you can have red-herrings and rum, in Demerara),—rum-bottle in his hand, no breeches on his body, pumpkin at discretion. . . .

> . . . Before the West Indies could grow a pumpkin for any Negro, how much European heroism had to spend itself in obscure battle; to sink, in mortal agony, before the jungles, the putrescences and waste savageries could become arable, and the Devils be in some measure chained there!

> . . . A bit of the great Protector's own life lies there; beneath those pumpkins lies a bit of the life that was Oliver Cromwell's. . . .

I have cited only a few passages out of this veritable procession of pumpkins, culminating in the vision of Carlyle's greatest hero pushing up the pumpkins so that unbreeched Blacks might exercise their potent teeth. Mere racism does not yield so pungent a phantasmagoria, and indeed I cannot credit it to Carlyle's likely impotence either. This pumpkin litany is Carlyle's demi-Gnosticism at its worst, for here time is no fair seed-bed but rather devouring time, Kronos chewing us up as so many pumpkins, the time of "Getting Under Way" in *Sartor Resartus:*

> . . . Me, however, as a Son of Time, unhappier than some others, was Time threatening to eat quite prematurely; for, strike as I might, there was no good Running, so obstructed was the path, so gyved were the feet. . . .

Emerson, in truth, did not abide in his own heroic stance towards Time and History. The great declaration of his early intensity comes in the 1838 Journals: "A great man escapes out of the kingdom of time; he puts time under his feet." But the next decade featured ebb rather than influx of the Newness. What matter? The American difference, however ill prepared to combat experience, had been stated, if not established. To come to that stating is to arrive fresh at Emerson's *Nature*, where the *clinamen* from Carlyle, and from Coleridge, is superbly turned.

IV

Deconstructing any discourse by Ralph Waldo Emerson would be a hopeless enterprise, extravagantly demonstrating why Continental modes of interpretation are unlikely to add any lustres to the most American of writers. Where there are classic canons of construction, protrusions from the text can tempt an unravelling, but in a text like *Nature* (1836) all is protrusion. Emerson's first book is a blandly dissociative apocalypse, in which everything is a cheerful error, indeed a misreading, starting with the title, which says

"Nature" but means "Man." The original epigraph, from Plotinus by way of the Cambridge Platonist Cudworth, itself deconstructs the title:

> Nature is but an image or imitation of wisdom, the last thing of the soul; nature being a thing which doth only do, but not know.

The attentive reader, puzzling a way now through Emerson's manifesto, will find it to be more the American Romantic equivalent to Blake's *The Marriage of Heaven and Hell* than to Coleridge's *Aids to Reflection* (which however it frequently echoes). At the Christological age of thirty-three (as was Blake in the *Marriage*), Emerson rises in the spirit to proclaim his own independent majority, but unlike Blake Emerson cheerfully and confidently proclaims his nation's annunciation also. Unfortunately, Emerson's vision precedes his style, and only scattered passages in *Nature* achieve the eloquence that became incessant from about a year later on almost to the end, prevailing long after the sage had much mind remaining. I will move here through the little book's centers of vision, abandoning the rest of it to time's revenges.

Prospects, and not retrospectives, is the Emersonian motto, as we can see by contrasting the title of the last chapter, "Prospects," to the opening sentences of the Introduction:

> Our age is retrospective. It builds the sepulchres of the fathers. It writes biographies, histories, and criticism. The foregoing generations beheld God and nature face to face; we, through their eyes. Why should we not also enjoy an original relation to the universe?

The "fathers" are not British High Romantics, Boston Unitarians, New England Calvinist founders, but rather an enabling fiction, as Emerson well knows. They are Vico's giants, magic primitives, who invented all Gentile mythologies, all poetries of earth. Emerson joins them in the crucial trope of his first chapter, which remains the most notorious in his work:

> Crossing a bare common, in snow puddles, at twilight, under a clouded sky, without having in my thoughts any occurrence of special good fortune, I have enjoyed a perfect exhilaration. I am glad to the brink of fear. In the woods, too, a man casts off his years, as the snake his slough, and at what period soever of life is always a child. . . . There I feel that nothing can befall me in life,—no disgrace, no calamity (leaving me my eyes), which nature cannot repair. Standing on the bare ground,—my head bathed by the blithe air and uplifted into infinite space,—all mean egotism vanishes. I become a transparent eyeball; I am nothing; I see all; the currents of the Universal Being circulate through me; I am part or parcel of God. . . .

This is not a "Spiritual Newbirth, or Baphometric Fire-baptism," akin to those of Carlyle's Teufelsdröckh or Melville's Ahab, because Emerson's freedom rises out of the ordinary, and not out of crisis. But, despite a ruggedly commonplace genesis, there is little that is ordinary in the deliberately outrageous "I become a transparent eyeball." Kenneth Burke associates Emerson's imagery of transparence with the *crossing* or *bridging* action that is transcendence, and he finds the perfect paradigm for such figuration in the Virgilian underworld. The unburied dead, confronted by Charon's refusal to ferry them across Stygia, imploringly "stretched forth their hands through love of the farther shore." Emersonian transparency is such a stretching, a Sublime crossing of the gulf of solipsism, but *not* into a communion with others. As Emerson remarks: "The name of the nearest friend sounds then foreign and accidental: to be brothers, to be acquaintances, master or servant, is then a trifle and a disturbance." The farther shore has no persons upon it, because Emerson's farther shore or beyond is no part of nature, and has no room therefore for created beings. A second-century Gnostic would have understood Emerson's "I am nothing; I see all" as the mode of negation through which the knower again could stand in the Abyss, the place of original fullness, *before* the Creation.

A transparent eyeball is the emblem of the Primal Abyss regarding itself. What can an Abyss behold in an Abyss?

The answer, in our fallen or demiurgical perspective, can be dialectical, the endless ironic interplay of presence and absence, fullness and emptiness; in Gnostic vocabulary, Pleroma and Kenoma. But the Emerson of *Nature* was not yet willing to settle for such a deconstruction. Not upon an elevation, but taking his stance upon the bare American ground, Emerson demands Victory, to his senses as to his soul. The perfect exhilaration of a perpetual youth which comes to him is akin to what Hart Crane was to term an improved infancy. Against Wordsworth, Coleridge, Carlyle, the seer Emerson celebrates the American difference of *discontinuity*. "I am nothing" is a triumph of the Negative Way; "I see all" because I am that I am, discontinuously present not wherever but whenever I will to be present. "I am part or parcel of God," yet the god is not Jehovah but Orpheus, and Emerson momentarily is not merely the Orphic poet but the American Orpheus himself.

Poetic Orphism is a mixed and vexed matter, beyond disentanglement, and it is at the center of Emerson, even in the rhetorically immature *Nature*. I will digress upon it, and then rejoin *Nature* at its Orphic vortices.

V

The historian of Greek religion M.P. Nilsson shrewdly remarked that "Orphicism is a book religion, the first example of the kind in the history of

Greek religion." Whatever it *may* have been historically, perhaps as early as the sixth century B.C.E., Orphism became the natural religion of Western poetry. Empedocles, an Emersonian favorite, shares Orphic characteristics with such various texts as certain Platonic myths, some odes of Pindar and fragments of poems recovered from South Italian Greek grave-sites. But later texts, mostly Neoplatonic, became the principal source for Emerson, who did not doubt their authenticity. W.K.C. Guthrie surmises a historical Orphism, devoted to Apollo, partly turned against Dionysus, and centered on a "belief in the latent divinity and immortality of the human soul" and on a necessity for constant purity, partly achieved through *ekstasis*.

Between the Hellenistic Neoplatonists and the seventeenth-century Cambridge variety, of whom Cudworth mattered most to Emerson, there had intervened the Florentine Renaissance mythologies, particularly Ficino's, which Christianized Orpheus. The baptized Orpheus lingers on in Thomas Taylor, whose cloudy account may have been Emerson's most direct source for Orphism. But from *Nature* on, Emerson's Orpheus is simply Primal Man, who preceded the Creation, and very little occult lore actually gets into Emerson's quite autobiographical projection of himself as American Orpheus. His final Orphic reference, in the 1849 Journals, has about it the authority of a self-tested truth though its burden is extravagant, even for Emerson:

> . . . Orpheus is no fable: you have only to sing, and the rocks will crystallize; sing, and the plant will organize; sing, and the animal will be born.

If Orpheus is fact in Emerson's life and work, this must be fact when seen in the light of an idea. The idea is the Central or Universal Man, the American More-than-Christ who is *to come*, the poet prefigured by Emerson himself as voice in the wilderness. In some sense he arrived as Walt Whitman, and some seventy years later as Hart Crane, but that is to run ahead of the story. In Emerson's mythopoeic and metamorphic conception, Central or Orphic Man is hardly to be distinguished from an Orphic view of language, and so breaks apart and is restituted just as language ebbs and flows:

> . . . In what I call the cyclus of Orphic words, which I find in Bacon, in Cudworth, in Plutarch, in Plato, in that which the New Church would indicate when it speaks of the truths possessed by the primeval church broken up into fragments and floating hither and thither in the corrupt church, I perceive myself addressed thoroughly. They do teach the intellect and cause a gush of emotion; which we call the moral sublime; they pervade also the moral nature. Now the Universal Man when he comes, must so speak. He must recognize by addressing the whole nature.

Bacon's Orpheus was a Baconian philosopher-natural scientist; Cudworth's a Neoplatonic Christian; Plutarch's and Plato's an image of spiritual

purification. It is sly of Emerson to bring in the not very Orphic Swedenborgians of the New Church, but he really means his Central Man to be
universal. The *sparagmos* of Orpheus is a prime emblem for the American
religion, whose motto I once ventured as: *Everything that can be broken should
be broken.* Emerson's all-but-everything can be given in a brief, grim list:

> February 6, 1831: death of his first wife, Ellen;
> May 9, 1836: death of his brother, Charles;
> January 27, 1842: death of his first son, Waldo.

These Orphic losses should have shattered the American Orpheus,
for all his life long these were the three persons he loved best. As losses they
mark the three phases in the strengthening of his self-reliant American
religion, an Orphism that would place him beyond further loss, at the high
price of coming to worship the goddess Ananke, dread but sublime Necessity.
But that worship came late to Emerson. He deferred it by a metamorphic
doctrine of Orpheus, best stated in his essay *History:*

> The power of music, the power of poetry, to unfix and as it were clap wings to
> solid nature, interprets the riddle of Orpheus. . . .

This sentence is strangely flanked in the essay, though since Emerson's unit of discourse tends more to be the sentence than the paragraph, the
strangeness is mitigated. Still, the preceding sentence is both occult and
puzzling:

> Man is the broken giant, and in all his weakness both his body and his mind
> are invigorated by habits of conversation with nature.

The Orphic riddle is the dialectic of strength and weakness *in Orpheus
himself.* Is he god or man? St. Augustine placed Orpheus at the head of poets
called theologians, and then added: "But these theologians were not worshipped as gods, though in some fashion the kingdom of the godless is wont to
set Orpheus as head over the rites of the underworld." This is admirably clear,
but not sufficient to unriddle Orpheus. Jane Harrison surmised that an actual
man, Orpheus, came belatedly to the worship of Dionysus and modified those
rites, perhaps partly civilizing them. Guthrie assimilated Orpheus to Apollo,
while allowing the Dionysiac side also. E.R. Dodds, most convincingly for my
purposes, associates Orpheus with Empedocles and ultimately with Thracian
traditions of shamanism. Describing Empedocles (and Orpheus), Dodds
might be writing of Emerson, granting only some temporal differences:

> . . . Empedocles represents not a new but a very old type of personality, the
> shaman who combines the still undifferentiated functions of magician and
> naturalist, poet and philosopher, preacher, healer, and public counsellor.
> After him these functions fell apart; philosophers henceforth were to be
> neither poets nor magicians. . . . It was not a question of "synthesising"

these wide domains of practical and theoretical knowledge; in their quality as Men of God they practised with confidence in all of them; the "synthesis" was personal, not logical.

Emerson's Orpheus and Empedocles, like those of Dodds, were mythical shamans, and perhaps Emerson as founder of the American religion is best thought of as another mythical shaman. His Orphism was a metamorphic religion of power whose prime purpose was divination, in what can be called the Vichian sense of god-making. But why Orphism, when other shamanisms were available? The native strain in Emerson rejected any received religion. I am unable to accept a distinguished tradition in scholarship that goes from Perry Miller to Sacvan Bercovitch, and that finds Emerson to have been the heir, however involuntary, of the line that goes from the Mathers to Jonathan Edwards. But I distrust also the received scholarship that sees Emerson as the American disciple of Wordsworth, Coleridge and Carlyle, and thus indirectly a weak descendant of German High Transcendentalism, of Fichte and Schelling. And to fill out my litany of rejections, I cannot find Emerson to be another Perennial Philosophy Neoplatonist, mixing some Swedenborgianism into the froth of Cudworth and Thomas Taylor. Since *Nature* is the text to which I will return, I cite as commentary Stephen Whicher's *Freedom and Fate*, still the best book on Emerson after a quarter-century:

> ... The lesson he would drive home is man's entire independence. The aim of this strain in his thought is not virtue, but freedom and mastery. It is radically anarchic, overthrowing all the authority of the past, all compromise or cooperation with others, in the name of the Power present and agent in the soul.
>
> Yet his true goal was not really a Stoic self-mastery, nor Christian holiness, but rather something more secular and harder to define—a quality he sometimes called *entirety*, or *self-union*. . . .
>
> This self-sufficient unity or wholeness, transforming his relations with the world about him, is, as I read him, the central objective of the egoistic or transcendental Emerson, the prophet of Man created in the 1830's by his discovery of his own proper nature. This was what he meant by "sovereignty," or "majesty," or the striking phrase, several times repeated, "the erect position." . . .

"This strain in his thought" I would identify as what, starting from Emerson, became the Native Strain in our literature. But why call Orphism a religion of "freedom and mastery," anarchic in overthrowing all the past and all contemporary otherness? The choice is Emerson's, as the final chapter of *Nature* shows, so that the question becomes: Why did Emerson identify his Primal, Central or Universal Man with Orpheus?

Hart Crane, Emerson's descendant through Whitman, provokes the same question at the formal close of *The Bridge*:

Now while thy petals spend the suns about us, hold
(O Thou whose radiance doth inherit me)
Atlantis,—hold thy floating singer late!
So to thine Everpresence, beyond time,
Like spears ensanguined of one tolling star
That bleeds infinity—the orphic strings,
Sidereal phalanxes, leap and converge:
—One Song, one Bridge of Fire!

The belated floating singer is still the metamorphic Orpheus of Ovid:

... The poet's limbs were scattered in different places, but the waters of the Hebrus received his head and lyre. Wonderful to relate, as they floated down in midstream, the lyre uttered a plaintive melody and the lifeless tongue made a piteous murmur, while the river banks lamented in reply. . . .

But beyond time, upon the transcendental bridge of fire that is his poem, Crane as American Orpheus vaults the problematics of loss even as Brooklyn Bridge vaultingly becomes the Orphic lyre bending, away from America as lost Atlantis, to whatever Crane can surmise beyond earth. If Coleridge could salute *The Prelude* as "an Orphic song indeed," then the American Crane could render the same salute to *The Bridge*. Emerson's Orphic songs, first in *Nature* and later in his essay *The Poet*, are Crane's ultimate paradigm, as he may not have known. To answer the question: Why an American Orpheus? I turn back now to *Nature*.

VI

Between "Nature" proper, the little book's first chapter, with its epiphany of the transparent eyeball, and the final chapter "Prospects," with its two rhapsodies of the Orphic poet, intervene six rather inadequate chapters, all of which kindle at their close. I give here only these kindlings:

A man is fed, not that he may be fed, but that he may work.

But beauty in nature is not ultimate.

That which was unconscious truth, becomes, when interpreted and defined as an obejct, a part of the domain of knowledge—a new weapon in the magazine of power.

. . . the human form, of which all other organizations appear to be degradations. . . .

. . . the soul holds itself off from a too trivial and microscopic study of the universal tablet. It respects the end too much to immerse itself in the means. . . .

The world proceeds from the same spirit as the body of man. It is a remoter and inferior incarnation of God, a projection of God in the unconscious. . . .

Perhaps Emerson might have kindled these kernels of his vision into something finer than the six chapters they crown. Their design is clear and impressive. Man's work moves beyond natural beauty through a power-making act of knowledge, which identifies the human form, beyond merely natural evidence, as the incarnation of God, an incarnation not yet elevated to full consciousness. That elevation is the enterprise of the Orphic poet, in the chapter "Prospects."

> ". . . Man is the dwarf of himself. Once he was permeated and dissolved by spirit. He filled nature with his overflowing currents. Out from him sprang the sun and moon; from man the sun, from woman the moon. The laws of his mind, the periods of his actions externized themselves into day and night, into the year and the seasons. But, having made for himself this huge shell, his waters retired; he no longer fills the veins and veinlets; he is shrunk to a drop. He sees that the structure still fits him, but fits him colossally. Say, rather, once it fitted him, now it corresponds to him from far and on high. He adores timidly his own work. Now is man the follower of the sun, and woman the follower of the moon. Yet sometimes he starts in his slumber, and wonders at himself and his house, and muses strangely at the resemblance betwixt him and it. He perceives that if his law is still paramount, if still he have elemental power, if his word is sterling yet in nature, it is not conscious power, it is not inferior but superior to his will. It is instinct." Thus my Orphic poet sang.

This "instinct" scarcely can be biological; like the Freudian drives of Eros and Thanatos it can only be mythological. Orphic, Gnostic or even Neoplatonic, it appears now in American colors and tropes. Call the Primal Man American, or even America (as Blake called him Albion, or Shelley, more misleadingly, Prometheus). America was a larger form than nature, filling nature with his emanative excess. Not Jehovah Elohim nor a Demiurge made the cosmos and time, but America, who thereupon shrunk to a drop. When this dwarf, once giant, starts in his sleep, then "gleams of a better light" come into experiential darkness. Very American is Emerson's catalog of those gleams of Reason:

> . . . Such examples are, the traditions of miracles in the earliest antiquity of all nations; the history of Jesus Christ; the achievements of a principle, as in religious and political revolutions, and in the abolition of the slave-trade; the miracles of enthusiasm, as those reported of Swedenborg, Hohenlohe, and the Shakers; many obscure and yet contested facts, now arranged under the name of Animal Magnetism; prayer; eloquence; self-healing; and the wisdom of children.

A contemporary Carlyle might react to this list by querying: "But why has he left out flying saucers?" I myself would point to "eloquence" as the crucial item, fully equal and indeed superior in Emerson's view to "the history of Jesus Christ" or "prayer." Eloquence is the true Emersonian instance "of

Reason's momentary grasp of the scepter; the exertions of a power which exists not in time or space, but an instantaneous in-streaming causing power." Eloquence is Influx, and Influx is a mode of divination, in the Vichian or double sense of god-making and of prophecy. Emerson, peculiarly American, definitive of what it is to be American, *uses* divination so as to transform all of nature into a transparent eyeball:

> . . . The ruin or the blank, that we see when we look at nature, is in our own eye. The axis of vision is not coincident with the axis of things, and so they appear not transparent but opaque. The reason why the world lacks unity, and lies broken and in heaps, is because man is disunited with himself. . . .

The American swerve here is from Milton, when in his invocation to Book III of *Paradise Lost* he lamented that to his literal blindness nature appeared a universal blank. But, more subtly, Emerson revises Coleridge's previous swerve from Milton's lament, in the despairing cry of *Dejection: An Ode*, where Coleridge sees literally but not figuratively: "And still I gaze— and with how blank an eye." The American transumption of Emerson's revisionary optics comes late, with the tragic self-recognition of the aged Wallace Stevens in *The Auroras of Autumn*, when Stevens walks the Emer- sonian-Whitmanian shores of America unable to convert his movements into a freshly American figuration, a new variation upon the tradition: "The man who is walking turns blankly on the sand."

What would it mean if the axis of vision and of things were to coincide? What would a transparent world be, or yield? Wordsworth's *Tintern Abbey* spoke of seeing into the life of things, while Blake urged a seeing *through* rather than *with* the eye. Is Emerson as much reliant upon trope as these British forerunners were, or do his optics prod us towards a pragmatic difference? I suggest the latter, because Emerson as American seer is always the shrewd Yankee, interested in what he called "commodity," and because we ought never to forget that if he fathered Whitman and Thoreau and Frost and (despite that son's evasions) Stevens, his pragmatic strain ensued in William James, Peirce and even John Dewey.

The optics of transparency disturb only the aspect of this text that marks it as a fiction of duration, while the topological residuum of the text remains untroubled. Most tropes, as Emerson knew, have only a spatial rather than a temporal dimension, metaphor proper and synecdoche and metonymy among them. Irony and transumption or metalepsis, which Emerson called the comic trick of language and Nietzsche the Eternal Recurrence, are the temporal as well as spatial modes. The Emersonian transparency or tran- scendence does not oppose itself to presence or spatial immanence, but to the burden of time and of historical continuity. As the quintessential American, Emerson did not need to transcend *space*, which for him as for Whitman, Melville and Charles Olson was the central fact about America. Transparency is therefore an agon with time, and not with space, and opacity thus can be re-defined, in Emersonian terms, as being fixed in time, being trapped in continuity. What Nietzsche called the will's revenge against time's "it was" Emerson more cheerfully sees as a transparency.

Pragmatically this did not mean, for Emerson, seeing things or people as though they were ectoplasm. It meant not seeing the fact except as an epiphany, as a manifestation of the God within the self-reliant seer:

> . . . We make fables to hide the baldness of the fact and conform it, as we say, to the higher law of the mind. But when the fact is seen under the light of an idea, the gaudy fable fades and shrivels. . . .

Why should Orpheus be incarnated again in America? Because he is the authentic prophet-god of discontinuity, of the breaking of tradition, and of re-inscribing tradition as a perpetual breaking, mending and then breaking again. The Orphic seer says of and to time: *It must be broken.* Even so, Emerson's own Orphic poet ends *Nature* by chanting a marvelous breaking:

> Nature is not fixed but fluid. Spirit alters, molds, makes it. The immobility or bruteness of nature is the absence of spirit; to pure spirit it is fluid, it is volatile, it is obedient. Every spirit builds itself a house, and beyond its house a world, and beyond its world a heaven. Know then that the world exists for you. For you is the phenomenon perfect. What we are, that only can we see. All that Adam had, all that Caesar could, you have and can do. Adam called his house, Rome; you perhaps call yours, a cobbler's trade; a hundred acres of ploughed land; or a scholar's garret. Yet line for line and point for point your dominion is as great as theirs, though without fine names. Build therefore your own world. . . .

The metaphoric-mobile, fluid, volatile is precisely the Orphic stigma. I discussed this passage in section 2, above, in terms of Abyss-radiance, but return to it now to venture a more radical interpretation. Pure spirit, or influx, is a remedial force not akin to what moved over the Abyss in merely demiurgical Creation, but rather itself the breath of the truly Primal Abyss. "Build therefore your own world" cannot mean that you are to emulate demiurgical creativity by stealing your material from the origin. Every man his own Demiurge hardly can be the motto for the Emersonian freedom. If seeing ranks above having, for Emerson, then knowing stands beyond seeing:

> The kingdom of man over nature, which cometh not with observation,—a dominion such as now is beyond his dream of God,—he shall enter without more wonder than the blind man feels who is gradually restored to perfect sight.

The crucial words are "now" and "gradually." If the dream of God were to be an Orphic and Gnostic dream of one's own occult self, then the reliance or religion would come now, and with great wonder. Emerson's

curiously serene faith, as he closes *Nature*, is that gradually we will be restored
to the perfect sight of our truly knowing self.

VII

Emerson's theology of being an American, his vision of *self*-reliance, has
nothing much in common with historical Gnosticism. In Gnosticism, this
world *is* hell, and both man's body and man's soul are the work of the
Demiurge who made this world. Only the *pneuma* or spark within the Gnostic
elect is no part of the false and evil Creation. Emerson's monism, his hope for
the American new Adam, and his Wordsworthian love of nature all mark him
as a religious prophet whose God, however internalized, is very distinct from
the alien God or Primal Abyss of Gnosticism.

I speak therefore not of Emerson's Gnosticism but of his Gnosis, of his
way of knowing, which has nothing in common with philosophic epistemology. Though William James, Peirce and Dewey, and in another mode,
Nietzsche, all are a part of Emerson's progeny, Emerson is not a philosopher,
nor even a speculator with a philosophic theology. And though he stemmed
from the mainstream Protestant tradition in America, Emerson is not a
Christian, nor even a non-Christian theist in a philosophic sense. But I am
not going to continue this litany of what our central man is not. Rather I will
move directly to an account of Emerson's Gnosis, of that which he was and is,
founder of *the* American religion, fountain of our literary and spiritual elite.

I will begin and end with my own favorite Emersonian sentence, from
the first paragraph of the essay *Self-Reliance:*

> In every work of genius we recognize our own rejected thoughts; they come
> back to us with a certain alienated majesty.

Emerson says "rejected" where we might use the word "repressed,"
and his Gnosis begins with the reader's Sublime, a Freudian Negation in
which thought comes back but we are still in flight from the emotional
recognition that there is no author but ourselves. A strong reading indeed is
the only text, the only revenge against time's "it was" that can endure.
Self-estrangement produces the uncanniness of "majesty," and yet we do
"recognize our own." Emerson's Gnosis rejects all history, including literary
history, and dismisses all historians, including literary historians who want to
tell the reader that what he recognizes in Emerson is Emerson's own thought
rather than the reader's own Sublime.

A discourse upon Emerson's Gnosis, to be Emersonian rather than
literary historical, itself must be Gnosis, or part of a Gnosis. It must speak of a
knowing in which the knower himself is known, a reading in which he is read.
It will not speak of epistemology, not even deconstructively of the epistemol-

ogy of tropes, because it will read Emerson's tropes as figures of will, and not figures of knowledge, as images of voice and not images of writing.

"Why then do we prate of self-reliance?" is Emerson's rhetorical question, halfway through that essay. Falling back, with him, upon power as agent and upon a rich internal "way of speaking," I repeat his injunction: "Speak rather of that which relies because it works and is." "Works" as an Emersonian verb has Carlyle's tang to it. Prate not of happiness, but work, for the night cometh. But Emerson's *clinamen* away from Europe, away even from Coleridge and Carlyle, is to be heard in "that which relies because it works and is." In the American swerve, tradition is denied its last particle of authority, and the voice that is great within us rises up:

> Life only avails, not the having lived. Power ceases in the instant of repose; it resides in the moment of transition from a past to a new state, in the shooting of the gulf, in the darting of an aim. . . .

There is no power in what already has been accomplished, and Emerson has not come to celebrate a new state, a gulf crossed, an aim hit. Power is an affair of crossings, of thresholds or transitional moments, evasions, substitutions, mental dilemmas resolved only by arbitrary acts of will. Power is in the traversing of the black holes of rhetoric, where the interpreter reads his own freedom to read. Or, we are read only by voicing, by the images for power we find that free us from the *already said*, from being one of the secondary men, traces of traces of traces.

I am suggesting that what a Gnosis of rhetoric, like Emerson's, prophetically wars against is every philosophy of rhetoric, and so now against the irony of irony and the randomness of all textuality. The Emersonian self, "that which relies because it works and is," is voice and not text, which is why it must splinter and destroy its own texts, subverting even the paragraph through the autonomy of sentences, the aggressivity of aphorisms. The sudden uncanniness of voice is Emerson's prime image for vocation, for the call that his Gnosis answers, as here in *Spiritual Laws:*

> Each man has his own vocation. The talent is the call. . . .
>   . . . It is the vice of our public speaking that it has not abandonment. Somewhere, not only every orator but every man should let out all the length of all the reins; should find or make a frank and hearty expression of what force and meaning is in him. . . .

Of this Emersonian spark or *pneuma*, this Gnostic true or antithetical self, as opposed to *psyche* or soul, we can observe that as an aggressive image of voice it will resist successfully all deconstruction. For this image is not a fiction *produced by* the original breaking-apart of the vessels of language but rather itself *tropes for* that primal breaking-apart. Emerson's image of voice is precisely a prophetic transumption of his son Nietzsche's image of truth as an army of figures of speech on the march, a march for which Heidegger gives us "language" or Derrida "writing" as a trope. The march keeps breaking up as voice keeps flowing in again, not as the image of presence but of Gnostic aboriginal absence, as here again in *Spiritual Laws* where the *thrownness* of all Gnosis returns in a forward falling:

> ... When the fruit is ripe, it falls. When the fruit is despatched, the leaf falls. The circuit of the waters is mere falling. The walking of man and all animals is a falling forward. All our manual labor and works of strength, as prying, splitting, digging, rowing and so forth, are done by dint of continual falling, and the globe, earth, moon, comet, sun, star, fall forever and ever.
> ... Place yourself in the middle of the stream of power and wisdom which flows into you as life, place yourself in the full centre of that flood, then you are without effort impelled to truth, to right, and a perfect contentment. ...

I gloss these Emersonian passages by the formula: every fall is a *fall forward*, neither fortunate nor unfortunate, but *forward*, without effort, impelled to the American truth, which is that the stream of power and wisdom flowing in as life is eloquence. Emerson *is* the fountain of our will because he understood that, in America, in the evening-land, eloquence *had* to be enough. The image of voice is the image of influx, of the Newness, but always it knowingly is a broken image, or image of brokenness. Whitman, still Emerson's strongest ephebe, caught the inevitable tropes for this wounded image of American voice:

> —and from this bush in the dooryard,
> With delicate-color'd blossoms and heart-shaped leaves of rich green,
> A sprig with its flower I break.
>
> In the swamp in secluded recesses,
> A shy and hidden bird is warbling a song.
> Solitary the thrush,
> The hermit withdrawn to himself, avoiding the settlements,
> Sings by himself a song.
>
> Song of the bleeding throat,
> Death's outlet song of life, (for well dear brother I know,
> If thou wast not granted to sing thou would'st surely die.)

The breaking of the tally, of the sprig of lilac, is one with the wounding of the hermit thrush's throat, the breaking of voice, of the call, of prophetic vocation. Because it is broken, castrated, it remains an image of voice and of life, not the unbroken image of writing and of death. Whitman *knows*, even *in extremis*, because his father Emerson *knew*, and both knowings are fallings forward. What any philosophical knowing necessarily is or isn't I scarcely know, but I can read Emerson because every knowing I do know is part of a thrownness, a synecdoche for what Emerson wanted to call "victory" or "freedom." Was it not Emerson's peculiar strength that what to me seems catastrophe was to him—by the mad law of Compensation—converted to victory? What made him free was his Gnosis, and I move now into its center, his center, the image of voice that is *self*-reliance, at the high place of that rhapsody:

> . . . It must be that when God speaketh he should communicate, not one thing, but all things; should fill the world with his voice; should scatter forth light, nature, time, souls, from the center of the present thought; and new date and new create the whole. Whenever a mind is simple and receives a divine wisdom, old Things pass away,—means, teachers, texts, temples fall; it lives now, and absorbs past and future into the present hour. All things are made sacred by relation to it,—one as much as another. All things are dissolved to their center by their cause. . . .

Let us apply Whitman, since he was the strongest of the Emersonians. In *Specimen Days* he wrote:

> . . . The best part of Emersonianism is, it breeds the giant that destroys itself. Who wants to be any man's mere follower? lurks behind every page. No teacher ever taught, that has so provided for his pupil's setting up independently—no truer evolutionist.

Emerson also then is a teacher and a text that must pass away if you or I receive the Newness, a fresh influx of the image of voice. On Emerson's precept, no man's Gnosis can be another's, and Emerson's images of voice are fated to become yet more images of writing. Surely this is part of the lesson of the Middle or Skeptical Emerson, warning us against all idolatries, including my own deep temptation to idolize Emerson. Here is the admonition of his greatest essay, *Experience:*

> . . . People forget that it is the eye which makes the horizon, and the rounding mind's eye which makes this or that man a type or representation of humanity, with the name of hero or saint. Jesus, the "providential man," is a good man on whom many people are agreed that these optical laws shall take effect. . . .

Emerson, unlike Whitman, hoped to evade the American version of that "providential man." If no two disciples can agree upon Emerson's doctrine, and they cannot, we can grant the success of his evasion. Yet there is the center: evasion. Emersonianism, indeed like any Gnosis, moves back and forth between negation and extravagance, and always by way of evasion rather than by substitution. I will digress from Gnosis to Gnosticism, before shuttling back to Emerson's passage through *Experience* to *Fate*, middle and late essays no less modes of Gnosis than *Self-Reliance* is.

The way of evasion for the Gnostics meant freedom, and this was freedom from the god of this world, from time, from text, and from the soul and the body of the universe. Such freedom was both knowledge and salvation, since the knowledge of saving self involved was one with the knowledge of the alien true God and the Primal Abyss. How could so large a knowing be known? Only by an image or trope of the self that transgressed language through the most positive of negative moments. What Coleridge, in his orthodox nightmare, dreads as the Positive Negation of *Limbo* is known by the Gnostics as a being-there in the Pleroma, in the Place of Rest. Coleridge's negative moment loses the self without compensation. Emerson, in his 1838 Journal, slyly turning away from Coleridge, achieves a Gnostic Sublime, a negative moment that is all gain and no loss, the truly American moment of *self*-reliance:

> In the highest moments, we are a vision. There is nothing that can be called gratitude nor properly joy. The soul is raised over passion. It seeth nothing so much as Identity. It is a Perceiving that Truth and Right ARE. Hence it becomes a perfect Peace out of the *knowing* that all things will go well. Vast spaces of nature the Atlantic Ocean, the South Sea; vast intervals of time years, centuries, are annihilated to it; this which I think and feel underlay that former state of life and circumstances, as it does underlie my present, and will always all circumstance, and what is called life and what is called death [my italics].

This passage is not so much an example of Gnostic rhetoric as it is part of a Gnosis of rhetoric, anti-epistemological without being vulnerable to the charge that it simply reverses an epistemological dilemma. In a transcendental hyperbole we mount beyond Coleridgean joy of the Secondary imagination because *we see nothing*. Instead, "we are a vision" and we know the identity between ourselves and our knowledge of ourselves. Space, time and mortality flee away, to be replaced by "the knowing." As always in Emerson, the knowing bruises a limit of language, and the impatient Seer transgresses in order to convey his "Perceiving that Truth and Right ARE," which compels the "ARE" to break through in capital letters. In its extravagance, this passage is nothing but tropological, yet its persuasive rhetoric achieves persuasion by the trick of affirming identity with a wholly discontinuous self, one which *knows* only the highest moments in which it *is* a vision. Emerson evades philosophy and chooses his Gnosis instead precisely because he is wary of the epistemological pitfalls that all trope risks. An image of voice is a fine tangle, well beyond logic, but it can testify only to the presence of things not seen, and its faith is wholly in the Optative Mood.

Yet if we move on from *Self-Reliance* first to *Experience* and then to *Fate*, we pass out of the Optative Mood and into the evidence of that world where men descend to meet, and where they cease to be a vision. But even in *Experience*, and then even more in *Fate*, we read not philosophy but Gnosis, a chastened knowing that is not chastened *as* knowing. Here is a single recovery from *Experience:*

... The partial action of each strong mind in one direction is a telescope for the objects on which it is pointed. But every other part of knowledge is to be pushed to the same extravagance, ere the soul attains her due sphericity. . . .

... And we cannot say too little of our constitutional necessity of seeing things under private aspects, or saturated with our humors. And yet is the God the native of these bleak rocks. That need makes in morals the capital virtue of self-trust. We must hold hard to this poverty, however scandalous, and by more rigorous self-recoveries, after the sallies of action, possess our axis more firmly.

Rather than comment upon this in isolation, I juxtapose it first with a more scandalous poverty of *Fate*:

... A man speaking from insight affirms of himself what is true of the mind: seeing its immortality, he says, I am immortal; seeing its invincibility, he says, I am strong. It is not in us, but we are in it. It is of the maker, not of what is made. . . .

The fragment of *Experience* makes imaginative need, epistemological lack, itself into potential Gnosis, the potentia of power. But the resting-point of *Fate* is a more drastic Gnosis, for there the mind and the self have dissociated, in order to win the compensation of the self as spark of the uncreated. And in a coda to this discourse I now abandon Emerson for the giant of Emersonianism, for the question that is a giant himself. What does Emersonianism teach us about an American Gnosis, and what is it which makes that Gnosis still available to us?

The primary teaching of any Gnosis is to deny that human existence is a historical existence. Emerson's American Gnosis denies our belatedness by urging us not to listen to tradition. If you listen hard to tradition, as Walter Benjamin said Kafka did, then you do not see, and Emersonianism wants you to *see*. See what? That is the wrong question, for Gnosis directs *how* to see, meaning to *see earliest*, as though no one had ever seen before you. Gnosis directs also in stance, in taking up a place from which to see earliest, which is one with the place of belated poetry, which is to say, American poetry in particular.

In poetry, a "place" is *where* something is *known*, while a figure or trope is *when* something is willed or desired. In belated poetry, as in any other Gnosis, the place where knowing is located is always a name, but one that comes by negation; an unnaming yields this name. But to un-name in a poem, you first mime and then over-mime and finally super-mime the name you displace. Emerson and Gnosticism alike seek the terrible burden of super-mimesis. The American poet must overthrow even Shakespeare, a doomed enterprise that shadows *Moby Dick*, despite our generous overpraise of the crippling of Melville's greatness by *King Lear*. Whitman must be the new Adam, the new Moses, and the new Christ, impossible aspirations that astonishingly he did not disappoint wholly. An imaginative literature that stems from a Gnosis, rather than a philosophy, is both enhanced and ruined by its super-mimetic teleologies. In every work of genius—in the Bible, Shakespeare, Spenser, Milton, Wordsworth—just there Hawthorne, Melville, Whitman, Thoreau, Dickinson, Henry James learned to recognize their own rejected thoughts. Frost, Stevens, Hart Crane, Faulkner and so many more later encountered their rejected thoughts coming back to them with a certain alienated majesty, when they read their American nineteenth-century precursors. Plato entered the agon with Homer to be the mind of Greece, but here in America we had no Homer. The mind of America perhaps was Emersonian even before Emerson. After him, the literary, indeed the religious mind of America has had no choice, as he cannot be rejected or even deconstructed. He *is* our rhetoric as he is our Gnosis, and I take it that his sly evasion of both Hegel and Hume deprived us of our philosophy. Since he will not conclude haunting us, I evade concluding here, except for a single hint. He was an interior orator, and not an instructor; a vitalizer and not an historian. We will never know our own knowing, through or despite him, until we learn the lesson our profession refuses. I end therefore by quoting against us an eloquence from the essay *History*, which the seer rightly chose to lead off his essays:

> ... Those men who cannot answer by a superior wisdom these facts or questions of time, serve them. Facts encumber them, tyrannize over them, and make the men of routine, the men of *sense*, in whom a literal obedience to facts has extinguished every spark of that light by which man is truly man. ...

That, in one dark epiphany, is Emerson's Gnosis.

BARBARA L. PACKER

"The Curse of Kehama"

How shall we face the edge of time? We walk
In the park. We regret we have no nightingale.
We must have the throstle on the gramophone.
Where shall we find more than derisive words?
When shall lush chorals spiral through our fire
And daunt that old assassin, heart's desire?
                                    —WALLACE STEVENS, "A Duck for Dinner"

"EXPERIENCE"

Emerson's final version of the Fall story is his shortest and most epigrammatic. It is remarkable not so much for its content as for its tone, and the startling nature of the "facts" it is invented to explain. The voice we hear in "Experience" has neither the rhapsodic intensity of the Orphic chants, nor the chill impersonality of the axis-of-vision formula, nor the militancy of "The Protest" or "Circles." It is instead the voice of a man of the world: urbane, rueful, a little weary. "It is very unhappy, but too late to be helped, the discovery we have made that we exist. That discovery is called the Fall of Man."

Equating self-consciousness with the Fall is of course one of the commonest Romantic ways of allegorizing the story of Genesis. And the myth of ossification, with its insistence that the conscious intellect was the enemy of that central power accessible only by surprise or abandonment, may be regarded as containing or at least implying this final myth (which we may call the myth of *reflection*).

But this new version differs from its predecessors in two significant respects. It is considerably more pessimistic in its implications (there is no suggestion that the catastrophe of self-consciousness is either potentially or temporarily reversible), and the evidence adduced to support it is more shocking, in its quiet way, than anything Emerson had ever written. In *Nature* he had based his argument for the original divinity of the Self on its surviving capacity for ecstasy; in "Circles," on its refusal to accept limitation. In "Experience" what is taken as proof of the "ill-concealed Deity" of the Self is neither its joy nor its zeal but simply its ruthlessness:

> There are moods in which we court suffering, in the hope that here at least we shall find reality, sharp peaks and edges of truth. But it turns out to be scene-painting and counterfeit. The only thing grief has taught me, is to know how shallow it is. That, like all the rest, plays about the surface, and never introduces me into the reality, for contact with which we would even pay the costly price of sons and lovers.
>
> We believe in ourselves as we do not believe in others. We permit all things to ourselves, and that which we call sin in others is experiment for us. It is an instance of our faith in ourself that men never speak of crime as lightly as they think; or that every man thinks a latitude safe for himself which is nowise to be indulged to another. . . . No man at last believes that he can be lost, or that the crime in him is as black as in the felon.

Emerson had once wanted to write a book like the Proverbs of Solomon; "Experience" sounds more like the *Maxims* of La Rochefoucauld.

The necessary ruthlessness of the Self had been a corollary of the doctrine of self-reliance from the beginning, of course; it is implicit in Emerson's exhortation to "shun father and mother and wife and brother" when genius calls, even if it causes them pain. And it is avowed even more frankly in "Circles," where Emerson argues that "men cease to interest us when we find their limitations. The only sin is limitation. As soon as you once come up with a man's limitations, it is all over with him." As individuals, we are always in the position of the disappointed child in "Experience" who asks his mother why the story he enjoyed yesterday fails to please him as much the second time around. And the only answer Emerson can give us is the one he offers the child: "will it answer thy question to say, Because thou wert born to a whole and this story is a particular?" This information is hardly an unmixed blessing. If our hunger for "sphericity" is on the one hand the only defense we have against the soul's tendency to ossification, it is on the other hand the restlessness that "ruins the kingdom of mortal friendship and of love."

Emerson's deliberate emphasis in essays like "Circles" and "Experience" on the ruthlessness and secret cruelty of the Self shocks us, and is meant to. It is not merely (as Firkins guesses) "that a parade of hardness may have seemed to him a wholesome counterpoise to the fashionable parade of sensibility," though that was doubtless an added attraction. Emerson says these unpleasant things chiefly because he thinks they are true. Of course it would be easier for us and for society as a whole if they were *not* true, if there were some way of living without the ruinous ferocity of desire, which never ceases to torment us in thought, even if our outward behavior is decorous. Our mortal condition would be easier to endure if the divine Providence had *not* "shown the heaven and earth to every child and filled him with a desire for the whole; a desire raging, infinite; a hunger, as of space to be filled with planets; a cry of famine, as of devils for souls"—as Emerson puts it in a memorable passage in "Montaigne." That desire sends us off on a perpetual quest through the world of experience, and at the same time foredooms the quest to failure, since each particular satisfaction can only frustrate a being whose desire is for the whole. As questers, we are partly like Tennyson's Ulysses—

> .... all experience is an arch wherethrough
> Gleams that untravelled world whose margin fades
> For ever and for ever when I move ...

but even more like Tennyson's Percivale—

> "Lo, if I find the Holy Grail itself
> And touch it, it will crumble into dust."

Romance—the glamour or beauty that could transmute life's baser metals into gold—is always somewhere else, somewhere just beyond our grasp. "Every ship is a romantic object, except that we sail in. Embark, and the romance quits our vessel and hangs on every other sail in the horizon." Or, as he had put it in the earlier essay "Love": "each man sees his own life defaced and disfigured, as the life of man is not, to his imagination."

Sensible people, hearing these confessions of frustration and despair, counsel renunciation of the Self's imperial ambitions. But Emerson denies that any permanent renunciation is possible. For one thing, that glimpse of the whole we were granted as children survives in adult life as more than a memory. Just when we have, as we think, managed to adjust our desires to reality, the old vision reappears to tantalize us:

> How easily, if fate would suffer it, we might keep forever these beautiful limits, and adjust ourselves, once for all, to the perfect calculation of known cause and effect. .... But ah! presently comes a day, or is it only a half-hour, with its angel-whispering,—which discomfits the conclusions of notions and years!

And this reminder, while it distresses us, calls to our attention something we cannot safely ignore. The desire that torments us is also the only "capital stock" we have to invest in the actions and relationships of life. The man who tried to conduct his business on the principles of common sense alone "would quickly be bankrupt. Power keeps quite another road than the turnpikes of choice and will; namely the subterranean and invisible tunnels and channels of life."

These meditations on power and ruthlessness are an important part of the essay "Experience." They constitute a sort of ground bass heard at intervals beneath the constantly varying melodies of the essay, and contribute not a little to the impression of toughness it makes on the reader's mind. Yet toughness is hardly the essay's most significant characteristic. What is strikingly new about "Experience" is the voice that is heard in its opening paragraph, a voice neither powerful nor ruthless, but instead full of bewilderment, exhaustion, and despair:

> Where do we find ourselves? In a series of which we do not know the extremes, and believe that it has none. We wake and find ourselves on a stair; there are stairs below us, which we seem to have ascended; there are stairs above us, many a one, which go upward and out of sight. But the Genius which according to the old belief stands at the door by which we enter, and gives us the lethe to drink, that we may tell no tales, mixed the cup too strongly, and we cannot shake off the lethargy now at noonday. Sleep lingers all our lifetime about our eyes, as night hovers all day in the boughs of the fir-tree. All things swim and glitter. Our life is not so much threatened as our perception. Ghostlike we glide through nature, and should not know our place again.

When Dr. Beard, in his *American Nervousness*, wanted a phrase that would convey to a popular audience an accurate sense of the new disease he had identified and named *neurasthenia*, he instinctively chose a metaphor Emerson would have admired: "nervous bankruptcy." In the peculiar lassitude of the prose here—so different from the militant assertiveness of "Circles" or "Self-Reliance"—Emerson has managed to create a stylistic correlative to the "Feeling of Profound Exhaustion" Dr. Beard found characteristic of the nervously bankrupt. Insufficiency of vital force is in fact Emerson's chief complaint in this opening passage.

> Did our birth fall in some fit of indigence and frugality in nature, that she was so sparing of her fire and so liberal of her earth that it appears to us that we lack the affirmative principle, and though we have health and reason, yet we have no superfluity of spirit for new creation? We have enough to live and bring the year about, but not an ounce to impart or invest. Ah that our Genius were a little more of a genius! We are like millers on the lower levels of a stream, when the factories above them have exhausted the water. We too fancy that the upper people must have raised their dams.

No reader of Emerson's journals can be unfamiliar with the mood described here. Recurrent laments over want of stamina and of animal spirits, over feelings of exhaustion and despair, punctuate the earliest notebooks. "I have often found cause to complain that my thoughts have an ebb & flow," he noted in one of them. "The worst is, that the ebb is certain, long & frequent, while the flow comes transiently & seldom." A few pages earlier, a pious composition intended as a meditation "Upon Men's Apathy to their Eternal interests" turns into a meditation upon apathy of a more personal sort—a meditation whose systematic hopelessness, coming from a youth of nineteen, almost raises a smile:

> In the pageant of life, Time & Necessity are the stern masters of ceremonies who admit no distinctions among the vast train of aspirants.... And though the appetite of youth for marvels & beauty is fain to draw deep & strong lines of contrast between one & another character we early learn to distrust them & to acquiesce in the unflattering & hopeless picture which Experience exhibits.

This grim lesson Emerson hastens to apply to his own disappointing life:

> We dreamed of great results from peculiar features of Character. We thought that the overflowing benevolence of our youth was pregnant with kind consequences to the world; that the agreeable qualities in the boy of courage, activity, intelligence, & good temper would prove in the man Virtues of extensive & remarkable practical effect.

The passage is revealing; it provides a glimpse of what Emerson's boyhood ambition had really been—not to become a reclusive scholar and occasional lecturer, but to be a public figure, an eloquent mover of men, like his hero Daniel Webster. The disinterest of his elders in his visionary schemes of regeneration had not dampened his personal ambitions; if anything, it had increased them. "The momentary ardour of childhood found that manhood & age were too cold to sympathise with it, & too hastily inferred that its own merit was solitary & unrivalled & would by and by blaze up, & make an era in Society." But this childhood ardor, like Wordsworth's "visionary gleam," eventually died away of its own accord.

> Alas. As it grew older it also grew colder & when it reached the period of manhood & of age it found that the waters of time, as they rolled had extinguished the fire that once glowed & there was no partial exemption for itself. The course of years rolls an unwelcome wisdom with them which forcibly teaches the vanity of human expectations.

And he concludes: "The dreams of my childhood are all fading away & giving place to some very sober & very disgusting views of a quiet mediocrity of talents & condition."

The intellectual revolution of the early 1830s—the discovery of the God within—liberated Emerson from the hopelessness that had oppressed his young manhood, but it could not do much for his stamina. He circumvented the limitations of his constitution by carefully husbanding his time and strength, and he learned to make the best of his alarming "*periods* of mentality" ("one day I am a doctor, & the next I am a dunce") by means of the unique method of composition he had already perfected by the mid-thirties. He spent his mornings barricaded in his study, writing isolated paragraphs in his journal when the spirit was upon him. When a longer composition was needed—a sermon or a lecture—he quarried in these journals for material and, as Chapman says, "threw together what seemed to have a bearing on some subject, and gave it a title." Chapman adds, correctly, I think, that what keeps this method from resulting in an "incomprehensible chaos" is Emerson's single-mindedness:

> There was only one thought which could set him aflame, and that was the unfathomed might of man. This thought was his religion, his politics, his ethics, his philosophy. One moment of inspiration was in him own brother to the next moment of inspiration, although they might be separated by six weeks.

What keeps this procedure from resulting in monotony for the reader, is first, the sheer power and felicity of Emerson's prose; next, the perpetual surprise of his observations (who else would have thought of comparing readers at the Boston Athenaeum to flies, aphids, and sucking infants?); and finally, his unflinching honesty, which will not let him rest until he has subjected his claim for the unfathomed might of man to every shred of negative evidence that can reasonably be urged against it. The combination of his single-mindedness and his insistence upon recognizing all the "opposite negations between which, as walls, his being is swung" is responsible for the curious fact about his work noticed long ago by Firkins. "Emerson's wish to get his whole philosophy into each essay tended toward sameness and promiscuity at once; it made the *essays similar* and the *paragraphs diverse*." (It is also responsible for the fact that while his paragraphs are extraordinarily easy to remember word for word, they can be almost impossible to locate. Anything can be anyplace. The most time-consuming feature of being a student of Emerson is the necessity it places one under of repeatedly rereading half the collected *Works* and *Journals* in the maddening pursuit of some paragraph one can remember but not find.)

But his habits of composition, though they enabled him to produce a body of written work that would be remarkable enough for even a vigorous man, probably contributed to his sense of the unbridgeable gap between the life of the soul and the life of the senses, between the Reason and the Understanding. His ecstasies were carefully reserved for his study; the price he paid for them was an abnormally lowered vitality for the acts and perceptions of everyday life. He repeatedly complains of the "Lethean stream" that washes through him, of the "film or haze of unreality" that separates him from the world his senses perceive. How to transfer "nerve capital" (as a follower of Dr. Beard termed it) from the column of the Reason to the column of the Understanding seemed to him life's chief insoluble problem. In "Montaigne" he writes:

> The astonishment of life is the absence of any appearance of reconciliation between the theory and practice of life. Reason, the prized reality, the Law, is apprehended, now and then, for a serene and profound moment amidst the hubbub of cares and works which have no direct bearing on it;—is then lost for months and years, and again found for an interval, to be lost again. If we compute it in time, we may, in fifty years, have half a dozen reasonable hours. But what are these cares and works the better? A method in the world we do not see, but this parallelism of great and little, which never discover the smallest tendency to converge.

Or, as he had once laconically observed: "Very little life in a lifetime."

Yet despite this discouraging arithmetic Emerson had always refused to abandon his insistence that the visionary moments constituted our *real* life, the one in which we felt most truly ourselves. This insistence is not quite as suicidal as it sounds, for the visionary moments, however brief they may be when measured by the clock, have a way of expanding while they are occurring into an eternal present that makes a mockery of duration. In a paragraph of "Circles" that looks forward to Thoreau's parable of the artist of Kouroo, Emerson had written:

> It is the highest power of divine moments that they abolish our contritions also. I accuse myself of sloth and unprofitableness, day by day; but when these waves of God flow into me, I no longer reckon lost time. I no longer poorly compute my possible achievements by what remains to me of the month or the year; for these moments confer a sort of omnipresence and omnipotence, which asks nothing of duration, but sees that the energy of the mind is commensurate with the work to be done, without time.

With this proviso in mind it is easier to understand why Emerson could speculate in his journal that "in the memory of the disembodied soul the days or hours of pure Reason will shine with a steady light as the life of life & all the other days & weeks will appear but as hyphens which served to join these."

In "Experience" Emerson tries for the first time in his career to describe life as it looks from the standpoint of the hyphens rather than the heights, from the "waste sad time" (as Eliot calls it) separating the moments of vision rather than from the moments themselves. It is his attempt to confront the only form of suffering he recognized as genuinely tragic, because it was the only one for which his imagination could discover no answering compensation—the haze of unreality that sometimes suggested to him that we were "on the way back to Annihilation."

Emerson had originally planned to call the essay "Life." At first glance the difference between the two titles does not seem very great. Everything that happens in life can be described as an experience: a visionary moment as much as a bump on the head. Emerson himself uses the word in this way in "The Transcendentalist" when he says that a transcendentalist's faith is based on a "certain brief experience" that surprises him in the midst of his everyday worries and pursuits.

Yet the word "experience" also had a technical meaning in empirical philosophy, where it refers to that portion of the world accessible to the senses, the world of time and space. This is the meaning it has in the works of Hume, whose skepticism had provoked the young Emerson into his first spiritual crisis during the decade of the 1820s. "Experience" is the weapon Hume uses to demolish belief in miracles and the argument for God's existence based on inferences from the evidence of design in the universe. If one accepted Hume's thesis—that "we have no knowledge but from Experience"—it was difficult to avoid his conclusion—that "we have no Experience of a Creator & therefore know of none." Hume could also use arguments from experience to shake belief in more fundamental assumptions: in the existence of matter, in the relationship of cause and effect, in the stability of personal identity. Emerson puzzled over these problems. In a high-spirited letter to his Aunt Mary written in 1823 he confessed that the doubts raised by this "Scotch Goliath" were as distressing to him as worries about the origin of evil or the freedom of the will. "Where," he asked rhetorically, "is the accomplished stripling who can cut off his most metaphysical head? Who is he that can stand up before him & prove the existence of the Universe, & of its Founder?" All the candidates in the "long & dull procession of Reasoners that have followed since" only proved, by their repeated attempts to confute Hume, that Hume had not been confuted.

Here, it is evident, Emerson is still accepting his teachers' argument that an attack on the existence of the material universe led inevitably to an attack on the existence of God. Whicher points out that "though Berkeley had denied the existence of matter independent of perception to confute sceptical materialism," to the Scottish Realists whose philosophical works dominated the Harvard scene in Emerson's youth, "the end product of the Ideal Theory was the scepticism of Hume."

Emerson's discovery of "the God within" released him from the necessity of clinging to proofs of the existence of matter, since once the confirmation of the truths of religion had been made a purely intuitive affair, no longer dependent for its ratification on miracles perceivable by the senses, the "Ideal Theory" no longer seemed dangerous. The endless, fussy debates about whether we could trust the testimony of the Apostles who claimed to have witnessed the miracles of Jesus, about how the immutable laws of nature could have been temporarily suspended (e.g., whether Jesus made the water he walked on temporarily solid or himself temporarily weightless), about whether the gospels in which these events were recorded were genuine or spurious, neutral historical records or (as the German Higher Critics alleged) legendary or mythological narratives, could all be dispensed with in one liberating gesture. "Internal evidence outweighs all other to the inner man," Emerson wrote in 1830. "If the whole history of the New Testament had perished & its teachings remained—the spirituality of Paul, the grave, considerate, unerring advice of James would take the same rank with me that now they do." It is the truth of the doctrine that confirms the truth of the miracle, not the other way round. If it were not so, Emerson frankly confesses, he would probably "yield to Hume or any one that this, like all other miracle accounts, was probably false."

Hume's argument against the possibility of miracles had rested on the observation that our opinions about the reliability of testimony and about the probability of matters of fact are both drawn from experience. We usually believe the testimony of honorable witnesses, because we have found from experience that such men usually tell the truth. But we also form our opinions about the probability of matters of fact from our experience: whether it is likely to snow in July, whether a man can walk on water or rise from the dead. "The reason, why we place any credit in witnesses and historians, is not derived from any *connexion*, which we perceive *a priori*, between testimony and reality, but because we are accustomed to find a conformity between them. But when the fact attested is such a one as has seldom fallen under our observation, here is a contest of two opposite experiences; of which the one destroys the other, as far as its force goes, and the superior can only separate on the mind by the force, which remains."

Emerson's mature position can best be characterized by saying that he accepts Hume's argument but reverses his conclusions. When the testimony involved is not the testimony of witnesses but the testimony of consciousness, the "superior force" clearly belongs to consciousness. Experience and consciousness are indeed in perpetual conflict: "life is made up of the intermixture and reaction to these two amicable powers, whose marriage appears beforehand monstrous, as each denies and tends to abolish the other." When an irreconcilable conflict occurs, it is consciousness, not experience, whose testimony we believe. Hence Emerson's delight in the "scientific" equivalent to this assertion: the law he attributed to the Swiss mathematician Euler and quoted in the "Idealism" chapter of *Nature*. "The sublime remark of Euler on his law of arches, 'This will be found contrary to all experience, yet it is true;' had already transferred nature into the mind, and left matter like an outcast corpse."

Idealism had always held a secret attraction for Emerson, which had survived unchanged even during the years when his teachers were telling him to regard it as dangerous. In a letter to Margaret Fuller in 1841 he writes: "I know but one solution to my nature & relations, which I find in the remembering the joy with which in my boyhood I caught the first hint of the Berkleian philosophy, and which I certainly never lost sight of afterwards." What Emerson means by the "Berkleian philosophy," as Whicher notes, is not Berkeley's particular system but

> simply the "noble doubt... whether nature outwardly exists." The seductive reversal of his relations to the world, with which the imagination of every child is sometimes caught, transferring his recurrent sense of a dreaminess in his mode of life to outward nature, and releasing him in his imagination into a solitude peopled with illusions, was scepticism of a special kind—

but a kind that increasingly seemed not the murderer of faith but rather its midwife. The man who believes that the mind alone is real, matter only a phenomenon, is easier to convince of spiritual realities than the empiricist who continually demands sensible proofs. "Idealism seems a preparation for a strictly moral life & so skepticism seems necessary for a universal holiness," Emerson noted in an early journal. Indeed, if what he asserts in "Montaigne" is correct—that "belief consists in accepting the affirmations of the soul; unbelief, in denying them"—it is the empiricist, not the idealist, who deserves the title of skeptic. With this in mind, the history of philosophy begins to look very different. The classical skeptics no longer look frightening—Emerson quotes with approval de Gerando's opinion that Sextus Empiricus' skepticism had been directed only at the external world, not at metaphysical truths. Even the Scotch Goliath begins to look less formidable. "Religion does that for the uncultivated which philosophy does for ~~Hume~~ Berkeley & Viasa;—makes the mountains dance & smoke & disappear before the steadfast gaze of Reason." Emerson crossed out Hume's name (enlisting Hume as an ally of religion was presumably too radical an idea for Emerson at this point in his career, though the Emerson of "Circles" would have found it plausible), but that he thought of Hume in context at all is significant enough.

But Idealism as a doctrine was more than philosophically important to Emerson; it was emotionally important as well. *Nature* as originally planned was to have ended with the chapter "Idealism"; and in that chapter he suggests some of the chief attractions the doctrine possessed. When "piety or passion" lifts us into the realm of Ideas, "we become physically nimble and lightsome; we tread on air; life is no longer irksome, and we think it will never be so. No man fears age or misfortune or death in their serene company, for he is transported out of the region of change." "The best, the happiest moments of life are these delicious awakenings of the higher powers, and the reverential withdrawing of nature before its God."

No wonder Emerson seized eagerly upon every philosopher whose system tended toward idealism of one kind or another: Plato, Plotinus, Berkeley, Kant, Fichte, Schelling. Religious doctrines, too, he tends to judge by their approximations to idealism. In an early journal he notes with approval that idealism seems to be a primeval theory, and quotes from the Mahabharata (one of the sacred books of India) a sentence that neatly inverts the Peripatetic formula (*nihil in intellectu quod non ante fuerit in sensu*) upon which Locke had based his philosophy. "The senses are nothing but the soul's instrument of action; *no knowledge can come to the soul by their channel*" (emphasis added).

I have made this digression into Emerson's philosophical interests for a reason: the essay "Experience" cannot, I think, be fully understood without some grasp of the metaphorical ways in which he employs the technical vocabulary of epistemology to talk about things like grief, guilt, ruthlessness, and isolation. Stanley Cavell sees in Emerson the only thinker who can be said to have anticipated the Heidegger of *Being and Time* in an attempt to "formulate a kind of epistemology of moods":

> The idea is roughly that moods must be taken as having at least as sound a role in advising us of reality as sense-experience has; that, for example, coloring the world, attributing to it the qualities "mean" or "magnani-mous," may be no less objective or subjective than coloring an apple, attribut-ing to it the colors red and green. Or perhaps we should say: sense-experi-ence is to objects what moods are to the world.

What makes this difficult subject more complicated still is Emerson's own recognition that the various epistemological theories proposed by every philosopher from Plato to Kant might themselves be little more than meta-phorical equivalents of moods or habitual ways of taking the world. "I fear the progress of Metaphysical philosophy may be found to consist in nothing else than the progressive introduction of apposite metaphors," Emerson had dryly remarked in an early journal. "Thus the Platonists congratulated themselves for ages upon their knowing that Mind was a dark chamber whereon ideas like shadows were painted. Men derided this as infantile when they afterwards learned that the Mind was a sheet of white paper whereon any & all characters might be written." The real difficulty in arriving at an epistemol-ogy of moods is that moods are likely to dictate beforehand the shape of one's epistemology. A soul in a state of exaltation will instinctively incline to the mystical idealism of the Mahabharata; a soul in a state of depression, to the skepticism of Hume. A healthy but nonreflective man might find the episte-mology of the Scottish Realists sufficiently convincing; a more introspective man might not rest content until he had seen the relation between subject and object given transcendental ground in the philosophy of Kant.

Words like "experience" and "idealism" have different meanings in each of these systems, and different from any are the meanings they have acquired in popular use, where "idealism" is taken to mean any rosy or elevated estimate of human possibilities, and "experience" the process by which that estimate is lost. In "Experience" Emerson does not so much attempt to introduce order into this confusion as to exploit its ironies. If the essay, like life itself, is a "train of moods" or succession of "many-colored lenses which paint the world their own hue," each showing only what lies in its focus, then one of the chief ways of arriving at an epistemology of moods is by studying the shadings these words take on as the paragraphs pass by. From some moods within the essay, "experience" looks like a neutrally descriptive word; from others, a term of bitterness or contempt; from others still, the most savage of ironies. And the same thing holds true for "idealism," as one can see from the sentence (which may be the bitterest Emerson ever wrote) taken from the paragraphs of the essay that deal with the death of his son: "Grief too will make us idealists."

From the beginning of the essay the concept of experience is already involved in ironies. The opening image, which compares life to the climbing of an endless staircase, has reminded more than one critic of a Piranesi engraving, and Porte has pointed out that Emerson's references to "lethe" and "opium" recall a passage in DeQuincey's *Confessions of an English Opium-Eater*, where Piranesi's *Carceri d'Invenzione* is explicitly mentioned. But DeQuincey was describing dreams induced by an actual drug; Emerson is describing the ordinary waking consciousness, life as it presents itself to the senses.

Hume, who thought that all knowledge came through experience, divided the contents of the mind into "IMPRESSIONS and IDEAS," the former derived from sensation (whether from external nature or the passions themselves), the latter the "faint images" of the former. Since the two are different not in kind but only in degree, he pauses at the beginning of the *Treatise of Human Nature* to consider whether the two can ever be confused. He admits that in madness or fever or dreams ideas may become almost as lively as impressions, and that conversely there are some states in which "it sometimes happens, that our impressions are so faint and low, that we cannot distinguish them from our ideas." What Emerson suggests in the opening paragraph of "Experience" is that the state Hume admitted as exceptional is in fact closer to being the norm: our impressions are most of the time as faint as our ideas, and a system of philosophy that separated one from the other according to the "degrees of force and liveliness, with which they strike upon the mind" would very shortly lose the power to tell reality from phantasmagoria. The first irony we can record about experience is that it chiefly menaces the very philosophical system supposed to revere it. The exhaustion that attends it numbs the mind so that all the things we perceive "swim and glitter" like apparitions—a condition that, as Emerson accurately says, threatens not so much our life as our perception.

The second paragraph of the essay lodges a different complaint: the fact that experience and whatever wisdom can be derived from it are never coincident. Our life becomes meaningful only retroactively. "If any of us knew what we were doing, or where we are going, then when we think we best know! We do not know to-day whether we are busy or idle. In times when we have thought ourselves indolent, we have afterwards discovered that much was accomplished and much was begun in us." The most valuable experiences Wordsworth discovered in his childhood as he looked back on it were not the incidents a biographer would be likely to record but rather certain uncanny moments of heightened perception that occurred unexpectedly in the midst of ordinary childish sports—ice skating, robbing birds' nests, going for a night ride in a stolen boat—just as the most significant experience during the European tour he made as a young man turned out to be not the visions of sublime Alpine scenery but the vague feeling of depression that had succeeded the peasant's revelation that he and his companion had passed the highest point on their Alpine journey without recognizing it. Life and the meaning of life can never be apprehended simultaneously; like Pandarus in *Troilus and Criseyde* we can all justly complain "I hoppe alwey byhynde."

Nor can any illumination ever prove final. "What a benefit if a rule could be given whereby the mind could at any moment *east* itself, & find the sun," Emerson had written in his journal. "But long after we have thought we were recovered & sane, light breaks in upon us & we find we have yet had no sane moment. Another morn rises on mid-noon." That final Miltonic allusion (along with its demonic counterpart, "under every deep a lower deep opens") may be regarded as a slightly more cheerful version of the staircase image that opens "Experience": it combines the suggestion of interminability with the suggestion that with each new layer of experience there is at least a widening of circumference or gain in wisdom. As Emerson says later on in the essay, "the years teach much that the days never know." Unfortunately, this wisdom clarifies only the past; each new situation finds us blundering like novices. "The individual is always mistaken." This melancholy but resigned conclusion resembles the opinion Yeats expresses in *Per Amica Silentia Lunae*, that since no disaster in life is exactly like another, there must always be "new bitterness, new disappointment"; it is perhaps even closer to the remark made by a contemporary Zen master, Shunryu Suzuki, to the effect that the life of a Zen master in pursuit of enlightenment "could be said to be so many years of *shoshaku jushaku*—'to succeed wrong with wrong,' or one continuous mistake."

It is important to realize that at this point in the essay Emerson is *not* contrasting the wisdom that comes from experience with the higher wisdom that comes from consciousness. He is exploring a curious paradox that exists within experience itself. "All our days are so unprofitable while they pass, that 'tis wonderful where or when we ever got anything of this which we call wisdom, poetry, virtue. We never got it on any dated calendar day." The contrast between the pettiness of our daily lives and the accumulated wisdom that somehow results from them is so vast that even a resolute empiricist will be driven to mythology or fiction to account for it. "Some heavenly days must have been intercalated somewhere, like those that Hermes won with the dice of the Moon, that Osiris might be born."

Yet the cruelest feature of experience is the power it possesses of alienating us not only from our perceptions and our interpretations but even from our own sorrows:

> What opium is instilled into all disaster! It shows formidable as we approach it, but there is at last no rough rasping friction, but the most slippery sliding surfaces; we fall soft on a thought; *Ate Dea* is gentle,—
>
> > "Over men's heads walking aloft,
> > With tender feet treading so soft."
>
> People grieve and bemoan themselves, but it is not half so bad with them as they say. There are moods in which we court suffering, in the hope that here at least we shall find reality, sharp peaks and edges of truth. But it turns out to be scene-painting and counterfeit. The only thing grief has taught me, is to know how shallow it is. That, like all the rest, plays about the surface, and never introduces me into the reality, for contact with which we would even pay the costly price of sons and lovers. Was it Boscovich who found out that bodies never come in contact? Well, souls never touch their objects. An innavigable sea washes with silent waves between us and the things we aim at and converse with. Grief too will make us idealists. In the death of my son, now more than two years ago, I seem to have lost a beautiful estate,— no more. I cannot get it nearer to me. If to-morrow I should be informed of the bankruptcy of my principle debtors, the loss of my property would be a great inconvenience to me, perhaps, for many years; but it would leave me as it found me,—neither better nor worse. So it is with this calamity; it does not touch me; something which I fancied was a part of me, which could not be torn away without tearing me nor enlarged without enriching me, falls off and leaves no scar. It was caducous. I grieve that grief can teach me nothing, nor carry me one step into real nature. The Indian who was laid under a curse that the wind should not blow on him, nor water flow to him, nor fire burn him, is a type of us all. The dearest events are summer-rain and we the Para coats that shed every drop. Nothing is left us now but death. We look to that with a grim satisfaction, saying, There at least is reality that will not dodge us.

I have quoted the whole of this magnificent passage because it is chiefly in its cumulative force that it achieves its great and disturbing power over us. I have never yet read a commentary on it that I thought did justice to the peculiar kind of shock it administers to the reader who is encountering the essay for the first time. The casual brutality of the sentence in which Emerson introduces the death of his son *as an illustration* is unmatched by anything I know of in literature, unless it is the parenthetical remark in which Virginia Woolf reports the death of Mrs. Ramsay in the "Time Passes" section of *To the Lighthouse.*

Not that the unreality or numbness Emerson reports is itself shocking. Many writers before and after Emerson have said as much. A similar experience forms the subject of Dickinson's chilling lyric, "After great pain, a formal feeling comes"; it is also analyzed in a passage of Sir Thomas Browne's *Hydrotaphia* from which Emerson had copied sentences into one of his early journals. "There is no antidote against the *Opium* of time," Browne reminds us, and then goes on to say:

> Darknesse and light divide the course of time, and oblivion shares with memory a great part even of our living beings; we slightly remember our felicities, and the smartest stroaks of affliction leave but short smart upon us. Sense endureth no extremities, and sorrows destroy us or themselves. To weep into stones are fables. Afflictions induce callosities, miseries are slippery, or fall like snow upon us, which notwithstanding is no unhappy stupidity. To be ignorant of evils to come, and forgetfull of evils past, is a mercifull provision in nature, whereby we digest the mixture of our few and evil dayes, and our delivered senses not relapsing into cutting remembrances, our sorrows are not kept raw by the edge of repetitions.

The whole passage, even down to the details of its tactile imagery, is a striking anticipation of "Experience." Yet the differences are as noteworthy as the similarities. The slipperiness of misery, which Browne calls "a mercifull provision in nature," is for Emerson "the most unhandsome part of our condition." And this is so because Emerson, unlike Browne, sees in the unreality of grief only an intensification of our normal state of alienation or dislocation from the world our senses perceive. This distance—the "innavigable sea" that washes between us and the world—is the real torture. If grief could relieve it, if suffering could introduce us to the reality behind the glittering and evanescent phenomena, we would welcome it. For contact with that reality we would be *willing* to pay (as Emerson says in what is surely the most chilling of all his hyperboles) "even the costly price of sons and lovers."

But grief proves to be as shallow as everything else. In a letter written a week after the death of his son Emerson laments: "Alas! I chiefly grieve that I cannot grieve; that this fact takes no more deep hold than other facts, is as dreamlike as they; a lambent flame that will not burn playing on the surface of my river. Must every experience—those that promised to be dearest & most penetrative,—only kiss my cheek like the wind & pass away? I think of Ixion

& Tantalus & Kehama." "Kehama" is an allusion to Robert Southey's long narrative poem *The Curse of Kehama*, in which a virtuous character named Ladurlad is laid under a curse by a wicked ruler Kehama, who, though himself a mere mortal, has learned to wrest such power from the gods that he is able to send a burning fire into Ladurlad's heart and brain, and at the same time order the elements to flee from him. As Ladurlad laments:

> The Winds of Heaven must never breathe on me;
> The Rains and Dews must never fall on me;
> Water must mock my thirst and shrink from me;
> The common earth must yield no fruit to me;
> Sleep, blessed Sleep! must never light on me;
> And Death, who comes to all, must fly from me,
> And never, never set Ladurlad free.

Ladurlad is the "Indian" mentioned in "Experience": in making him a "type of us all" Emerson gives us his grimmest assessment of the human condition: an endless, goalless pilgrimage, driven by an inner but unquenchable fire through a world that recedes perpetually before the pilgrim. The bitter lesson we learn from experience is the soul's imperviousness to experiences. The traumas are not traumatic. "The dearest events are summer-rain, and we the Para coats that shed every drop." If we look forward with a "grim satisfaction" to death, it is because it is the one event in life that we can be sure will not slip through our fingers. "There at least is reality that will not dodge us."

Yet the central portion of the passage is the most explicitly self-lacerating. In observing that grief, like poetry or religion, convinces us of the insubstantiality of the phenomenal world, in offering as evidence for this assertion his own imperviousness to the death of his son, whose loss he likens, with deliberate vulgarity, to the loss of an estate, Emerson is indulging in a candor so "dreadful" (as Bishop puts it) that it has driven more than one critic to suppose that he either did not mean what he said or else was unaware of his meaning.

Part of the problem comes from the difficulty of determining Emerson's tone in the passage. Bishop has pointed out Emerson's fondness for what he calls "tonal puns." He instances a sentence from *The Conduct of Life*: "Such as you are, the gods themselves could not help you." Bishop says: "One can hear a voice that says this insultingly and another voice, intimate and quiet, that says it encouragingly." But he confesses that sentences like "*Ate Dea* is gentle" and "Grief too will make us idealists" and "I cannot get it nearer to me" leave him puzzled. Are they straightforward or ironical, desperate or resigned? The answer, I think, is that we *can* imagine a voice that says all of these things with bitter irony, but that we can also imagine them being said in a voice as toneless and detached as that of a witness giving evidence in a war crimes trial, or that of the wasted and suffering discharged soldier whom Wordsworth questions about his experiences in Book IV of *The Prelude*:

> . . . in all he said
> There was a strange half-absence, as of one
> Knowing too well the importance of his theme
> But feeling it no longer.

Emerson is driven to offer his testimony by an inner necessity. I admire Maurice Gonnaud's fine remark about this compulsion: "The greatness of an essay like 'Experience' lies, I suggest, in our sense of the author's being engaged in a pursuit of truth which has all the characters of faith except its faculty of radiating happiness."

What sharpens the sting of the revelations is Emerson's tacit acknowledgment, through his phrasing and imagery, that fate itself has retroactively conferred upon some brave assertions of the past the one kind of irony it was beyond his power to intend. Thus "grief too will make us idealists" both echoes and answers a journal entry of 1836 in which Emerson was working out the concepts that later became part of the sixth chapter of *Nature*: "Religion makes us idealists. Any strong passion does. The best, the happiest moments of life are these delicious awakenings of the higher powers & the reverential withdrawing of nature before its god." His remark that his relationship to his son proved to be "caducous" recalls a happy declaration, made after the departure of some friends in August of 1837, that he had faith in the soul's powers of infinite regeneration: "these caducous relations are in the soul like leaves . . . & how often soever they are lopped off, yet still it renews them ever." Even more chilling is the prophetic remark he made to Jones Very during the latter's visit in 1838: "I told Jones Very that I had never suffered, & that I could scarce bring myself to feel a concern for the safety & life of my nearest friends that would satisfy them: that I saw clearly that if my wife, my child, my mother, should be taken from me, I should still remain whole with the same capacity of cheap enjoyment from all things." There is a kind of self-contempt in this passage; Emerson had already survived so many losses that he felt confident in predicting his response to more. But this passage was written when little Waldo was barely two. In the intervening years—years in which Emerson had delightedly recorded his small son's doings and sayings in his otherwise austerely intellectual journal—he had evidently come to hope that this relationship was somehow different, that it was something that "could not be torn away without tearing me nor enlarged without enriching me."

Alas. Though Elizabeth Hoar's brother Rockwood "was never more impressed with a human expression of agony than by that of Emerson leading the way into the room where little Waldo lay dead," Rusk tells us, Emerson discovered to his sorrow that the prophecy he had made in 1838 was true. In his young manhood he had been greatly stirred by the remark of a Methodist farmer he worked with one summer that men were always praying and that their prayers were always answered. "Experience" records Emerson's grim awareness that the price you pay for invulnerability is invulnerability.

The passages here recounted were all confined to Emerson's private journals—a fact that helps explain why the opening pages of "Experience," almost alone among Emerson's works, give the impression of being not heard but overheard. But these privately recorded passages are not the only ones to be so retracted. Nearly every critic of the essay has pointed out the connection between some detail of its imagery or argument and those of an earlier work that it systematically recants or retracts. Thus the opening question—"Where do we find ourselves?"—when compared to the boldness of *Nature*'s opening—"Let us inquire, to what end is nature?"—suggests the bewilderment that has overtaken this latter-day Oedipus as he turns from riddle solving to self-examination. The opening image of an endless staircase recalls the "mysterious ladder" of "Circles," but where the latter saw a new prospect of power from every rung, "Experience" sees only repetition and exhaustion. Idiosyncrasy or subjectivity, which in "Self-Reliance" was felt to be the source of one's chief value, now becomes part of the limitation of temperament, which shut us out from every truth our "colored and distorting lenses" cannot transmit. The horizon that in "Circles" was a promise of perpetual expansion has now become merely a metaphor for frustration: "Men seem to have learned of the horizon the art of perpetual retreating and reference." In *Nature* Emerson was a Transparent Eye-ball; in "Experience" he is shut in "a prison of glass which [he] cannot see." The "noble doubt" whether nature outwardly exists, the exhilarating suggestion that perhaps the whole of the outward universe is only a projection from the apocalypse of the mind, has become in "Experience" the Fall of Man.

But if "Experience" is in one way a palinode, it is in another way a continuation, under grimmer conditions, of the faith Emerson had never relinquished. That faith first enters the essay only as a kind of recoil against the reductiveness of the argument in the section devoted to temperament. Life is a string of moods, each showing only what lies in its focus; temperament is the iron wire on which these beads are strung. "Men resist the conclusion in the morning, but adopt it as the evening wears on, that temper prevails over everything of time, place, and condition, and is inconsumable in the flames of religion."

Yet in the midst of this determinism Emerson suddenly pauses to note the "capital exception" every man makes to general or deterministic laws—that is, himself. Although every man believes every other to be "a fatal partialist," he never sees himself as anything other than a "universalist." (In a similar passage later on in the essay Emerson will observe that we make the same exception to moral laws, which is why no man can believe that "the crime in him is as black as in the felon.") In "Circles" Emerson had noted that "every man supposes himself not to be fully understood; and if there is any truth in him, if he rests at last on the divine soul, I see not how it can be otherwise. The last chamber, the last closet, he must feel was never opened; there is always a residuum unknown, unanalyzable. That is, every man believes that he has a greater possibility." However much we may appear to one another as creatures limited by a given temperament, bound by the "links of the chain of physical necessity," the very fact that our consciousness rebels utterly at such a description of *ourselves* is the best evidence we have of the falsity of the doctrine. On its own level—the level of nature, of experience— temperament may be final, relativism inescapable.

> But it is impossible that the creative power should exclude itself. Into every intelligence there is a door which is never closed, through which the creator passes. The intellect, seeker of absolute truth, or the heart, lover of absolute good, intervenes for our succor, and at one whisper of these high powers we awake from our ineffectual struggles with this nightmare. We hurl it into its own hell, and cannot again contract ourselves to so base a state.

Yet this recovery, though it suggests the direction the essay will take, is by no means a final triumph over the lords of life. After Temperament there is Succession, by which Emerson means both the succession of "moods"— which he has already discussed—and the succession of "objects." The succession of moods is something we suffer; the succession of objects is something we choose. "We need change of objects." Our hunger for the whole keeps us restlessly searching through the world of experience in pursuit of a final consummation forever denied us. But if there are no final satisfactions, there are at least partial ones. In *The American Scholar* Emerson had compared inspiration to the "one central fire which flaming now out of the lips of Etna, lightens the capes of Sicily; and now out of the throat of Vesuvius, illuminates the towers and vineyards of Naples." The image he uses in "Experience" is considerably less apocalyptic, but the faith it expresses is the same: "Like a bird which alights nowhere, but hops perpetually from bough to bough, is the Power which abides in no man and no woman, but for a moment speaks from this one, and for another from that one."

The essay by this point seems to have established a pattern—a dip into despair, followed by a recoil of hope. But suddenly and unexpectedly Emerson turns on himself and his method: "what help from these fineries or pedantries? What help from thought? Life is not dialectics." This yawing back and forth between despair and hope is not, after all, how we spend most of our time. "Life is not intellectual or critical, but sturdy." Some way must be found to redeem the time, to treat it as something other than an emptiness separating moments of vision. "To fill the hour,—that is happiness; to fill the hour and leave no crevice for a repentance or an approval. We live amid surfaces, and the true art of life is to skate well on them." In these sentences we hear a different voice emerging, a voice that will become stronger in "Montaigne" and dominant in a book like *English Traits*. It is the voice of strong common sense, giving a view of the world Emerson had indeed expressed earlier, in things like the "Commodity" chapter of *Nature* and in essays like "Prudence" and "Compensation," but had never before offered as a serious *alternative* to the world of Reason. Now, for the first time, he proposes the "mid-world" as something other than a step on the way to vision.

Yet the mid-world offers no permanent anchorage either; moments of illumination *will* return whether we want them to or not, upsetting all our resolutions to keep "due metes and bounds." "Underneath the inharmonious and trivial particulars, is a musical perfection, the Ideal journeying always with us, the heaven without rent or seam." This region is something we do not make, but find, and when we find it all the old exhilaration returns. We respond with joy and amazement to the opening of "this august magnificence, old with the love and homage of innumerable ages, young with the life of life, the sunbright Mecca of the desert. And what a future it opens! I feel a new heart beating with the love of the new beauty. I am ready to die out of nature and be born again into this new yet unapproachable America I have found in the West."

For a vision of life that assessed man only from the platform of "experience" would leave out half his nature. "If I have described life as a flux of moods, I must now add that there is that in us which changes not and which ranks all sensations and states of mind." This something is the "central life" mentioned at the end of "Circles," the center that contains all possible circumferences. "The consciousness in each man is a sliding scale, which identifies him now with the First Cause, and now with the flesh of his body; life above life, in infinite degrees." Different religions have given this First Cause different names—Muse, Holy Ghost, *nous*, love—but Emerson confesses that he likes best the one ventured by the Chinese sage Mencius: "vast-flowing vigor." Asked what he means by this, Mencius describes it as the power that can "fill up the vacancy between heaven and earth" and that "leaves no hunger." With this definition we have come as far as possible from the terminal exhaustion and depletion of the essay's opening paragraphs: "we have arrived as far as we can go. Suffice it for the joy of the universe that we have arrived not at a wall, but at interminable oceans. Our life seems not so much present as prospective; not for the affairs on which it is wasted, but as a hint of this vast-flowing vigor."

But if this is the end of the dialectic, it is not the end of the essay, which—like life itself—will not let us remain in any state of illumination for long. We are brought back to the mid-world in a paragraph that summarizes all that has come before:

> It is very unhappy, but too late to be helped, the discovery we have made that we exist. That discovery is called the Fall of Man. Ever afterwards we suspect our instruments. We have learned that we do not see directly but mediately, and that we have no means of correcting these colored and distorting lenses which we are, or of computing the amount of their errors. Perhaps these subject-lenses have a creative power; perhaps there are no objects. Once we lived in what we saw; now, the rapaciousness of this new power, which threatens to absorb all things, engages us. Nature, art, persons, letters, religions, objects, successively tumble in, and God is but one of its ideas.

As Michael Cowan notes, this investigation of Subjectiveness in some ways "represents a spiralling back to the lord of Illusion, but now seen from the viewpoint of the saved rather than the damned imagination." What has made the difference is the discovery that there is an irreducible something in the soul that rebels fiercely at any attempt to reduce it to a mere "bundle of perceptions," and that is hence the best proof that any such definition is false. Knowing that the soul retains even in its grimmest moments "a door which is never closed, through which the creator passes" is the saving revelation that transforms the hell of Illusion into the purgatory of Subjectiveness. We are still unable to transcend the limitations of our vision, but now we seem not so much cut off from the real as the unconscious progenitors of it. Our "subject-lenses," unlike the object-lenses of a telescope or microscope, do not merely magnify reality, they determine its characteristics: "the chagrins which the bad heart gives off as bubbles, at once take form as ladies and gentlemen in the street, shopmen or bar-keepers in hotels, and threaten or insult whatever is threatenable or insultable in us." This is a trivial example of a principle, anything but trivial, whose gradual triumph one can witness in the history of the race. Realism is the philosophical system of every primitive tribe, but as civilization advances, men come gradually to suspect that as it is the eye that makes the horizon, so it is the beholder who creates the things he perceives.

It is not to be denied that there is something melancholy about such self-awareness. In a lecture entitled "The Present Age," delivered in 1837, Emerson expresses the traditional Romantic envy of those luckier ages that lived in what they saw:

> Ours is distinguished from the Greek and Roman and Gothic ages, and all the periods of childhood and youth by being the age of the second thought. The golden age is gone and the silver is gone—the blessed eras of unconscious life, of intuition, of genius. . . . The ancients were self-united. We have found out the difference of outer and inner. They described. We reason. They acted. We philosophise.

The act of reflection severs us as with an "innavigable sea" from the "things we aim at and converse with," and at the same time plants in our minds the suspicion that these things, which *feel* so distant, may not be "out there" at all. On this point modern empiricism and idealism coincide. Hume wrote: "Let us fix our attention out of ourselves as much as possible: let us chase our imagination to the heavens, or to the utmost limits of the universe; we can never really advance a step beyond ourselves, nor can conceive of any kind of existence, but those perceptions, which have appear'd in that narrow compass." As Emerson remarked of a similar passage from the materialist Condillac, "what more could an idealist say?"

This imprisonment has some lamentable consequences, as Emerson is the first to acknowledge, for the kingdoms of mortal friendship and of love. "Marriage (in which is called the spiritual world) is impossible, because of the inequality between every subject and every object. . . . There will be the same gulf between every me and every thee as between the original and the picture." For the soul, though it incarnates itself in time as an ordinary mortal with ordinary limitations, is in fact "of a fatal and universal power, *admitting no co-life*" (emphasis added). To say this is to push one's philosophy considerably beyond antinomianism; it ought logically to lead to a state in which everything—theft, arson, murder—is permitted. Emerson does not attempt to refute this objection. Instead (in what is surely one of the more audacious gestures in American literature) he coolly embraces it. That crime occurs at all is the best evidence we have of our unshakable belief in the divinity of the self. "It is an instance of our faith in ourselves that men never speak of crime as lightly as they think. . . . Murder in the murderer is no such ruinous thought as poets and romancers will have it; it does not unsettle him or fright him from his ordinary notice of trifles; it is an act quite easy to be contemplated." Our reasons for abstaining from murder are (by a nice irony) purely empirical, derived from experience: "in its sequel [murder] turns out to be a horrible confounding of all relations." Emerson's own version of the categorical imperative derives from the same ontology. Just as the highest praise we can offer any artist is to think that he actually possessed the thought with which he has inspired us, so the highest tribute we can pay to a fellow human being is to assume that his exterior—which must remain to us merely a part of the phenomenal—conceals a Deity as central to itself as our own. "Let us treat the men and women well; treat them as if they were real; perhaps they are."

We have here reached the shadowy ground where philosophy and psychology merge. In the letter to Margaret Fuller quoted earlier Emerson had claimed that the Berkleian philosophy was the clue to his nature *and relations*. Idealism as a philosophical doctrine appealed to him partly because it offered a credible way of accounting for the loneliness and isolation to which he felt temperamentally condemned. In 1851, after a rambling talk with Thoreau in which both of them had "stated over again, to sadness, almost, the Eternal loneliness," Emerson exclaimed, "how insular & pathetically solitary, are all the people we know!" We are inclined to try to find excuses for our separation from others, but in more honest moments we admit the grimmer truth: "the Sea, vocation, poverty, are seeming fences, but Man is insular and cannot be touched. Every man is an infinitely repellent orb, and holds his individual being on that condition." Existence for each of us is a drama played out in a private theater that admits only one spectator:

> Men generally attempt early in life to make their brothers first, afterwards their wives, acquainted with what is going forward in their private theater, but they soon desist from the attempt on finding that they also have some farce or perhaps some ear- & heart-rending tragedy forward on their secret boards on which they are intent, and all parties acquiesce at last in a private box with the whole play performed before him *solus*.

The same haunting notion prompts the question that closes this section of "Experience": "How long before our masquerade will end its noise of tambourines, laughter and shouting, and we will find it was a solitary performance?"

It is true, as Emerson says, that the muses of love and religion hate these developments. But our inescapable subjectivity has its own compensations. The "sharp peaks and edges of truth" we had hoped to find in reality we discover at last in the soul. God himself is "the native of these bleak rocks," an insight that "makes in morals the capital virtue of self-trust. We must hold hard to this poverty, however scandalous, and by more vigorous self-recoveries, after the sallies of action, possess our axis more firmly. The life of truth is cold and so far mournful; but it is not the slave of tears, contritions, and perturbations. It does not attempt another's work, nor adopt another's facts." As James Cox notes, "if 'Self-Reliance' was a ringing exhortation to trust the self, 'Experience' turns out to disclose that, after the last disillusion, there is nothing to rely on *but* the self."

And the sunbright Mecca of the West? The New Jerusalem, the kingdom of man over nature? What has become of it? In a journal Emerson had once noted sadly that "it takes a great deal of elevation of thought to produce a very little elevation of life. . . . Gradually in long years we bend our living to our idea. But we serve seven years & twice seven for Rachel." In "Experience" Emerson admits that he has served his time—"I am not the novice I was fourteen, nor yet seven years ago"—and still must be content only with Leah. "Let who will ask, Where is the fruit? I find a private fruit sufficient." This private fruit is, as Yoder says, "consciousness without correspondent results"—but I think it is not quite true to say that it is the only paradise offered us after the circuitous journey of "Experience." The view from Pisgah is as clear as it ever was.

In a letter to Margaret Fuller written to mark the second anniversary of his son's death Emerson declared himself no closer to reconciling himself to the calamity than when it was new, and compared himself to a poor Irishman who, when a court case went against him, said to the judge, "I am not satisfied." The senses have a right to perfection as well as the soul, and the soul will never rest content until these "ugly breaks" can be prevented. The attitude of defiance and the feeling of impotence recall a famous journal entry written a few months after his son's death. Speaking of Christ's sacrifice, he says:

> He did well. This great Defeat is hitherto the highest fact we have. But he that shall come shall do better. The mind requires a far higher exhibition of character, one which shall make itself good to the senses as well as the soul. This was a great Defeat. We demand Victory.

If it is not clear how long we will have to wait for this victory, how wide is the distance between ourselves and the Promised Land, Emerson refuses to give up hope. "Patience and patience, we shall win at the last." Experience may counsel only despair, "but in the solitude to which every man is always returning" there is a "sanity" that gives a very different kind of advice. "Never mind the ridicule, never mind the defeat; up again, old heart!—it seems to say." The "romance" that fled from our ship at the beginning of "Experience" returns at the end to become the goal of our weary but still hopeful pilgrimage. The "true romance which the world exists to realize"—the point at which desire and fact, the pleasure principle and the reality principle, will coincide—"will be the transformation of genius into practical power."

Yet the ending of "Experience," if it restates the old hope—or at least restates the impossibility of giving it up—hardly leaves us cheered. As Firkins says, "the victory is gained in the end, idealism is reëstablished, but the world in which its authority is renewed looks to the common eye like a dismantled, almost a dispeopled, universe." After such knowledge, what consolation?

Emerson develops two main answers to his question in the decade of the 1840s, one of them given in "The Poet," the other in "Montaigne." Both are attempts to find some sort of "paradise within" to compensate the individual for his loss of Eden and for his failure to reach the New Jerusalem. One is designed to satisfy the Reason, the other the Understanding. (The very fact that this distinction still remains is a sign that the conclusions offered are clearly thought of as *second bests*.) And both essays, in their imagery and structure, show that by now Emerson's four fables—contraction, dislocation, ossification, and reflection—have become a system of significances as useful to him as the Biblical stories had been to his ancestors: a series of types or analogies by which the chaotic impressions of experience could be ordered and understood.

JULIE ELLISON

Detachment and Transition

I have followed Emerson's example in describing in Romantic terms the sensations produced by reading his prose. For just as he knowingly reflects on his anti-authoritarian hermeneutics in certain of his fables, so he represents, in other parables, ideas about composition and style that utilize a variety of Romantic aesthetic notions. The relationship between the drama of interpretation enacted throughout the essays and the thematic values Emerson ascribes to stylistic features is very close. His fluctuating emotions about the nature and extent of the author's intellectual control of his tradition are repeated in allegories about the interaction between words and thoughts, discontinuity and teleology, purposiveness and surprise. He manages to convince me, at least, that his style successfully gratifies his desire for both conscious power over his material and the feeling of being surprised by it. He addresses our sense of the apparent randomness of his prose by repeatedly telling us what randomness signifies; he advances but also skeptically criticizes periodic claims to order. Such meditations focus on the metaphoric opposition of objects and energy and, analogously, of detachment and transition.

These patterns emerge in a characteristic fable. Emerson justifies his own practice of assembling essays from journal entries by attributing this method to all artists. Initially, he praises stylistic discontinuity resulting from the separate origins of a work's parts:

> by a multitude of trials & a thousand rejections & the using & perusing of what was already written . . . a poem made that shall thrill the world by the mere juxtaposition & interaction of lines & sentences that singly would have been of little worth & short date. Rightly is this art named composi-

tion & the composition has manifold the effect of the component parts. The orator is nowise equal to the evoking on a new subject of this brilliant chain of sentiments, facts, illustrations whereby he now fires himself & you. Every link in this living chain he found separate; one, ten years ago; one, last week; some of them he found in his father's house or at school when a boy; some of them by his losses; some of them by his sickness; some by his sins. The Webster with whom you talk admires the oration almost as much as you do, & knows himself to be nowise equal, unarmed, that is, without this tool of Synthesis to the splendid effect which he is yet well pleased you should impute to him.

No hands could make a watch. The hands brought dry sticks together & struck the flint with iron or rubbed sticks for fire & melted the ore & with stones made crow bar & hammer these again helped to make chisel & file, rasp & saw, piston & boiler, & so the watch & the steam engine are made, which the hands could never have produced & these again are new tools to make still more recondite & prolific instruments. So do the collated thoughts beget more & the artificially combined individuals have in addition to their own a quite new collective power. The main is made up of many islands, the state of many men. The poem of many thoughts each of which, in its turn, filled the whole sky of the poet was day & Being to him.

(*JMN.* V. 39–40)

Journal keeping—"the using & perusing of what was . . . written . . . ten years ago" or "last week"—initiates the "art named composition." Sentences record "sentiments, facts, illustrations" that have been lifted out of the continuum of experience, have "filled the whole sky of the poet," were "day & Being to him." The author must link these in a "living chain" without diminishing their individual integrity as moments. The separate genesis of "lines & sentences" makes possible juxtaposition, in which they creatively clash with each other and generate the "power" that "fires" the reader or listener.

This parable metaphorically represents the interaction of subject matter and imagination as the symbiotic relationship between objects and energy. Fragments of experience ("sentiments, facts, illustrations") and of prose ("lines & sentences") correspond to raw materials: dry sticks, flint, iron, stones, tools. Authorial intelligence is represented by energy: hands, fire, steam. The "living chain" of imaginative prose is a chain reaction between the two. Later in the passage, the ocean's flow, a collective political will, the poet's active mind transform into new wholes isolated islands, men, and thoughts. But Emerson's metaphor undergoes a significant change as he feels his way through this meditation. "Mere juxtaposition" gives way to "Synthesis" and an allegory of technological progress. He begins by celebrating the "splendid effect" of random combination. But open-ended process becomes teleological through shifts in metaphor. Oscillation becomes progressive, as in the famous dictum from "Self-Reliance": "Power . . . resides in the moment of transition from a past to a new state, in the shooting of the gulf, in the darting to an aim" (*CW*. II.40). The privileged term ceases to be "transition" and becomes "aim."

In a lecture of the same year as the "tool of Synthesis" passage, Emerson criticizes Bacon's failure to use that tool:

> Bacon's method is not within the work itself, but without. This might be expected in his *Natural History* but . . . in his *Essays* it is the same. All his work lies along the ground a vast unfinished city. He did not arrange but unceasingly collect facts. His own Intellect often acts little on what he collects. Very much stands as he found it—mere lists of facts. . . . The fire has hardly passed over it and given it fusion and a new order from his mind. It is sand without lime . . . thrown together; the order of a shop and not that of a tree or an animal where perfect assimilation has taken place and all the parts have a perfect unity. (*EL*.I.335)

Again we find the dichotomy between matter and fire, "facts" and intellect. Their ideal relationship is the organic fusion of a tree's or an animal's "perfect assimilation." The opposite image of a "vast unfinished city" bears witness to repeated beginnings never completed, a nightmare vision of the technological miracles praised in the other passage. Nostalgia for the organic enters in response to an unending series like the desire for the unifying absolute of the sublime. We glimpse the anxiety that frequently leads Emerson to recommend organic synthesis rather than the contrived alternation that potentially leads to "mere lists."

The impulse to sheer away from the constructed nature of his own work surfaces in his equivocations on the writer's self-consciousness. The idea that "composition" involves "a multitude of trials & a thousand rejections & the using & perusing of what was already written" implies that revision is the most creative phase of writing. Our examination of Emerson's own methods bears this out. Yet he then claims that his successes are inadvertent. The author "admires the oration almost as much as you do & knows himself to be nowise equal . . . to the splendid effect which he is yet well pleased you should impute to him." The passage shuffles between method and accident, intention and automatism, as he attributes energy to the artist's own mind, then to a spirit within or behind things. "Juxtaposition" generates sparks that surprise even the author. Tools—emblems of human inventiveness—produce effects beyond his control. The brilliant synopsis of technological development from the Stone Age to the Industrial Revolution conveys our perpetual unpreparedness in the face of our "recondite and prolific instruments."

The journal entry written at Nantasket Beach in July 1841 and partly quoted in my introduction brings together with marvelous complexity Emerson's simultaneous desire for knowledge and power, which he represents as repetition and surprise:

We have two needs. Being & Organization. See how much pains we take here in Plato's dialogues to set in order the One Fact in two or three or four steps & renew as oft as we can the pleasure the eternal surprise [sic] of coming at the last fact as children run up steps to jump down or up a hill to coast down on sleds or run far for one slide or as we get fishing tackle & go many miles to a watering place to catch fish and having caught one & learned the whole mystery we still repeat the process for the same result though perhaps the fish are thrown overboard at the last. The merchant plays the same game on Change, the card lover at whist, and what else does the scholar? He knows how the poetry he knows how the novel or the demonstration will affect him no new result but the oldest of all, yet he still craves a new book & bathes himself anew with the plunge at the last. The young men here this morning who have tried all the six or seven things to be done, namely, the sail, the bowling alley, the ride to Hull, and to Cohasset, the bath & the spyglass, they are in a rage just now to *do* something these itching fingers, this short activity, these nerves, this plasticity or creativeness accompanies forever & ever the profound Being. (*JMN*. VIII. 12–13)

Emerson's explanation posits an economy of psychic forces. The last sentence suggests that repetition is a discharge of energy. Young men "in a rage . . . to *do* something" are flooded with the suprapersonal force of Being, of which they are not conscious and which is consequently beyond their control. They "rage" because they have not yet discovered the pleasures of recurrence. But if they are governed by involuntary motion ("itching fingers" and "nerves"), the scholar "organizes" the pure dynamism of Being by *electing* to repeat himself. Repetition is a complex episode in which consciousness manages to surprise itself—a perfectly ironic and perfectly sublime event. As always in Emerson's writings, surprise is a conscious strategy to replicate unself-consciousness, a borderline state contained in the oxymoron, "eternal surprize." The reader "knows the poetry . . . will affect him" with "the oldest of all results" yet "bathes himself anew." An instantaneous change of state yields a split second of illusory newness which, later, he knows as renewal. It is as though there is a momentary lag when memory has not yet caught up to sensation.

As Nietzsche proclaimed in "The Use and Abuse of History" (1873), one of his most Emersonian polemics, "Forgetfulness is a property of all action." Emerson was quite right to assert, in "Memory," "We forget . . . according to beautiful laws" (*W*.XII.107): He clearly attributes repetition to the workings of a pleasure principle; he repeats to "renew . . . the pleasure, the eternal surprize." "This metonymy, or seeing the same sense in things so diverse, gives a *pure pleasure*," he writes elsewhere. "Every one of a million times we find a charm in the metamorphosis" (*W*.VIII.25; emphasis added). Pleasure is a compound of motion and power. The mind's leap in repeated transition is play for its own sake. As with the card player's or financier's calculations, the winnings are irrelevant; "perhaps the fish are thrown overboard at last." Stevens, writing against Freud, would later celebrate the same pleasure in repetition and difference: "Two things of opposite nature seem to depend / On one another. . . . This is the origin of change / . . . cold copulars embrace / and forth the particulars of rapture come" ("Notes toward a Supreme Fiction," Part II, canto iv, 11.1–6).

Emerson's need for a distance or difference between subject and object, mind and world, reveals how unlike Coleridge he was. Despite the importance of Coleridge to his intellectual development, he never absorbed the English Romantic's desire to inter-involve subject and object organically; rather, he thrives on the almost conflictual difference between them. In another parable, which favors teleology over sheer transition, the action of energy on matter once again represents imaginative process. "Is not poetry the little chamber in the brain," he asks, "where is generated the explosive force which, by gentle shocks, sets in action the intellectual world?" He answers himself by illustrating how consciousness takes up nature and converts it into words in a process which both requires and frees the mind's energy:

> the beholding and co-energizing mind sees the same refining and ascent to the third, the seventh or the tenth power of the daily accidents which the senses report, and which make the raw material of knowledge. It was sensation; when memory came, it was experience; when mind acted, it was knowledge; when mind acted on it as knowledge, it was thought.

"Explosive force" acts on "raw material." When objects are "melted" in the Promethean alembics" of the mind, they "come out men, and then, melted again, come out words, without any abatement, but with an exaltation of power!" (W.VIII.64, 24, 16).

Emerson summarizes his metaphoric system in "Experience": "A subject and an object,—it takes so much to make the galvanic circle complete." The authorial subject is "the conductor of the whole river of electricity" (W.III.80, 40). His objects are fragments of writing, the "boulders" or "infinitely repellent particles" that he knows make for his "lapidary style" (CEC.185, 303). Emerson's journal entries are substantial, even material, entities. Each of his sentences is "a cube, standing on its bottom like a die, essential and immortal" (J.IX.423). It is while writing to Carlyle that he most often objectifies his language. Usually these metaphors are self-deprecating, part of the exchange of apologies and curiously mutual stylistic insults sprinkled throughout their letters. "I dot evermore in my endless journal," he reports, "a line on every unknowable in nature; but the arrangement loiters long, & I get a brick kiln instead of a house." The "little raft" of *Essays, First Series* is "only boards & logs tied together." Carlyle agrees. His correspondent's sentences do not "rightly stick to their foregoers and their followers: the paragraph [is] not as a beaten *ingot*, but as a beautiful square bag of *duck-shot* held together by canvas!" (CEC.278, 291, 371).

Emerson restates the metaphor of objects and energy cognitively in terms of the mind's acts of "detachment" and "transition," two of the key terms of his poetics. His artist's first task is identifying and fixing the points between which he will move. "And thou shalt serve the god Terminus, the bounding Intellect, & love Boundary or Form," he instructs the poet (*JMN*.VIII.405). In the following selection from "Art," the starting point can be object, thought, or word, so long as it be detached:

> The virtue of art lies in detachment, in sequestering one object from the embarrassing variety. Until one thing comes out from the connection of things, there can be enjoyment, contemplation, but no thought. . . . It is the habit of certain minds to give an all-excluding fulness to the object, the thought, the word, they alight upon, and to make that for the time the deputy of the world. . . . The power . . . to magnify by detaching is the essence of rhetoric in the hands of the orator and the poet. (CW.II.211)

Rhetorical power originates in an epiphanic experience of the object when the poet's attentiveness climaxes in a moment of "all-excluding fulness." Having made "a pigment of thought . . . palpable and objective," the artist can launch himself toward another position. The "fact" created by objectification becomes a "fulcrum": "Transition is the attitude of power. A fact is only a fulcrum of the spirit. It is the terminus of a past thought, but only a means now of new sallies of the imagination and new progress of wisdom" (W.XII.59).

Emerson's ambivalence about detachment is characteristic of Romantic notions of creative thought. Coleridge attributes something like the powers of detachment and transition to the imagination. The secondary imagination, we recall,

> dissolves, diffuses, dissipates, in order to re-create; or where this process is rendered impossible, yet still, at all events, it struggles to realize and to unify. It is essentially *vital*, even as all objects (as objects) are essentially fixed and dead.

Coleridge is pessimistic about the possibility of total "recreation." He implies (more darkly than is usually noticed), that "this process" is frequently "rendered impossible." Still, when the imagination cannot win, it should "at all events" struggle with its material. If the Coleridgean imagination fails, what remains is Emerson's terminology of energy (vitality), "fixed and dead" objects, and the continuous oscillation (struggle) between them. Coleridge prefers to focus on the successful acts of re-creation that effect unity in poems, nations, and Christians. But his vision of what happens when the secondary imagination breaks down seems to prophesy the poet who detaches objects rather than dissolves them and juxtaposes thoughts and things instead of "diffusing" them. Emerson's habit of distinguishing objects from energy reverses the strategy of most English Romantics, who envisioned language as living matter or incarnate spirit. He desires the contest between idealizing mind and recalcitrant objects which, to Coleridge, was a poor second best. Like a good American, he identifies power with struggle, self-reliance with rebellion. The poet as liberator cannot afford to "diffuse" his adversary.

In his emphasis on detachment and objectification, Emerson comes closer to the German Romantics than to the English. Detachment was frequently discussed as both a perceptual and an historical phenomenon, "the path along which the individual, as well as the race, must pass." For Schiller, disunity is the moral equivalent of the fall of man. In the naïve state, man enjoyed "an undivided sensuous unity." But "once [he] has passed into the state of civilization," art "divides and cleaves him in two." Detachment is agonizingly felt as self-division but is absolutely essential for art. For Schelling, detachment, "definiteness of form," is "never negation but always an affirmation." It is not an historical process but an attribute of nature and the works that seek to represent her: "without bound the boundlessness could not be manifested . . . if unity is to be made palpable, this can only be done through singularity, isolation and conflict."

The notion of the detached fragment leads Emerson, as it led Schlegel, to a celebration of irony. Emerson's translation of "Witz" is "whim of will." He characterizes the fragment as an aggressive, self-reliant individual. It is no accident that in "Fate," his exemplar of the sublime is a human fragment, a baby. "I know not what the word *sublime* means," he writes in that essay, "if it be not the intimations, in this infant, of a terrific force. . . . A little whim of will to be free gallantly contending against the universe of chemistry!" (W.VI.29). Compression increases energy, and diminution is an index of heroism, it seems, in people as in prose. The speaker of "Experience" expects to be admired for telling us, "I know better than to claim any completeness for my picture. I am a fragment, and this is a fragment of me" (W.III.83). Emerson's irony informs the peculiarly blithe tone of many passages in "Fate": "The way of Providence is a little rude." "The more of these drones perish, the better for the hive." "[I]t would be . . . the speediest way of deciding the vote, to put the selectmen or the mayor and aldermen at the hay-scales." "The German and Irish millions, like the Negro, have a great deal of guano in their destiny" (W.VI.7, 14, 16). This essay, which is supposed to express the darkening mood of Emerson's middle and later years, is, in fact, dryly humorous. The tension between the themes of repetition (the determinism of fate) and of discontinuity (the human will that defies necessity) results in a celebration of sublime irony:

here they are, side by side, god and devil, mind and matter, king and conspirator, belt and spasm, riding peacefully together in the brain of every man.

A man must ride alternately on the horses of his private and his public nature, as the equestrians in the circus throw themselves nimbly from horse to horse, or plant one foot on the back of one and the other foot on the back of the other. (W.VI.22–23, 47)

In "The Comic," we recall, the "double consciousness" exposes "the radical joke of life, and then of literature." The simultaneous perception of freedom and fate is a "radical joke," not tragic knowledge.

In intensifying the struggle between mind and matter, Emerson drew on quite a different set of sources, nineteenth-century varieties of linguistic fundamentalism and primitivistic conceptions of the word. In Sweden-borgian cosmology, ideas and words tend toward the condition of matter but remain sharply distinguished from each other, for correspondence requires a triple parallelism of nature, thought, and language. The French Sweden-borgian, Oegger, for example, advanced a theory of literal correspondence between nature and Scripture, even providing a table of "Hieroglyphic Keys" to facilitate a reading of nature's text. Sampson Reed dreamed of an ideal state of language in which ideas are one with words and words "one with things." Human language "being as it were resolved into its original ele-ments, will lose itself in nature." It is but a short step from the correspondence of words and things to conceiving of words as thinglike. Attributing substance to words implies that ideas, too, are discrete entities.

Emerson's conception of detachment combines or reacts to elements of all these speculations. From the philosophers, he receives the fundamental notion of detachment as the origin of art and, like them, regards it as both loss and gain. In order to emphasize transition between detached perceptions, he increases the materiality of thoughts and words. Swedenborgianism provides a convenient vocabulary for this, although Emerson's "transition," as a differentiating movement, undoes the Swedenborgians' correspondential links. The demand for objects to react against comes from an antithetical rather than synthetic or Coleridgean imagination. Emerson's need to repre-sent the unlikeness of words and mind (objects and energy) reveals the crucial role of difference in repetition. What is repeated is the "struggle" between different qualities, which strongly suggests that the motive for repetition is antagonism.

One result of Emerson's conception of the encounter between mind and matter is that every object comes to stand for the term, "matter." The aggressive imagination turns the world into a collection of metaphors, all vehicles for the same tenor. The alternating current of transition can take place between any two places, things, or persons, if sufficiently detached:

Our strength is transitional, alternating; or, shall I say, a thread of two strands. The sea-shore, sea seen from shore, shore seen from sea; the taste of two metals in contact; and our enlarged powers at the approach and at the departure of a friend; the experience of poetic creativeness, which is not found in staying at home, nor yet in travelling, but in transitions from one to the other, which must therefore be adroitly managed to present as much transitional surface as possible. (W.IV.55–56)

Sea and shore, two metals, two persons must be separate. When the artist moves through the spaces created by detachment, he cannot be precisely located. He evades those who would define him and in this elusive freedom discovers the "enlarged powers" which make possible "the experience of poetic creativeness." Yet his termini are related by resemblance. Intellect masters an "embarrassing variety" of objects by discovering that they typify the same thing. Intense scrutiny transforms the object into a figure for the world's "central nature." The underlying affinity between the end points of transition permits Emerson to conceive of transition as metaphor making.

The metamorphosis of nature shows itself in nothing more than this that there is no word in our language that cannot become typical to us of nature by giving it emphasis.... The world is a Dancer; it is a Rosary; it is a Torrent; it is a Boat; a Mist; a Spider's Snare; it is what you will, and the metaphor will hold, and it will give the imagination keen pleasure.... [T]he ear instantly hears, & the spirit leaps to the trope. (JMN.VIII.23)

"Emphasis"—that is, detachment or objectification—makes any word "typical . . . of Nature." Detachment entails the perception of the inherently metaphoric character of words and things which, thus fixed, become the objects between which "metamorphosis" occurs. (We remember the connection, in the "Transition" collection, between "transit" and "trope" in the mind of the reader [JMN.X.160].) In "Prospects" at the end of Nature, Emerson announces that the mystery of man's life lies in the "tyrannizing unity in his constitution, which evermore separates and classifies things, endeavoring to reduce the most diverse to one form" (CW.I.39–40). This splendidly succinct definition, which ricochets between unity and separation, reduction and diversity, under the pressure of his drive to embrace them simultaneously, shows us what metaphor does. A unifying impulse separates in order to conform what has been sundered to its own vision of unity. Imagination thus generates discontinuities that only it can heal, a solipsist exulting in its own deconstructive and reconstructive powers. We can see how metaphor fits into the paradigm of language as objectification that "separates and classifies" and as "tyrannizing, endeavoring" energy. This energy enables the writer to contain opposites in the close verbal quarters of a metaphor, where their interaction generates the "explosive force" of language (W.VIII.64).

The physics of detachment and transition replicates the strategy we observed at the outset of "The Poet" and other essays. Emerson sets himself against one figure in order to propel himself toward another. He attacks, we found, not in order to attain the object of his desire, but to restore or strengthen his self-regard. In opposition, he feels free, distinct, and individual. His theory of transition accomplishes the same thing. With a remarkable awareness of the thematics of style, he makes fixity a necessary attribute of figurative language. The sensation of power comes in the transition between one momentarily frozen percept and the next, in the instant of undoing their artificial importance. "Man is made for conflict, not for rest," he exclaims. "In action is his power; not in his goals but in his transitions man is great" (W.XII.60). In acting to connect two objects, intellect becomes aware of its own energy. Self-consciousness, in turn, brings on "an exaltation" or redundancy "of power" (W.VIII.16). The mind discovers that it is greater than the thoughts it entertains; between two ideas is a field of force that contains them both. By continuously separating and rejoining consciousness and its contents, energy and matter, Emerson simultaneously enjoys freedom from and mastery of facts.

The association of transition with power is, of course, conventional. Sudden, even violent transitions between the parts of the ode (turn, counterturn, stand) had long been thought to be essential to the reader's astonishment and wonder. In the Romantic lyric, the association between discontinuity and greatness persists. Blair found it difficult to condone the fact that the sublime poet is "so abrupt in his transitions; so eccentric and irregular in his motions." But Wordsworth hoped his readers would find in "the transitions and the impassioned music of the versification" of "Tintern Abbey" "the principal requisites" of the ode.

Although in Emerson's formula perpetual transition seems to be brought about by an unlimited supply of metaphoric vehicles, the availability of these vehicles actually depends on the author's "ulterior intellectual perception": "*once seen* . . . [metamorphosis] does not stop" ((W.III.20, 30; emphasis added). Metaphor is not a property of the object but of the observer who

> perceives the independence of the thought on the symbol, the stability of the thought, the accidency and fugacity of the symbol. As the eyes of Lyncaeus were said to see through the earth, so the poet turns the world to glass, and shows us all things in their right series and procession. (W.III.20)

The metaphoric chain reaction is an ongoing act of mastering the object world. Once things are seen through, we are free from them; that is why symbols have the "power of emancipation" and "liberty" for all men (W.III.30, 32). Since any word or image can "represent the world," and since transition can occur between any two words or images, the chain reaction can go on forever, fueled by an infinite number of possible substitutions. Emerson "deprives himself of any brake on the transmutation of form," but this is not what bothers him. When he knows himself capable of transition, he can contemplate the possibility of its endless repetition with perfect equanimity. But a series of unrelated objects not bound by organizing energy, the "vast unfinished city" that "lies along the ground," is a different matter. At one moment, detachment is "the measure of all intellectual power" (W.XII.39) and at another, an "immense deduction from power" (W.XII.44). Pessimistic versions of his fable of mind show us detachment without transition. In these passages, we can trace how he alters his parable to compensate for transit's frequent cessation.

In the absence of energy, solid objects become oppressive. "[I]t is the inert effort of each thought having formed itself into a circular wave of circumstance . . . to heap itself on that ridge, and to solidify and hem in the life." The writer cannot muster sufficient force to overcome the inertia of his raw material. "Alas for this infirm faith," Emerson laments, "this will not strenuous, this vast ebb of a vast flow!"(CW.II.180–82). He feels that enormous intervals, as well as hypostasis, prevent him from making contact with his material and thus from manipulating it in transitional play. For example, the writings that make up "Natural History of Intellect," from which I cited passages that show his delight in the mind's detaching power, also contain passages like these:

> the discontinuity which perception effects between the mind and the object paralyzes the will. . . . That indescribably small interval is as good as a thousand miles, and has forever severed the practical unity. . . . Affection blends, intellect disjoins subject and object. For weal or woe we clear ourselves from the thing we contemplate. We grieve but are not the grief; we love but are not love.
>
> [C]ontinuity is for the great. . . . what we want is consecutiveness. 'T is with us a flash of light, then a long darkness, then a flash again. Ah! could we turn these fugitive sparkles into an astronomy of Copernican worlds.
>
> (W.XII.44, 52–53)

In good Romantic fashion, he blames self-consciousness ("perception" or "intellect") for his debility. An "indescribably small interval" appears immense ("as good as a thousand miles") because the will to span it is paralyzed. The verbal result of this condition is the remoteness of words from things; its visual effect, the lack of coincidence between "the axis of vision" and "the axis of things" (CW.I.43).

Frequently, he represents the curse of detachment in compressed synopses of the passage from a naïve to a sentimental condition. In his little cosmogony in *Nature* ("Man is the dwarf of himself"), the Orphic poet describes an "interval" that is both spiritual and temporal:

> having made for himself this huge shell, his waters retired; he no longer fills the veins and veinlets; he is shrunk to a drop. He sees that the structure still fits him, but fits him colossally. Say, rather, once it fitted him, now it corresponds to him from far and on high. (CW.I.42)

The same parable that describes the poor fit of man to nature illustrates his linguistic predicament:

> Language clothes nature as the air clothes the earth, taking the exact form & pressure of every object. Only words that are new fit exactly the thing, those that are old like old scoriae that have been long exposed to the air & sunshine have lost the sharpness of their mould & fit loosely. (JMN.V.246)

The yearning to eliminate all distance whatsoever by taking "the exact form and pressure" of the world is the opposite of the enjoyment of voluntary detachment Emerson recommends elsewhere.

These last two passages exhibit the structure of the "alienated majesty" motif in its diachronic manifestations (CW.II.27). When Emerson longs for something, he tends to locate it in the past or future. He may draw, in the first instance, on fables of the Fall, Romantic primitivism, and theories of an original language in which words were one with things. In the second case, he makes use of the prophetic conventions and millennial imagery found in the closing paragraphs of "The Poet." He is fully aware that these mythic projections are representations of inaccessible mental states. With considerable humor, he pictures the nostalgic impulse as a mildly senile but benevolent old man:

> The Spirit of Humanity finds it curious & good to leave the arm-chair of its old age . . . & go back to the scenes of Auld Lang Syne, to the old mansion house of Asia . . . where the faculties first opened, where youth first triumphed in the elasticity of strength & spirits & where the ways of Civilization & thought (*then* deemed *infinite*) were first explored.

"It may be," he comments after this flight of fancy, this emotion will be only occasionally felt for though the grandeur is real, it is ever present, as the firmament is forever magnificent but is only felt to be so when our own spirits are fresh" (JMN.II.218). Even as a very young man (this was written when he was twenty-one) he understood the dynamics of desire well enough to know that it projects its objects in time and space: "the world lacks unity and lies broken and in heaps . . . because man is disunited with himself" (CW.I.43). But this awareness does not defend him against feeling that the condition of detachment unredeemed by transition is one of loss. Loss, in turn, activates the desire for future resolution he has criticized as a wishful illusion. He compensates for the failure of transitional energy by introducing teleology into his fables, as we have already seen. Separate insights, images, and sentences are defined, not as the termini of energetic oscillation, but as parts evolving in the direction of wholeness. The unifying element is an anticipated retrospection, as hope replaces power:

> I write anecdotes of the intellect; a sort of Farmer's Almanac of mental moods. . . .
>
> I cannot myself use that systematic form which is reckoned essential in treating the science of the mind. But if one can say so without arrogance, I might suggest that he who contents himself with dotting a fragmentary curve, recording only what facts he has observed, without attempting to arrange them within one outline, follows a system also—a system as grand as any other, though he does not interfere with its vast curves by prematurely forcing them into a circle or ellipse, but only draws that arc which he clearly sees, or perhaps at a later observation a remote curve of the same orbit, and waits for a new opportunity, well assured that these observed arcs will consist with each other. (W.XII.11)

Keeping an "Almanac" of daily "anecdotes" demonstrates his faith that life is taking shape, that time itself bestows form. When self-reliance wavers, future closure gives the present its significance. Transition originates in freely willed detachment. Its reward is the sensation of mastery that occurs in the rapid apprehension of unlikeness when, as in all forms of the sublime, the mind recognizes its superiority to its objects. When incapable of transition, Emerson feels that he has lost control. Detachment has been imposed, not elected. The movement between dissimilar elements is not his own, aggressive and quick, but the impersonal, slow purposiveness of nature or of the soul's instinct.

The fluctuation between the two versions of detachment and transition repeats the alternating moods of desire and power analyzed. . . . Emerson is proud of his bravely unconventional prose and scorns the critic who would protest. In this he is right in line with theorists and practitioners of the sublime who, beginning with Longinus, have legitimated breaking the rules of style. But at times, he looks on discontinuity as failure. To the extent that he shares them, he feels himself at the mercy of his readers' expectations of thematic unity and stylistic continuity. One of the most complex manifestations of Emerson's ambivalence occurs in a journal entry recorded in the fall of 1841. The heading indicates that its purported theme is "Criticism," not the act of criticizing, as it turns out, but the effect of criticism on the writer (one is tempted to say "victim"). The passage begins by recounting a dream or dreamlike fable and proceeds to interpret it:

Into one of the chambers of hell came a man with his head under his arm, then several men carrying their heads under their arms. Well I suppose a man will come to that in his time also to put up his brain & his heart neatly in a box to carry, and put his irritabilities aloof from him as a fact, out of which the interpretation of the dream was also to be extorted. But why do I write another line, since my best friends assure me that in every line I repeat myself? Yet the God must be obeyed even to ridicule. The criticism of the public is, as I have often noted, much in advance of its invention. The ear is not to be cheated. A continuous effect cannot be produced by discontinuous thought and when the eye cannot detect the juncture of the skilful mosaic, the Spirit is apprised of disunion simply by the failure to affect the Spirit. This other thing I will also concede,—that the man Fingal is rather too swiftly plastic, or, shall I say, works more in the spirit of a cabinet maker, than of an architect. The thought which strikes him as great & Dantesque, & opens an abyss, he instantly presents to another transformed into a chamber or a neat parlor, and degrades ideas. (*JMN*. VIII.95–96)

The passage exhibits two kinds of detachment or "disunion" which correspond to two visions of hell. The effect of criticism is the same as the effect of man's fall into self-consciousness. "[A]n intellectual man has the power to go out of himself and see himself as an object," he writes in "Powers and Laws of Thought." "Intellectual perception severs once for all the man from the things with which he converses" (*W*.XII.44). Criticism exacerbates these operations and causes the artist to perform them on himself. He literally contains himself, boxing up his brain, his heart, and his anger. He has betaken himself voluntarily to a hell where his punishment reenacts his sin. Assuming that style is a true image of spirit, he accepts decapitation as an image of psychic "disunion" that no rhetorical surface can mask. He attempts to excise the organ that he blames for provoking criticism by disassociating himself from his irritabilities (putting them "aloof"), but this only creates more drastic division. Having been censured for excessive repetitiveness, he confronts duplicates of himself: "a man with his head under his arm" turns into "several men carrying their heads under their arms."

Emerson defends himself against criticism by agreeing with it. He accepts the judgment of his "best friends" and "the public," which he credits with critical astuteness "much in advance of its inventions." The irritability which he disavows is almost certainly exasperation at such friendly advice. The question "why do I write another line," and his answer, "The God must be obeyed," show him to be restless in his acquiescence. But the reference to Fingal (a figure for Emerson) occasions more self-criticism, and he confesses to being fanciful rather than imaginative. But even as he chastises his "too swiftly plastic" talent, his "god" inspires "the thought which strikes him as great and Dantesque and opens an abyss." Having imagined the hell of criticism, he recalls the hell Dante created. The wish to match Dante's powers, suppressed throughout as he tries to make concessions to his critics, breaks out in an acknowledgment of the thrill of disunion and the sublimity of the abyss. But what came to him as a sublime image, he receives "in the spirit of a cabinet maker." In the end, he boxes up inspiration as he boxed up his brain and heart in the "dream."

Two models of imagination, composition, and reading, each with radically different criteria for success, are implicit in this entry. According to the dominant conventional view, "discontinuous thought," an imaginative flaw, produces a regrettably discontinuous prose. Even where disjunction is not manifested stylistically, the "failure to affect the reader's Spirit" betrays the author's spiritual condition. Penetrating the rhetorical surface, spirit speaks to spirit; the reader is disappointed and the writer exposed. Reacting to this condition, the artist goes to the other extreme, producing graceful, "plastic" prose with all the aesthetic virtues of a "neat parlor." The reference to a "Dantesque thought" suggests an opposite interpretation of the same facts. The poet does indeed think discontinuously—his idea "opens an abyss." But as Dante's readers find his abyss to be sublime, so Emerson recognizes his thought as "great." In this light, the urge to domesticate and decorate with an excessively continuous style "degrades" the vision of the abyss. Both reader and writer would prefer less unity and more power.

This exercise in defensive self-interpretation is a meditation on the compositional habits we examined [previously.] Repetition and discontinuity are genetically related, and their effects are clearly intentional. But they result in a form of sublimity that defies conventional expectations of continuity and resolution. The thought of failing in the judgment of his public and anxiety about his mind's power to control and organize its material (which is to say, the thought of failure, period) makes sublimity a source of distress as well as of gratification. Emerson works out his mixed feelings by inventing elaborate metaphoric representations of his style which are alternately defensive and desirous. In the reading of his dream, he rebels against the expectations of the conventional reviewer and insists that his text is inspired. The author turns interpreter and retroactively makes the dream in which he was damned represent an imaginative victory; he changes it from an image of his failure into a figure for his will.

RICHARD POIRIER

The Question of Genius

THE CHALLENGE OF EMERSON

The question of "genius" is simply put: where is it and whose is it? If it is in a text like *King Lear* or in the composition of Mozart's Symphony No. 40, then why is it that we never feel quite satisfied with efforts to locate its presence in specific features of a work? And even when the efforts are to some degree successful, is it not the case that the findings are so awesome in their complication that we are then reluctant to attribute them to the agency of one person, an author or a composer? There is nearly always a sense in which the work of "genius" seems to have a more mysterious emanation, one that puts in doubt the idea of authorship and even the idea of texts as an accountable source for the experiences we have when listening to music or poetry or watching a work like, say, Balanchine's *Concerto Barocco*. Perhaps one explanation for this difficulty is that in a real sense we want to attribute "genius" to ourselves, to that mysterious part of ourselves that may lack only the talent for expression. "The great poet," Emerson writes in "The Over-Soul," "makes us feel our own wealth, and then we think less of his compositions. His greatest communication to our mind is to teach us to despise all he has done. Shakespeare carries us to such a lofty strain of intelligent activity as to suggest a wealth which beggars his own; and we then feel that the splendid works which he has created and which in other hours we extol as a sort of self-existent poetry, take no stronger hold of real nature than the shadow of a passing traveller on the rock."

In considering the question of "genius" I will be guided by Emerson for several reasons. First, because he seems to me, of those who address the subject, to have the best, which is to say the most uncompromised and troubled sense of its elusive identity. Second, because his corresponding idea of the over-soul inclines him to the view that what attracts us to "genius" has less to do with particular works and authors than with something we want to discover in ourselves, something that resides not in sentiments and pieties but in corporate human power. And third, because the strongest evidence for me of Emerson's genius as a writer is that he wrote in such a way as simultaneously to affirm and to call into doubt his own individual authority over language, the language he himself chooses to use, and to call also into doubt the very existence in language of the individual self even while he famously affirms it.

When he talks about that self, there is frequently something peculiar and unsettling about the bravado of his aphorisms, as if they are meant to transcend the occasion of their utterance and also of our reading. "All that Adam had, all that Caesar could, you have and can do," he tells us at the end of *Nature*. Is anyone supposed to believe this or to act upon the conviction that it is true? Emerson himself did not expect us to, and the carelessness of his references indicate as much. Anyone who has "all that Adam had" would scorn all that Caesar did and would hardly need or care to do it. But Emerson never means to be taken at his word. He is in fact not proposing either figure as a model but is dismissing them in favor of whatever version of their "genius" may exist in each of us, now. "Why, then," he asks a bit later in "The Over-Soul," "should I make account of Hamlet and Lear, as if we had not the soul from which they fell as syllables from the tongue?"

Emerson is forever dissolving figures and texts of the past in order to transpose them into an indefinite future. So, too, with his own writing. More important than any specific claims he makes on our behalf is the fact that he speaks the claims, writes them, as if, nearly a century and a half later, he intended still to be a living exhortatory presence on the scene, not someone trapped in the writings left behind. "It avails not, time nor place—distance avails not, / I am with you, you men and women of a generation, or ever so many generations hence." Whitman was to write this in "Crossing Brooklyn Ferry," and it is an Emersonian plea away from the poem itself, from the textuality of the poem, all as much as Emerson intends his aphorisms to stand clear of his essays. No wonder we can never remember for sure from which specific essays they come. Emerson has always had a precarious hold on literary immortality, as distinct from the immortality of *Bartlett's Familiar Quotations*, because he so nearly succeeds in persuading us that to have read him once is to have read him forever, that he is himself an example of the kind of "genius" he believed in: "a large imbibing of the common heart . . . not anomalous, but more like and not less like other men" ("The Over-Soul").

Emerson encourages quotation and thrives on it, to the point where many of the best known passages in the essays are already being remembered by him and cited, without mention, from the *Journals*. Often written years before, they then find themselves in the frequently confusing and sometimes confounding contexts of his published writings. There, in the shifty, devious, tortured movements of essays and lectures, the aphorisms have a very different career not only from the one originally provided for them but from the one they pursue in the enclosure of the reader's memory. The aphorisms rest in a corrosive swirl of other sentences, and Emerson seems to look upon them half in awe at his powers of clarification, half in dismay. He already knew what others have since claimed to have learned about the burdens and beguilements of language. The poignancy of his style is to be found in his half-articulated conviction that in a paradoxical way language is detrimental to that "genius" which is everyone's potential birthright, so that what survives of "genius" in language is only the deprivation of its having to express itself there. "Much of the wisdom of the world is not wisdom," remarks this renowned giver of wisdom, "and the most illuminated class of men are no doubt superior to literary fame, and are not writers" ("The Over-Soul").

Emerson's proverbial wisdom is an embarrassment to us and, I think, to him, and I am so far from suggesting that it manifests his genius that I would instead recall what he says in "The Poet": that "every thought is also a prison," that "the quality of imagination is to flow and not to freeze," and that "all language is vehicular and transitive, and is good, as ferries and horses are, for conveyance, not as farms and houses are, for homestead." Famous, nonetheless—and glad to be—for sentences that moor or fix him and the reader to a thought, a thought usually meant to serve a hortatory purpose, he is excited by this into an almost immediate counter-movement, within the same sentence or paragraph, an effort at disjunction, fracture, and dispersal. The aphorisms that must have thrilled him when he discovered their pointedness and power, their promise to echo down the centuries, are, he seems at once to fear, potentially deadening. The very sound of them presumed or called for the kind of conformity to "the truth" which was what had already made society "everywhere in conspiracy against the manhood of every one of its members."

Emerson is an example of a phenomenon made all the more rare and intriguing by the claims to exclusivity of literary modernism—he is the type of popular writer and at the same time a genius who escapes all of his own platitudes. He is a kind of writer, and so is Shakespeare, whose pact with the common reader is made out of a true sense of social kinship, but who meanwhile intends to break that pact so as to bring the reader into the realms of genius where he naturally belongs. It gives him pleasure as a writer to know what will also give pleasure to the reader, but he wants thereby to induce another kind of commonality, a shared feeling radically different from socially accredited ones, feelings that belong to what Wordsworth calls "the native and naked dignity of man," something before and after society. This process, by which a relatively superficial commonality drifts into a much more mysterious one, is felt by any reader of Wordsworth poems or of Shakespeare's plays.

It is possible that Emerson is the kind of writer who invested too heavily in his bargain with the common reader—his inheritor Frost is surely another—so that he has somehow dissuaded his own countrymen from taking him as complexly as, say the Germans take their Goethe or the English their Dr. Johnson. The failure of institutional criticism to see what Emerson is deeply about—a failure despite the efforts of several remarkably good studies in the last few decades—has had damaging consequences for intellectual life in America in this century. All of the Southern and, with a few exceptions like Alfred Kazin and Quentin Anderson, the New York intellectual contingents were either totally neglectful of Emerson or never took him seriously, any more than do most academic theorists of the present time. To have centralized the Emersonian inheritance, William James as well as John Dewey, would have meant, I suspect, that the New York intelligensia would not, for the span of decades from the 30's to the present, have convulsed themselves over the single issue of anti-Communism, and it would have made the New Critics less obsequious before modernist claims both about the specialness of the contemporary plight and the consequent necessity of certain forms of artistic difficulty.

These are distortions that can be modified when we begin to learn from Emerson's style how it is possible to sustain some tough measure of hope for the future. That hope is buttressed, curiously enough, by Emerson's own historical skepticism. His dream of human freedom did not, in the final analysis, look for authentication to anything unique in America's historical circumstance. Had his idea of freedom depended on practical realizations in American life, then all he could have left us is nostalgia and bitterness for a chance irretrievably lost. America was an "idea." "That idea which I approach & am magnetized by," he wrote in his *Journal* in 1844, "is my country"; America, he said, is always "a poem in our eyes." In the prospect of the country's actual achievements he could be quite mordantly funny: "Look at literary New England, one would think it was a national fast." "We are all," he said, "dying of miscellany." Contemplating what he called the country's "bareness," he was capable of finding there an opportunity but also a threat. In the *Journal* (for October 27, 1851) he offers a particularly affecting example:

It would be hard to recall the rambles of last night's talk with H.T. but we started over again, to sadness, almost, the Eternal loneliness. . . . how insular & pathetically solitary, are all the people we know! Nor dare we tell what we think of each other, when we bow in the street. 'Tis mighty fine for us to taunt men of the world with superficial & treacherous courtesies. I saw yesterday, Sunday, whilst at dinner my neighbor Hosmer creeping into my barn. At once it occurred, 'Well, men are lonely, to be sure, & here is this able, social, intellectual farmer under this grim day, sidling into my barn, in hope of some talk with me, showing me how to husband my cornstalks. Forlorn enough!' It is hard to believe that all times are alike & that the present is also rich. When this annual project of a Journal returns, & I cast about to think who are to be contributors, I am struck with a feeling of great poverty; my bareness! my bareness! seems America to say.

More than Cooper in *Home as Found*, more even than James in the book on *Hawthorne*, Emerson saw that the nation's bareness did not make America innocent of inherited culture but actually more complicit with it, as if what he called the country's "enormous disproportion of unquickend earth" was totally exposed to foreign radiations without the protection of any cultural cloud layers of its own. "We are not the first born," he admits at one point, "but the latest born . . . we have no wings . . . the sins of our predecessors are on us like a mountain of obstruction." He means that there was nothing in America to resist the overwhelming cultural force already implicit in language, and especially in that shape of it called literature:

Literature has been before us, wherever we go. When I come in the secretest recess of a swamp, to some obscure and rare, & to me unknown plant, I know that its name & the number of its stamens, every bract & awn, is carefully described & registered in a book in my shelf. So is it with this young soul wandering lonely, wistful, reserved, unfriended up & down in nature. These mysteries which he ponders, which astonish & entrance him, this riddle of liberty, this dream of immortality, this drawing to love, this trembling balance of motive, and the centrality whereof these are rays, have all been explored to the recesses of consciousness, to the verge of Chaos & Neant, by men with grander steadfastness & subtler organs of search than any now alive; so that when this tender philosopher comes from his reverie to literature, he is alarmed (like one whose secret has been betrayed) by the terrible fidelity, with which, men long before his day, have described all & much more than all he has just seen as new Continent in the West.

If Emerson's America was bare of native culture, one paradoxical consequence was that everywhere European art preceded you to perception. America may be "a poem in our eyes" but that is because in our eyes there are already so many poems. The invisible and therefore the most unavoidable and voracious instrument of inherited culture was language itself. That, I think, is what Emerson means by the wonderful phrase "this riddle of liberty." He was ready to teach us, long before Foucault, that if we intend ever to resist our social and cultural fate, then we must first see it for what it is, and the form of that fate, ultimately, is the language we use and by which we learn to know ourselves. Language is also, however, the place wherein we can make our most effective inflections of dissent. These consist of acts of writing, reading, speaking by which language gets modified to individual purpose. Through such acts as these, more than by directly political actions, consciousness might be altered and, if only on occasion, a truer self, or "genius," might be discovered. Language was the way; language was also the obstruction, and in his management of this dilemma Emerson shows why he is so important to us.

I want now to explore these matters by considering the relation in his writing between, on the one hand, what he calls "genius" and, on the other, the institutions represented for him by the word "culture." How could "genius" propose to survive in language? How could Emerson himself hope to survive in his writing when, as he saw it, language already belongs to a cultural and literary inheritance which "genius," by its very nature, wants to resist? How, with respect to culture or to literary textuality, does "genius" find itself, and, indeed, can it find itself in language at all?

Consider what he has to say, for instance, about cultural change. "The things which are dear to men at this hour," he writes in "Circles," "are so on account of the ideas which emerged on their mental horizon, and which cause the present order of things. . . . A new degree of culture would instantly revolutionize the entire system of human pursuits." Such a proposition could be expected from Nietzsche or from Foucault, but not in a tone at once so gingerly and placid, so confident—and so confused by its own geniality. The passage has a characteristically Emersonian blur or density. The tempo is polite and yet a little on edge, as it passes rapidly through quite subversive proposals, proposals which are hurried along against a number of inferable resistances. In a manner characteristic of Emerson, enthusiastic utterances come into being from the foreknowledge of their implausibility. Thus the excitement at the prospect of "a new degree of culture," with its instantaneous revolutionary results, has as a prior condition, what he calls "the present order of things." But this "present order" has already been described in a phrase ("dear to men at this hour") which ought to preclude the emergence of any such "new degree," especially one which would at once change "the entire system of human pursuits."

When a writer heads into confusions of this kind the reader should, I think, simply follow him there. Any classroom effort at clarification, any tidying up in the interest of what he is supposedly trying to say, is in fact misleading. Why not let the confusion be the experience? Having followed the writer into the maze, the reader may at any time decide simply to leave him there, particularly if the confusions and stalemates turn out to be the results of incompetence or laziness or a limp dependence on someone else's terminology.

But why, on many occasions, do we decide to stay in the thick of it? For the reason, I suspect, that we feel ourselves in tandem with a writer for whom language has, at some crucial moment, become an antagonist. How has this happened? By virtue, oddly enough, of the writer's keenest attentions to it. Thanks to his placations and seductions, language has finally had to reveal that it is devoted also, forever and always, to someone or something else. It is at such moments that a writer touches upon some nerve center in the culture which, by his writing, he may be trying to reform. And he discovers at that moment that the culture, as it is embodied in language, is all the while *de*forming him and what he is trying to say. Emerson is continually arriving at this discovery, and he is then at his most appealing. He lets us know by movements of style that he intends to keep at it, to court the rebuffs of language in the hope of turning it, troping it, if ever so slightly, to his purposes. The infidelities of language—Santayana called them it will be remembered, "the kindly infidelities"—in no way persuade him to resentments or to resignations. He pushes ahead, into the next sentence—it will be a detour, likely as not, from the one he has just written—confident that he is leaving behind a sign that will mark for the future yet another stroke, though never a victory, against that fate which, for him, is embodied in the institutional force of language.

No wonder it is at times extraordinarily hard to know how to take Emerson. The uncertainty has only partly to do with his tendency to indulge in profuse illustrations or in shifts and substitutions of terminology. Except to hapless paraphrase, his terminological vagaries are less a problem in his writing than its very substance. Any greatly ambitious writer is subject to the same sort of slippage, as Leo Bersani shows in his readings of Freud, though Emerson, unlike the Freud who had at least early aspirations to science, is not the victim so much as the instigator of his own driftings. He wants to evade formulas even while announcing them; he wants to say things, as Frost once remarked of his own writing, "that suggest formulae but won't formulate— that almost but don't quite formulate."

Beyond these complications, however, is Emerson's predeliction for what he calls in "The Poet," "abandonment," "abandonment to the nature of things," a habit of evacuating rhetorical positions in pursuit of a truth that is only suspected. He gets almost audibly exasperated with the prospect that his reader might actually believe what he is saying, that the writer really is expected to mean what he is saying. He gets uncomfortable even with such concessions as he makes to the propriety of sentences and paragraphs, with their implicit commitment to ideas of duration, sequence, and logical progression. Obviously I am not describing what a dreary criticism likes to call "verbal strategies," as if language were passively available to an author's already premeditated intentions. His, rather, is a design *upon* language and syntax, an exploratory and never completed effort which the reader is asked to join. He struggles, and he knows he struggles, within the mediations which consciousness creates for itself through language. "The Emersonian self . . . is voice and not text," Harold Bloom remarks "which is why it must splinter and destroy its own texts." The voice—or what Barbara Packer aptly calls "Emerson's many voices"—this, too, is of course splintered and blurred, and the language that issues from it refers us back not to a consistently structured moral or psychological self. It refers us rather to a presence on the periphery of any humanistically conceived individual, scrutinizing it, wondering at it, performing, playing off against it, joking with and about it, a voice from the margin. To recall Thoreau's nice little joke which unites this kind of writing posture with idiomatic postures of everyday life, Emerson is always "beside" himself "in a sane way," or, with Whitman, "Both in and out of the game and watching and wondering at it."

These reflections on the destiny of writing and reading are inseparable from a consideration of that aspect of individualism called "genius." "Genius" is commonly assumed to involve a mastery of the codes and signs by which a culture structures itself. It therefore also offers a clue to any latently subversive content that these codes and signs might have accumulated during their long passage through many histories. Marvell's punning is an example of subversiveness, as is Thoreau's (a sometimes too cute one for my taste), so, too, are Shakespeare's troping of words within different contexts. Shakespeare manages to establish hidden identities (which the surface of the historical plays would not politically dare to support) between characters otherwise wholly different, like Falstaff and Bolingbroke, both "portly" gentlemen, one with a fat gut, the other with a swelled head, one a glutton for sack, the other for power and expropriated inheritance, both of them thieves and, taken together, an indictment of the insatiable appetite let loose at all levels of society as England passed from the medieval into the capitalist period.

By such examples I want to suggest that when "genius" finds itself in language the result is a productive multiplication, a thickening of possibilities which are a challenge to those clarifications of purpose and design on which public and institutional life prides itself. The density or thicket in which "genius" moves thereupon often stimulates something nearly the reverse: an idealization of simplicity, as in Wordsworth, or transparency, as in Emerson. And since in these cases "genius" is associated not with writing merely but with a kind of power available to all human beings who do not write or even read, the discovered plight of "genius" in the clutches of language becomes coexistent with a recognition of a need for cultural change of great magnitude, a change, let us say, as would bring about an end to man as that figure is now represented to ourselves. Such need is likely to be felt most profoundly, after all, by someone who, in the act of writing and as a condition of everyday life, has already experienced the enormous sloth and intractibility of the languages which the culture makes most readily available to him, languages which represent those very "ideas" which a writer like Emerson may want to dislodge, but which have infiltrated every facet of the culture.

On this issue of cultural reformation, Emerson has already confronted the difficulties whose discovery is nowadays credited to his admirer Nietzsche and, after him, to Foucault. This is evident, for instance when Nietzsche wants both to affirm and deny the burdens of historical consciousness, or when Foucault arrives at the conclusion that man came into being, came to knowledge of himself, by virtue of previous discursive formations whose source is not determinable and whose power is therefore to be resisted only indirectly. Can this power be resisted at all? That is the inevitable and probably unanswerable question. If it is assumed that life is totally subordinated to language systems, then resistance to them can come only by some species of troping, only from within the discourse already believed to be utterly ubiquitous and, in its effects, claustrophobic. So much so that it must wholly determine the self-knowledge, the self-representation, and the affiliations even of those who propose to elude these things. Arguing that "it is in discourse that power and knowledge are joined together," Foucault, for example, proposes, apropos homosexuality, that:

> There is no question that the appearance in nineteenth century psychiatry, jurisprudence, and literature of a whole series of discourses on the species and subspecies of homosexuality, inversion, pederasty, and 'psychic hermaphrodism' made possible a strong advance of social controls into this area of 'perversity'; but it also made possible the formation of a 'reverse' discourse: homosexuality began to speak in its own behalf, to demand that its legitimacy or 'naturality' be acknowledged, often in the same vocabulary, using the same categories by which it was medically disqualified.

Resistance and the possibility of reform find a voice, in this view, only after and by virtue of submissive compliance. This same discovery can be credited to Emerson without its being the incentive, as it is in Foucault, for proposals to do away altogether with the idea of the human. Emerson's alienation is of a kind which George Kateb, in his study of Hannah Arendt, calls "practiced." Kateb has in mind a peculiar American form of alienation in which "the moral unit . . . is the individual, not humanity or masses of people heaped together traumatically. The individual is the democratic individual, not some unconditioned and unsituated ghost." Thus imagined, the self is "loose fitting," indifferent to social identification, and capable (as I demonstrate at some length in *A World Elsewhere*) of that "doubleness" by which it is possible to be inside and outside society all at once, inside and outside the self. The self becomes a form of the Other. Thus, Emerson will often use words having to do with the enterprise of American capitalism (the self "relies because it works and is," for example) in order to claim virtues for exactly those human attributes which the business ethic finds antithetical. He does this so unaffectedly that it is sometimes mistakenly suggested that he is promoting not the soul but the idea of property. Emerson conducts a raid on the opposition party of Property, he steals its language for purposes it would find ulterior. His own position, within this complex operation, is explained, with quite startling candor, in "New England Reformers":

> It is handsomer to remain in the establishment better than the establish-
> ment, and conduct that in the best manner, than to make a sally against evil
> by some single improvement, without supporting it by a total regeneration.
> Do not be so vain of your one objection. Do you think there is only
> one? . . . Do you complain of the laws of Property? it is pedantry to give such
> importance to them. Can we not play the game of life with these counters,
> as well as with those? in the institution of property as well as out of it? . . . No
> one gives the impression of superiority to the institution, which he must
> give who will reform it. It makes no difference what you say, you must make
> me feel that you are aloof from it; by your natural and supernatural ad-
> vantages do easily see to the end of it—do see how man can do without it.

I have put Foucault in a field with Emerson so as to indicate, as sharply and briefly as possible, that the problems the reader may and ought to have with Emerson's writing are indistinguishable from the problem of cultural reformation, possibilities for which are presumably inherent in the idea and promise of "genius." One reason Emerson is so hard to read is that he refuses to separate the problem of language from the problem of culture or either of these from the problem of the relation of "genius" to culture and, specifically, to textuality. Instead, he willingly submits to the contradictions and questions that result when these problems are put into active conjunction. In the passage quoted at the beginning, for example, what is the inferable source for any "new degree of culture" and how could its source, if located in individual "genius," also provide the authority for its being centered on any "mental horizon" and made subject to consensus? Assuming, nonetheless, that the "new degree of culture" were promulgated, how could it dislodge or encircle the present one, especially when it is the present "order of things" which allows man to make sense of the world, to find a home in it? And, if, as he further claims, "all [our] facts are classified in accordance with a governing idea, a 'circle' or 'mental horizon,'" how is it possible for an individual, except vaguely or intermittently, even to recognize those other facts which presumably either call for or are created by "a new order of things," a new "circle" or discursive formation?

Problems of this kind beset any proposal for cultural reformation, and Emerson's efforts to negotiate among them depend heavily on his use of the term "genius." These same efforts also help account for his effusions, fractures, and mobilities, which are for me testimony both to his own "genius" and to a further complication, which is that "genius," instead of being a solution to the problem of language is, again, itself confounded by it. What he calls the "influx of divinity into the world," does not and cannot reach us unobstructed by language, by history, by materiality, the "things" already in place from which "genius" might commonly be supposed to free us. "Genius" is itself interrogated by "the present order of things," so that it does not necessarily move to the "center" of the horizon; it can be deformed, put to one side, made to disappear. "When God lets loose a thinker on this planet," he says, "then all things are at risk"—including, it should be added, the "thinker." Because when "genius" enters history, when it articulates itself so as to expand or embrace existing "circles," it thereby submits to the distortions that are a precondition, apparently, of its being seen or heard at all. Any "circle" produced by an act of "genius" soon begins, like the ones that precede it, to "heap itself," as he puts it, "to solidify and hem in life."

Emerson carries on against the odds, but it is no wonder that his praise of specific examples of "genius," especially historically credited ones, is frequently edged with a flickering and disconcerting sarcasm. A telling instance occurs in "Experience" when he refers to that great example of "an influx of divinity" or "genius," namely Jesus, a figure who was great according to Keats, partly because he did *not* write. As it is read and re-read, the passage becomes not more firm but more slithery, and for the reason that you begin to hear in the voice the pressure of something wanting to be articulated— namely an exasperation with any cultural *location* of genius—in excess of what is being directly put to you, and in conflict with it:

> People forget that it is the eye which makes the horizon, and the rounding mind's eye which makes this or that man a type or representative of humanity, with the name of hero or saint. Jesus, the 'providential man,' is a good man on whom many people are agreed that these optical laws shall take effect. By love on the one part and by forbearance to press objection on the other part, it is for a time settled that we will look at him in the centre of the horizon, and ascribe to him the properties that will attach to any man so seen. But the longest love or aversion has a speedy term. The great and crescive self, rooted in absolute nature, supplants all relative existence and ruins the kingdom of mortal friendship and love.

Time and again his approbations for a figure like Jesus are preyed upon by his critical aloofness about the process by which "genius" gets appropriated to and recognized within cultural hierarchies. Though Jesus is not put into a list with several others, which is Emerson's usual way of modifying his enthusiasm for anyone in particular, the claim that he is the "providential man" is accompanied by the curious suggestion that "the type of humanity" who is hero or saint is actually the beneficiary of "the *name* hero or saint," and that even Jesus got that "name" thanks not to indisputable merit, but because "many people [were] agreed that these optical laws shall take effect." It is as if while being earnest with us and with himself Emerson were plagued with the after thoughts and misgivings that language, as it takes shape, begets in him. Since he has so often insisted that any man may aspire to be Jesus, it is perhaps incumbent on him to say that this "type" of humanity may be seen in "this or that man." But why and how? The workings of such "optical laws" may for example, result from special interests, so that not all but only "many men agreed" on Jesus. If everyone is called, how are the very few chosen, unless the choice proceeds from local historical necessity? And if to be chosen means that you are convenient to necessity, then what is the relative importance, if any, of the personal attributes of "genius"? How is "genius" kept from being sullied by its need to shape itself (if it is to be recognized at all) into particular "circles"? At issue, then, is not Emerson's idea of "genius," or any of his ideas in the abstract, but rather the career, the status, the plight of the term as it twists itself into time and history. What happens to "genius" as it tries—this is the central question—to transmit itself to later times through the medium of language?

It is this—the necessary textuality of "genius"—which puts immense strain on Emerson's discourse and on his voice. There is, for instance, something like surly, even competitive resentment in his going on to say of Jesus that "By love on the one part and by forbearance to press objection on the other part, it is for a time settled that we look at him in the centre of the horizon, and ascribe to him the properties that will attach to any man so seen." This kind of talk is familiar enough if translated into formulaic Emerson: do not, he keeps telling us, be overawed by cultural tradition. What is apt to be unfamiliar is the derisive undertone—"it is for a time settled," "forbearance to press objection," "we will look at him" (as if someone else had already placed him there), and we will "ascribe" virtues, which implies that the same virtues might accrue to "any man so seen" or implaced. And yet, implicit disenchantment, close to contempt, for the very forms of cultural and historical ascription is never allowed fully to assert itself, and it is immediately deflected in a maneuver, quite characteristic of him, by which he reaffirms the value of that same human power whose practices have just provoked him to skepticism. His near disdain for the processes by which culture structures itself gives way to an ecstatic evocation of "the great and crescive self"—which "ruins the kingdom of mortal friendship and love." But the transition is accomplished by the innocuous linking remark that "the longest love or aversion has a speedy term." Jesus does not last forever at "the centre of the horizon," but neither, he suggests, do our affectionate attachments, which are cleverly given a statutory or institutional weight by calling them "kingdoms." Before the reader lets himself be flattered by such glamorous excuses for domestic flare-ups, he should notice that "the order of things" is being manipulated here merely in Emerson's tactical interests. He wishes to evade, or at least he wishes not to push further into, the remarkable suggestion that all cultural artifacts which achieve historical celebrity, all persons who attain the title of "genius," all works which can be called "classic," are products not so much of the influx of God or Intellect or Omniscience or Soul but of the prior needs of what Hawthorne calls "artificial system."

When "genius" enters history, when it becomes textualized, then at that point for Emerson it is also likely to become blurred or entrapped. This is even truer for writers than for those he calls providential people who do not write at all, like Jesus or Socrates, and it helps account for the crankiness of some of Emerson's literary judgements. "When we adhere to the ideal of the poet," he says, "we have our difficulties even with Milton and Homer. Milton is too literary, and Homer too literal and historical" ("The Poet"). Shakespeare and Dante are, he grants, "geniuses," and while he knows this by virtue of their work as it has been written, transcribed and read, the implication of his larger position is that access to their "genius" is in fact obscured by their writing and by any reading of it, since both activities are subject to the historical conditions within which they occur. In appreciating a writer of "genius," then, it is not necessarily always required by Emerson that there be a reader of "genius," or, for that matter, any sustained act of reading. "The genius is a genius by the first look he casts on objects," as he says in his essay "Montaigne," "his thought has dissolved the works of art and nature into their causes, so that the works appear heavy and faulty."

When we inquire after "genius," we are required, then, to imagine a criticism that follows after the demolition of texts, the disappearance of writing, the collapse into itself of the historicity of composition. The difficulties of imagining this can be alleviated, and usually are, by releasing Emerson's terminology from any of the binds into which it puts itself, so that "man," "reader," and "poet" might be allowed at difficult junctures to stand duty for one another, as would the "work of art" for "natural objects." But while this is loyal to his theory of tropes it is also a way of not admitting those radical challenges and contradictions that are in evidence in his work wherever we choose to look. In his essay on "Art," for example, he means both on the one hand to approximate a position Eliot will take in "Tradition and the Individual Talent," and, on the other, to dismiss all works of art as "hypocritical rubbish" unless "it opens our eyes to the mysteries of eternal art." Similarly, when he grants that the artist functions within "the thought amidst which he grew" and which "he cannot avoid or wipe out of his work," he wants still to maintain that "the reference of all production is at last"—"at last" being a teleological phrase of which he is inordinately but understandably fond—"to aboriginal Power." It is this "Power," in turn, which explains "the traits common to all works of the highest art—that they are universally intelligible; that they restore us to the simplest states of mind." How any work of "genius," especially in language, can possibly be "universally intelligible," leaving aside the issue of literacy, is a question to which there is no satisfactory answer. It is not resolved by his saying in "The Poet" that "the man is half himself, the other half is his expression" or that "every man should be so much an artist that he can report in conversation what has befallen him," especially when he says in "The Over-Soul" that "the soul answers never with words," that "an answer in words is delusive," and, in "Intellect," that "silence is a solvent that destroys personality and gives leave to be great and universal."

What is required so that art would be "universally intelligible"? On balance, it would seem to be the disappearance of the media, the means by which art comes into existence as a public event. It would yield to a transparency in which reader and writer, viewer and painter would share in the executant power, as Wordsworth would call it, that is still making its ghostly transits through the work of art. The ideal reader of literature would in that sense be supremely competent or of no competence whatever, a person of "simple tastes and susceptibility to all great human influences" which "overpower the accidents of local and special culture" ("Art"). We are thus left with the peculiar prospect that works of "genius" may enhance and create human life by the degree to which they make their own materiality inconspicuous. A particularly engaging example, in the essay "Art," describes, if that is the right word, an experience in Rome:

> When I came at last to Rome and saw with eyes the pictures, I found that genius left to novices the gay and fantastic and ostentatious, and itself pierced directly to the simple and true: that it was familiar and sincere; that it was the old eternal fact I had met already in so many forms—unto which I lived, that it was the plain *you and me* I knew so well—and left at home in so many conversations.

This "Plain *you and me*" that shouts at us in italics, what is to be said of them? "Seen with eyes" (is there another way of seeing them?) can they really be the same "plain *you and me*" "left at home in so many conversations," especially when "the soul never answers with words"? Is it not more likely that "plain *you and me*" resembles the friends he imagines for himself in the essay "Friendship," of which Evan Carton has written so astutely, "friends" with whom he prefers *not* to have real talk, but rather what he calls "this evanescent conversation"? "I will receive from them not what they have but what they are," is how he oddly puts it. To bring the issue of representation more directly into line with the question of "genius," "plain *you and me*" are meant to be joined not on "the thread of talent" ("talent makes counterfeit ties," he warns us in "Montaigne"), but on "the thread" of "genius" (which "makes real ones"). "Talent," according to the 1843 *Journals* "is applicability. A human body, an animal is an applicability" but "the Life, the Soul, is Genius." Not for him, then, the colorful surface, "the figures of exaggeration." Instead, like the painters of genius whose work he sees in Rome, he will "pierce directly" to some kind of pentimento behind the visible surface of the paint, or he will let some "aboriginal Power" emerge through the color, dissolving as it does so the extravagance, the animal figures, the "applicable" representations of the human. What comes through to him as he stands there in Rome or sits there writing in Concord is not the image of a human figure but the images of a "stroke," a "stroke" as of the brush or of the pen as it makes the figure. We are left to suppose that what he sees in the painting is an inscription or a hieroglyph, as John Irving might put it, emanating from some "gigantic hand" which guides the hand of the artist. "The whole extant product of the plastic arts," he writes, " has herein its highest value, *as history*; as a stroke drawn in the portrait of that fate, perfect and beautiful, according to whose ordinations all beings advance to their beatitude" ("Art"). The product of art is not the work you read or look at, much less the animal figures it tries to represent; instead, it is the inferable "stroke" which, by its own forever unsatisfied anticipations, at once creates, passes through and banishes the solidified aspects of the work.

"The transparent eyeball" is an example of such a "stroke" both as an occurrence in life, and as an occurrence in writing. It has also notoriously resisted interpretive rendering, any translation into "applicability." As a figure it epitomizes Emerson's anatomy of man at the moment when he is possessed by "genius," when he is in it and it is in him. It is only one of many related instances, however, where there is a precipitation in the writing which paradoxically is the sign that "genius" is to emerge as a figure of radiant clarity, much as revelation has traditionally signaled itself by obscurity. In life, however, such moments are few, and Emerson is especially sardonic when the promised advent of "genius" in the Concord area turns into something less, as when in the *Journals* he discovers that "Alcott is a tedious archangel" who "can as little as any man separate his drivelling from his divining," or, in "The Poet," where, in a possible comment on the "transparent eyeball" passage, he comically describes a local versifier as "this winged man" who instead of "carrying me into the heavens," takes me "like a fowl or a flying fish, a little way from the ground or water." The day he and the world truly "discover a poet," he adds, "shall be better than my birthday; then I became an animal; now I am invited into the science of the real."

An inquiry could be made, but not here, into some tortured affiliation between Emerson, in the moods I have been describing, and some later figures mentioned sympathetically in A *Pluralistic Universe* by William James. Referring first to the Mills, James and John Stuart (presumably for the latter's entry called "Mental Chemistry" in A *System of Logic*) and to Wilhelm Wundt's "psychic synthesis," James goes on to list such writers as "Spencer, Taine, Fiske, Barratt and Clifford [who] had promoted a great evolutionary theory in which, in the absence of souls, selves, and other principles of unity, primordial units of mind-stuff or mind-dust were represented as summing themselves together in successive stages of compounding and re-compounding, and thus engendering our higher and more complex states of mind." These, like still later "genetic codes," are secularized versions of the over-soul, and Emerson is to me often most intriguing when he proposes a structure for man that reduces his animal and sentimental features to a field of energy wherein he himself would often act, as he says when speaking of slavery in the *Journals*, as a "geometer of [man's] forces."

THE PROBLEM FOR CRITICISM

Emerson's constant troping of himself, from poet to farmer, from transparent eyeball to "a geometer of forces," is a way of suggesting that any work a man does, any stance he honestly assumes, offers a momentary, partial glimpse of his potential for "genius." And even this will be denied us if, instead of emulating the actions prompted by the example of genius, we merely admire what it has in the past already produced. Recall that in "The Over-Soul" he advises that "the best communication to our mind," by a great poet "is to teach us to despise all he has done." This reluctance to let "genius" take a permanently measurable form in language or in any sort of text, literary or otherwise, has made Emerson largely incompatible with critical and interpretive practice in and, perhaps even more, outside the academy. Why is it that even those like myself who think of him, in William James's phrase, as "the divine Emerson," and who would give endorsement to what he says about "genius" and about language are nonetheless unable to conduct a critical argument in a manner that would fully satisfy his notions of how writing ideally gets written and how ideally it ought to be read? One obvious reason, which he himself acknowledges, is that writing and reading do not ever get produced under ideal circumstances but are always conditioned by the historical and institutional factors under which they proceed.

There are contradictions in Emerson between his optative theory of "genius" and his worldly recognitions of the restrictive circles of any available discourse. These contradictions are not resolved by his rhetorical insistence that the circles can be broken, especially since the result is then only a new circle which will ultimately hem in life. When it comes to the value of human culture as it has so far evolved, especially literary culture, Emerson is quite disconcertingly mistrustful. Why would we read works of reputed "genius," much less anything else that is not of an immediately utilitarian nature, if the reason for doing so is only that we may "despise" them? Does he mean to suggest that the work is good only for the exercise it affords our faculties while we read it? Probably so, but if that is the case, then how are the benefits of works of "genius" ever transformed from individual experience of reading into those values presumably beneficial to the commonwealth? These questions are made inevitable precisely by the circle of discourse within which Emerson himself wrote and within which he necessarily is read, and they suggest how close he comes to proposing that literary culture, including the Western idea of man as the object of its concern, is in fact an obstruction to true self-realization. Once again he anticipates Nietzsche and Foucault while proposing an alternative to the latter's incipient hopelessness. Through his concept of "genius" he manages to hold onto an idea of the self, but it is a self far more shadowy than his rhetoric of individualism has led people to suppose. The self in Emerson is not an entity, not even a function; it is an intimation of presence that comes from the very act by which the self eludes definition.

It is not surprising, then, that Emerson has not lent himself to any of the institutional forms of criticism in the last or in this century, including the current fashion of deconstruction. The reasons take on a particular interest, however, if we compare him to another massive figure of the nineteenth century, the source and sustenance of a still prevailing humanistic thrust in Anglo-American criticism, Matthew Arnold. Why did Arnold and not Emerson become the dominant figure in literary-cultural criticism in America up to the present moment? I mean Arnold as he is generally understood, rather than the Arnold made congenial to contemporary theory by, for instance, George Levine in *Critical Inquiry*. Arnold's predominance probably has something to do with the slow, begrudging acceptance of American literature as a fit subject for study in colleges and universities. More important, however, are stubborn convictions that language exists as a servitor to established ideas of the self, and, as a result, that there always can be a fairly direct relation between some version of that self and any voice located in the language of a literary text. Where language proves nonetheless recalcitrant to clarity, or where narrative appears to disperse or fracture expectations, then criticism has chosen to take these things not as in themselves constituting a reality but only as a deviation from it. The job of criticism is thereby and quite erroneously imagined to be fairly simple: it is to make these deviations consistent with humanistic assumptions about the self, and consistent also with the self's presumed desire to exist and be redeemed in ways already paradigmatically familiar. Allowance is made, that is, for fracturings, disloca-tions, and like manner of literary behaviour, but these are taken as a communication of longings for lost continuities; Molly Bloom's soliloquy in *Ulysses* makes perfect sense, a renowned expert once assured me, if you add the punctuation which Joyce (for good reason) left out. The effort of Anglo-American criticism has been in large part to perpetuate the cultural traditions which Emerson chose to write against, and his oppositions extended well beyond that relatively benign version of the anxiety of influence which he proposes in the essay "Intellect." "Take thankfully and heartily all they can give," he remarks of writers of genius. "Exhaust them, wrestle with them, let them not go until their blessing be won, and after a short season the dismay will be overpast, the excess of influences withdrawn, and they will be no longer an alarming meteor, but one more bright star shining serenely in your heaven and blending its light with all your day."

This sort of advice can be put effectively into practice, though even here established academic criticism has been until quite recently hostile to Harold Bloom's demonstrations of this. But the advice comes from a writer who more frequently recommends practices that cannot be acted upon at all. If, for example, one set out with Emerson's help to discover the evidence of "genius" in a text it would immediately be apparent that the text itself was to surrender its materiality, was instead to become volatile. "Criticism," accord-ing to a remarkable passage in the *Journals*, "must be transcendental, that is, must consider literature ephemeral and easily entertain the supposition of its entire disappearance." Here as everywhere Emerson means to detextualize, to dehistoricize, to un-authorize "genius," leaving in place only an activity, and a barely traceable one at that. It is this phenomenon—"genius" as an activity, an influx, a movement, "genius" as energy—that has always, with or without Emerson, posed problems for humanistic criticism and the culture it looks to for support. As a phenomenon of energy, "genius" in Emerson lays waste to generally perceived humanistic images of authorial and therefore of individual human purpose and intent. "Genius" is antithetical to the proposi-tion that "all human values, all human emotions, are of social growth if not of social origin . . . and that much of what man does for himself depends on what society allows him to do." This is a remark by Lionel Trilling in his study of

Arnold, though any of Trilling's subsequent works would offer a comparable illustration. Even in its general stylistic deportment, it illustrates why Trilling became the most urbane of the American successors to Arnold, and why he tried to cultivate "a mind never entirely his own," to recall Blackmur's characterization of it, "a mind always deliberately to some extent what he understands to be the mind of society, and also a mind always deliberately to some extent the mind of the old European society taken as corrective and as prophesy."

I am using Trilling here, not I think unfairly, so that yet another question might be posed. And that is, *how* is the "mind of society" to be "cultivated," especially "the old European society," of which Emerson wrote with ambivalent yearning? Principally, of course, by immersion in the texts produced by it. So that while humanistic criticism has always been suspicious of "genius" as a possibly disruptive force, a force that brings into question even the idea of authorship, it has all the while found the products of "genius"—the writing, the texts, and what Arnold called "touchstones"—indispensable to its larger cultural purposes, though needless to say these products are transformed by the function they are thereby asked to serve. By contrast, the implication of Emerson's position is that "genius," as it transmits itself into writing, is thereby to a degree repressed and deformed, even before it is adulterated still further by institutions of reading.

To emphasize how antithetical is the Emersonian to any Arnoldian aesthetic, consider the famous preface of 1869 to *Culture and Anarchy*: "the whole scope of the essay is to recommend culture as the great help out of our present difficulties; culture being a pursuit of our total perfection by means of our getting to know, on all matters which most concern us, the best which has been thought and said in the world." Culture may be "the pursuit of our total perfection" but it is being recommended at the same time for reasons more immediately practical ("a great help out of our present difficulties"). And while in the 1865 preface to *Essays in Criticism*, first series, criticism has been defined as "a Disinterested endeavor to learn and propagate the best that is known and thought in the world," it gets to sound somewhat less "disinterested" when, four years later, we are asked to know the "best" rather more selectively ("on all matters that most concern us"). A criticism that proposes to find in literature things "to know," "to learn," "to propagate," has already decided that literature is not to "flow," as Emerson would have it, but to "freeze" ("The Poet"), a kind of immobilized treasure trove out of which "thoughts" and "sayings" and ideas might be lifted, allowing for the concession that each age will have somewhat different preferences.

Consider, in contrast, a few comparatively unfamiliar aphorisms of Emerson, all of them filled with a sense of the vehicular, transitive, mobile nature of "something" passing through writing. This, from the *Journals* for 1835, "The truest state of mind rested in becomes false," or this from the *Journals* for 1830, "genius . . . finds its end in the means," or this, from "The Poet," "art is the path of the creator to his work," or this, "an imaginative book renders us much more service at first by stimulating us through its tropes than afterwards when we arrive at the precise sense of the author," (though it must be added that nowhere does he suggest that we ever can arrive at this "precise sense"). And, finally, in the essay on "Plato," this: "the experience of poetic creativeness . . . is not found in staying at home, nor yet in travelling, but in transitions from one to the other, which must therefore be adroitly managed to present as much transitional surface as possible."

In "the present order of things" it would, I think, be impossible to plan either a literary history or a course of study whose purpose would be to account for the initial "stimulation" offered by tropes or by the movements on a text's "transitional surface." And the difficulty of doing so attests to the chasm which has always separated the history or pedagogy of literature from the moment by moment experience of reading it. "Genius," and not only as it is conceived by Emerson, disrupts the prevalent humanistic design of—and upon—literature.

The quality of debate on these issues is now so coarse, and the chance of being misunderstood so likely, that I want to clarify my position a little more carefully. I think that a truly disinterested effort to trace the workings of "genius" in literature, no less than in the musical structures of Bach, would severely challenge, and in many instances reveal as a mere come-on or flirtation, the humanistic intentions ascribed to the arts. At the same time it would be absurd to deny or in any way begrudge the existence in literature, or other artistic forms, of traditional humanisms. Humanism is not, after all, merely a school of criticism; it is, in its many variations, a way of believing in the world, of finding how life might offer some moments of clarification and purpose, and most works of literature, necessarily and for obvious historical reasons, are compelled to represent it. I would argue, however, that humanistic representation in, say, a novel by Dickens or a play by Shakespeare, a poem by Wordsworth or Frost, or Stevens, may not be the purpose of a work but instead a part of its process, its operation, its method. Humanism is often the straight man of performative "genius"; it is the material which genius works in and not necessarily for. Emerson says repeatedly of "genius" what he says in "Self-Reliance" about the soul: "This is one fact the world hates; that the soul *becomes*; for that forever degrades the past, turns all riches to poverty, all reputation to shame, confounds the saint with the rogue, shoves Jesus and Judas equally aside." To focus on performance or the work of troping will therefore seem a trivialization of literature only to politicians of high culture for whom taking literature seriously consists in finding how it might function in an already determined scheme of things.

I trust this political aside will not seem irrelevant in view of the fact that criticism has so often been covertly political in its efforts to scramble the power of "genius" so that it can be made to conform to the order of things. Criticism customarily assigns the effects of "genius" to various moral or semiotic, numerological or historical functions. In opposing such assignments, Emerson insists on the utter indifference of "genius" to them, its indifference to standards of good and evil, its refusal to participate even in the assumption absolutely central to humanistic interpretation and its continuities; namely, that some subjects are necessarily of greater magnitude than others. In this regard, it would be instructive, he tells us in "Experience," to watch what might be called a "circle" in action: a "kitten chasing so prettily her tail."

In elaborating this appealing suggestion he again attacks, to recall the discussion of the paintings at Rome, "the gay and fantastic and ostentatious" and carries forward the implications that when performance is "simple and true" it is by nature also solitary:

> Do you see that kitten chasing so prettily her tail? If you could look with her eyes you might see her surrounded with hundreds of figures performing complex dramas, with tragic and comic issues, long conversations, many characters, many ups and downs of fate—and meantime it is only puss and her tail. How long before our masquerade will end its noise of tambourines, laughter and shouting, and we shall find it was a solitary performance? A subject and an object—it takes so much to make the galvanic circuit complete, but magnitude adds nothing. What imports it whether it is Kepler and the sphere, Columbus and America, a reader and his book, or puss with her tail?

"Genius" in Emerson is linked in its manifestations to an awesome indifference to preferences likely to have been created in the reader by conventional representations, even while at the same time "genius" may be using these very things as the materials on which it works its transformations. In this passage, the metaphors combine in a way that reiterates the connections he frequently makes between reading a book, scientific inquiry, geographical explorations into the unknown, and the comfortingly dense familiarity that is the substance of domestic conversation, including the soliloquies and conversations of our cats. Moral strictures are not much help to a reading of any of these nor are any of them usually initiated by moral imperatives. It is this fact which especially disappoints the votaries of talent, who are committed to the already known, the already represented.

A particularly arresting instance of Emerson's astringent sense of things occurs just before "puss and her tail," in a brief discussion of "murder." "Murder," he remarks, is not a crime to the intellect, "for there is no crime to the intellect." He means "intellect constructive" which, as he says in the essay "Intellect," "we properly designate by the word Genius," and he calls it "constructive" because it produces systems, designs, poems, sentences like his own. To this "intellect," "the world is a problem in mathematics or the science of quantity, and it leaves out praise and blame and all weak emotions." Thus, "murder" is susceptible less to moral than to some quantitative or geometric measure of always evolving human possibility. It is a factor in what Henry James, while discussing his responsibilities to his characters, calls "compositional resource." For Emerson, the reading of life or of art is not a search for morally stabilizing moments or summary but for infusions and diffusions of energy, for that constant redistribution of forces called troping, including the troping of the self. His own drift within an essay is obedient only to an alert extemporizing, a readiness to meet the contingencies that the writing itself will unexpectedly throw up.

For example, the two paragraphs I have been discussing in "Experience" bring him to a point of exceptional bleakness, but there is always at such moments, in life or in writing, a kind of abandon, as if, with so much given up already, caution can be put aside, making it possible to say that "murder is no crime" or that "puss and her tail" are some version of Columbus and America. The next paragraph is one of the most dramatically powerful in Emerson, as he draws back from tentative speculations before pushing on to resolutions which have been opened up and made inevitable by the behavior of his own language. He begins by saying that the "muses and love and religion hate these developments," and then goes on in a rather distraught comparison to say that these interested parties "will find a way to punish the chemist who publishes in the parlor the secrets of the laboratory." He hesitates for another sentence, uncertain as to his motives—perhaps he has only revealed the "institutional necessity of seeing things under private aspects"?—and then finds himself in the sort of bind he confronted earlier in "Self-Reliance," where he discovered how the terms of his very title had betrayed him. "To talk of reliance," he wrote, "is a poor external way of speaking," (rather like "speaking" of "chemists" or ill humors). "Speak rather of that which relies because it works and is." We are, in "Experience," at a similar moment, one in which Emerson himself is most audibly dramatizing the struggle of writing, of finding his way perilously through the currents of his own language, which means of course also through other people's language. It is appropriate that one of the images of himself near the end of the paragraph is of a swimmer "among drowning men, who all catch at him, and give so much as a leg or a finger they will drown him." He turns therefore from talk of chemists and humors to what "works and is," to his own lonely genius and its costs:

> And yet is the God the native of these bleak rocks. That need makes in morals the capital virtue of self-trust. We must hold hard to this poverty, however scandalous, and by more vigorous self-recoveries, after the sallies of action, possess our axis more firmly. The life of truth is cold and so far mournful: but it is not the slave of tears, contritions and perturbations.

All active "genius" is an instance of "self-reliance" but not all self-reliance is an instance of "genius." Indeed, the exercise of "genius" puts self-reliance not just continually but continuously at risk, as it moves within the unrelenting, the constantly disconcerting and distorting pressures of cultural discourses. That is why Emerson associates "genius" with so strong a counter-power of effacement, transparency, reduction, all of which dangerously consort with idealizations of silence, of flowers born to blush unseen. That is why, too, it is inadvisable to press him too hard for a working definition of "genius." The term is essential to him, and to all of us, not because it means this or that, or because it puts "talent" in its place. It is an essential word for the very reason that it is vague and can stand for a dream of human power and mastery that is a challenge to other Gods. People have always been obsessed with "genius" for reasons that are in every sense good ones. No matter what its source, no matter how supremely human or strangely non-human it might be thought to be, it has had results ascribed to it which make people truly excited by the possibilities of human life. Ideally, the idea of the "human" and of "genius" are tolerant and wary of their mutual incursions, and the task set by Emerson (and no less by Shakespeare or Melville) is to prevent the usurpations of the one idea by the other in what Emerson derisively calls "manipular efforts to realize the world of thought." The proper destiny of "genius" and of the "human" is to claim the other as a field of resisted and never to be completed action. The two words belong to that syntax of possibility which moves with serial grandeur through and beyond the last sentence of "Experience": "the true romance which the world exists to realize will be the transformation of genius into practical power."

It is impossible to say what this transformation would mean, or how in our present state we would even be able to recognize it. We would have to be there already in a future that seems to recede as we approach it, thanks to Emerson's accumulated terms of postponement. We cannot project ourselves into this future from a present wherein we are fractured into partialities, where even the language we would have to use to describe such a future is, as Emerson would have it, also flawed and partial. It is therefore appropriate that the sentence makes no mention of humans at all; it is "the world" that exists to realize this "true romance." We are left instead, by the immediately preceding sentence, in "the solitude" to which "every man is always return-ing," there to have "revelations" which can be carried, it is said, into "new worlds." A "revelation" is, alas, far short of a "transformation"; it is some-thing that might occur for a moment in our present condition. And while in that condition, all we can do to change the world is to get to "work," in the special sense in which he uses that term. "Do your work and I shall know you," he says in "The Poet"; "Do your thing," was the way he put it earlier in the *Journals* (1835) "and I shall know you." "Work" is a way to confront the essential facts of existence and to discover in doing so the power of human desire which turns facts into mythologies and mythologies into facts, as in Thoreau's hoeing of beans in *Walden* or Frost's "apple-picking" or the occupa-tion of love-making in Shakespeare's *Antony and Cleopatra*. Let me end with a charming and simpler instance from Emerson himself, as when in the section of *Nature* called "Commodity" he remarks that man "no longer waits for favoring gales, but by means of steam, he realizes the fable of Aeolus's bag, and carries two and thirty winds in the boiler of his boat." Typically, Emerson chooses an example which combines poetry and industry, an example, too, in which transport is an aspect of transformation and of transition from one state to another. Criticism is enjoined by him not to stop or slow this perpetual process in the hope of some sort of clarity or extractable wisdom. Language must conform not to any God of tradition but to the still emergent "genius" of the race. And yet if Emerson must admit that "I look in vain for the poet whom I describe," we need not wonder that we still look in vain for such a criticism as he proposes.

Chronology

1803	Born May 25, in Boston.
1821	Graduates from Harvard.
1826	Approbated as Unitarian minister.
1829	Accepts ordination as minister at Second Church, Boston on March 11. Marries Ellen Tucker on September 30.
1831	Death of Ellen on February 8.
1832	Resigns from Second Church in October, after refusing to celebrate the Lord's Supper. Leaves for European tour in December.
1833	Travels in France, Italy, England. Meets Coleridge, Wordsworth and befriends Carlyle. Returns to Boston in October.
1834	Death of his brother Edward. Moves to Concord, where ancestors had lived.
1835	Begins career as secular lecturer. Marries Lydia ("Lidian") Jackson on September 14.
1836	Death of his brother Charles on May 9. First book, *Nature*, published on September 9. First child, Waldo, born on October 30.
1837	National business and bank crisis in the spring. Oration at Harvard on August 31: "The American Scholar."
1838	Oration at Harvard Divinity School on July 15: "The Divinity School Address."
1839	Birth of daughter Ellen on February 24.
1840	Founding of *The Dial*.
1841	*Essays, First Series* published on March 20. Birth of daughter Edith on November 22.
1842	Death of son Waldo on January 27.
1843	Lecture tour to Washington, Baltimore, Philadelphia and New York City.
1844	Birth of son Edward on July 10. *Essays, Second Series* published on October 19.
1846	Publication of *Poems* on December 25.
1847–48	Travels in France and England.
1850	Webster's Seventh of March speech. Publication of *Representative Men*.

1856   *English Traits* published on August 6.

1860   Publication of *The Conduct of Life*.

1862   Death of Thoreau.

1867   Publication of *May-Day and Other Pieces*.

1872   Burning of Emerson's house on July 24. Travels in Europe and Egypt from October 1872 until May 1873, but returns much diminished in mind.

1882   Emerson dies in Concord on April 27.

Contributors

HAROLD BLOOM, Sterling Professor of the Humanities at Yale University, is the author of *The Anxiety of Influence, Poetry and Repression* and many other volumes of literary criticism. His forthcoming study, *Freud: Transference and Authority*, attempts a full-scale reading of all of Freud's major writings. He is the general editor of *The Chelsea House Library of Literary Criticism.*

The late STEPHEN E. WHICHER taught at Swarthmore College and Yale University. His study of Emerson's "inner life," *Freedom and Fate* (1953) was his largest achievement in a lifetime devoted to the study of American literature.

SACVAN BERCOVITCH is a Professor of English and American Literature at Harvard University. His books include *The American Jeremiad* and *The Puritan Origins of the American Self.*

JAMES M. COX is Professor of American Literature at Dartmouth College. He is widely known for his critical writings upon Mark Twain, Robert Frost, and American autobiography.

DAVID PORTER is Professor of English at the University of Massachusetts, Amherst. His books include *The Art of Emily Dickinson's Early Poetry* and *Emerson and Literary Change.*

BARBARA L. PACKER has taught at Yale and at the University of California, Los Angeles, where she is Associate Professor of English. Her book, *Emerson's Fall*, has been acclaimed as one of the best studies of the sage since those of Firkins and Whicher.

JULIE ELLISON teaches in the English Department of the University of Michigan, Ann Arbor. Her book, *Emerson's Romantic Style*, is part of her ongoing study of the Sublime and the relation between nineteenth and twentieth century critical theory.

RICHARD POIRIER is Professor of English at Rutgers University. He edits the magazine *Raritan*, and is one of the editors of the Library of America. His critical work includes *A World Elsewhere, The Performing Self*, and influential books on Robert Frost, Henry James, and Norman Mailer. He is also well known as a critic of ballet, and of the contemporary cultural scene.

Bibliography

Allen, Gay Wilson. *Waldo Emerson: A Biography*. New York: The Viking Press, 1981.

Anderson, Quentin. *The Imperial Self: An Essay in American Literary and Cultural History*. New York: Alfred A. Knopf, 1971.

Bishop, Jonathan. *Emerson on the Soul*. Cambridge, Mass.: Harvard University Press, 1964.

Bloom, Harold. *The Ringers in the Tower*. Chicago: University of Chicago Press, 1971.

_____. *A Map of Misreading*. New York: Oxford University Press, 1975.

_____. *Figures of Capable Imagination*. New York: Seabury Press, 1976.

_____, ed. *Ralph Waldo Emerson: Poetry and Later Writings*. New York: The Library of America, 1985.

Bode, Carl, ed. *Ralph Waldo Emerson: A Profile*. New York: Hill and Wang, 1969.

Buell, Lawrence. *Literary Transcendentalism*. Ithaca: Cornell University Press, 1973.

Burke, Kenneth. "I, Eye, Ay—Emerson's Early Essay 'Nature': Thoughts on the Machinery of Transcendence." In *Transcendentalism and its Legacy*, edited by Myron Simon and Thornton H. Parsons, pp. 3–24. Ann Arbor: The University of Michigan Press, 1966.

Cabot, James Elliot. *A Memoir of Ralph Waldo Emerson*. 2 vols. Boston and New York: Houghton Mifflin & Co., 1895.

Cavell, Stanley. "An Emerson Mood" and "Thinking of Emerson." In *The Senses of "Walden": An Expanded Edition*. San Francisco: North Point Press, 1981.

Chapman, John Jay. "Emerson." In *The Selected Writings of John Jay Chapman*, edited by Jacques Barzun. New York: Funk and Wagnalls, Minerva Press, 1968.

Cheyfitz, Eric. *The Trans-Parent: Sexual Politics in the Language of Emerson*. Baltimore: The Johns Hopkins University Press, 1981.

Cowan, Michael. *City of the West: Emerson, America, and Urban Metaphor*. New Haven, Conn.: Yale University Press, 1967.

Ellison, Julie. *Emerson's Romantic Style*. Princeton: Princeton University Press, 1984.

Emerson, Edward Waldo, ed. *The Complete Works of Ralph Waldo Emerson*. 12 vols., Centenary Edition. Boston and New York: Houghton Mifflin Co., 1903–04.

Emerson, Edward Waldo, and Forbes, Waldo Emerson, eds. *The Journals of Ralph Waldo Emerson*. 10 vols., Centenary Edition. Boston and New York: Houghton Mifflin Co., 1910–14.

Firkins, O.W. *Ralph Waldo Emerson*. Boston and New York: Houghton Mifflin & Co., 1915.

Gillman, William, et al., eds. *The Journals and Miscellaneous Notebooks of Ralph Waldo Emerson*. Cambridge, Mass.: Harvard University Press, Belknap Press, 1960–.

Hopkins, Vivian. *Spires of Form: A Study of Emerson's Aesthetic Theory*. Cambridge, Mass.: Harvard University Press, 1951.

Hughes, Gertrude. *Emerson's Demanding Optimism*. Baton Rouge: Louisiana State University Press, 1984.

Konvitz, Milton R., ed. *The Recognition of Ralph Waldo Emerson: Selected Criticism Since 1837*. Ann Arbor: The University of Michigan Press, 1972.

Konvitz, Milton R., and Whicher, Stephen E., eds. *Emerson: A Collection of Critical Essays*. Englewood Cliffs, N.J.: Prentice-Hall, Inc., 1962.

Levin, David, ed. *Emerson: Prophecy, Metamorphosis, and Influence: Selected Papers from the English Institute*. New York: Columbia University Press, 1975.

Loving, Jerome. *Emerson, Whitman, and the American Muse*. Chapel Hill: The University of North Carolina Press, 1982.

Lowell, James Russell. "Emerson the Lecturer." In *The Literary Criticism of James Russell Lowell*, edited by Herbert F. Smith. Lincoln: University of Nebraska Press, 1969.

Matthiessen, F.O. *American Renaissance: Art and Expression in the Age of Emerson and Whitman*. New York: Oxford University Press, 1941.

McAleer, John. *Ralph Waldo Emerson: Days of Encounter*. Boston: Little, Brown and Company, 1984.

McGiffert, Arthur Cushman, Jr., ed. *Young Emerson Speaks: Unpublished Discourses on Many Subjects*. Boston: Houghton Mifflin Co., 1938.

Miller, Perry. "From Edwards to Emerson." In *Errand into the Wilderness*. New York: Harper, 1964.

Packer, Barbara L. *Emerson's Fall*. New York: Continuum, 1982.

Paul, Sherman. *Emerson's Angle of Vision*. Cambridge, Mass.: Harvard University Press, 1952.

Poirier, Richard. *A World Elsewhere*. New York: Oxford University Press, 1966.

Porte, Joel. *Representative Man: Emerson in His Time*. New York: Oxford University Press, 1979.

_____, ed. *Emerson in his Journals*. Cambridge, Mass.: Harvard University Press, Belknap Press, 1982.

_____, ed. *Ralph Waldo Emerson: Essays and Lectures*. New York: The Library of America, 1983.

Porter, David. *Emerson and Literary Change*. Cambridge, Mass.: Harvard University Press, 1978.

Richardson, Robert D., Jr. *Myth and Literature in the American Renaissance*. Bloomington: Indiana University Press, 1978.

Rusk, Ralph L., ed. *The Letters of Ralph Waldo Emerson*. 6 vols. New York: Columbia University Press, 1964.

_____, ed. *The Life of Ralph Waldo Emerson*. New York: Columbia University Press, 1949.

Slater, Joseph, ed. *The Correspondence of Emerson and Carlyle*. New York: Columbia University Press, 1964.

Spiller, Robert; Fergusen, Alfred, et al., eds. *The Collected Works of Ralph Waldo Emerson*. Cambridge, Mass.: Harvard University Press, Belknap Press, 1971–.

Waggoner, Hyatt H. *Emerson as Poet*. Princeton: Princeton University Press, 1974.

Whicher, Stephen E. *Freedom and Fate: An Inner Life of Ralph Waldo Emerson*. Philadelphia: University of Pennsylvania Press, 1953.

————, ed. *Selections from Ralph Waldo Emerson: An Organic Anthology*. Boston: Houghton Mifflin, 1957.

Whicher, Stephen; Spiller, Robert, et al., eds. *The Early Lectures of Ralph Waldo Emerson*. 3 vols. Cambridge, Mass.: Harvard University Press, Belknap Press, 1960–72.

Wilson, Edmund, ed. "Emerson and Whitman: Documents on Their Relations (1855–58)." In *The Shock of Recognition*. New York: Doubleday, Doran and Co., 1943.

Winters, Yvor. *In Defense of Reason*. Denver: Alan Swallow, 1943.

Woodbury, Charles J. *Talks with Ralph Waldo Emerson*. New York: Baker and Baker, 1890.

Yoder, R.A. *Emerson and the Orphic Poet in America*. Berkeley and Los Angeles: University of California Press, 1978.

Acknowledgments

"Mr. America" by Harold Bloom from *The New York Review of Books* 31, no. 18, copyright © 1984 by *The New York Review of Books*. Reprinted by permission.

"The Question of Means" by Stephen E. Whicher from *Freedom And Fate: An Inner Life of Ralph Waldo Emerson* by Stephen E. Whicher, copyright © 1953 by The University of Pennsylvania Press. Reprinted by permission.

"Emerson the Prophet: Romanticism, Puritanism, and Auto-American-Biography" by Sacvan Bercovitch from *Emerson: Prophecy, Metamorphosis, and Influence* edited by David Levin, copyright © 1975 by Columbia University Press. Reprinted by permission.

"R. W. Emerson: The Circles of the Eye" by James M. Cox from *Emerson: Prophecy, Metamorphosis, and Influence* edited by David Levin, copyright © 1975 by Columbia University Press. Reprinted by permission.

"The Muse Has a Deeper Secret" by David Porter from *Emerson and Literary Change* by David Porter, copyright © 1975 by Harvard University Press. Reprinted by permission.

"Emerson: The American Religion" by Harold Bloom from *Agon* by Harold Bloom, copyright © 1982 by Oxford University Press. Reprinted by permission.

"'The Curse of Kehama'" by Barbara L. Packer from *Emerson's Fall* by Barbara L. Packer, copyright © 1982 by Continuum. Reprinted by permission.

"Detachment and Transition" by Julie Ellison from *Emerson's Romantic Style* by Julie Ellison, copyright © 1984 by Princeton University Press. Reprinted by permission.

"The Question of Genius" by Richard Poirier from *Making a Difference: Emersonians and Modernists* by Richard Poirier, copyright © 1985 by Random House. Reprinted by permission.

Index